SUCCESSFUL FUND RAISING FOR HIGHER EDUCATION
The Advancement of Learning

Edited by Frank H.T. Rhodes

Sponsored by Council for Advancement and
Support of Education

AMERICAN COUNCIL ON EDUCATION ★
ORYX PRESS ★
Series on Higher Education
1997

The rare Arabian Oryx is believed to have inspired the myth of the unicorn. This desert antelope became virtually extinct in the early 1960s. At that time several groups of international conservationists arranged to have 9 animals sent to the Phoenix Zoo to be the nucleus of a captive breeding herd. Today the Oryx population is over 1,000 and over 500 have been returned to the Middle East.

© 1997 by The American Council on Education and The Oryx Press
Published by The Oryx Press
4041 North Central at Indian School Road
Phoenix, Arizona 85012-3397

Published simultaneously in Canada
Printed and Bound in the United States of America

∞ The paper used in this publication meets the minimum requirements of American National Standard for Information Science—Permanence of Paper for Printed Library Materials, ANSI Z39.48, 1984.

Library of Congress Cataloging-in-Publication Data

Successful fund raising for higher education : the advancement of
   learning / edited by Frank H.T. Rhodes : sponsored by Council for
   Advancement and Support of Education
      p.   cm.
   Includes bibliographical references and index.
   ISBN 1-57356-072-3 (alk. paper)
   1. Educational fund raising—United States.   2. Education, Higher—
United States—Finance.   I. Rhodes, Frank Harold Trevor.
II. Council for Advancement and Support of Education.
LB2336.S86   1997
378.1'06-0973—dc21   97-22597
                                                            CIP

This book is dedicated to all those who, by their partnership, have become champions for the advancement of learning, and to one champion—the late Richard M. Ramin, former vice president for public affairs at Cornell University—whose life and career embodied those values that true learning promotes.

CONTENTS

LIST OF
CONTRIBUTORS

Editor and Contributor

Frank H.T. Rhodes, President Emeritus, Cornell University, Ithaca, NY

Contributors

Peter McE. Buchanan, Former President, Council for Advancement and Support of Education, Washington, DC

Rev. Jonathan DeFelice, O.S.B., President, Saint Anselm College, Manchester, NH

Paul A. Dowd, Director of Public Relations, Saint Anselm College, Manchester, NH

James J. Duderstadt, President, University of Michigan, Ann Arbor, MI

Michael C. Eicher, Associate Vice Chancellor for Development, University of California, Los Angeles, Los Angeles, CA

Alfred Gibbens, Vice President of Development, Pomona College, Claremont, CA

William R. Harvey, President, Hampton University, Hampton, VA

Herman James, President, Rowan University, Glassboro, NJ

Robert J. Kopecek, President, Northampton County Area Community College, Bethlehem, PA

Susan K. Kubik, Vice President, Institutional Advancement, Northampton County Area Community College, Bethlehem, PA

Lori D. Marshall, Director of Publications, Rowan University, Glassboro, NJ

Mary Patterson McPherson, President Emeritus, Bryn Mawr College, Bryn Mawr, PA

T. Edward Mercer, Vice President, Institutional Advancement, The University of Texas-Pan American, Edinburg, TX

Miguel A. Nevárez, President, The University of Texas-Pan American, Edinburg, TX

Janice Odom, Director of University Relations, The University of Texas-Pan American, Edinburg, TX

James W. Osterholt, Former Associate Vice Chancellor for Development, University of California, Los Angeles, Los Angeles, CA; currently Executive Director of Development, RAND

David G. Pond, Assistant Headmaster—Alumni Afrairs and Development, Deerfield Academy, Deerfield, MA

Inge T. Reichenbach, Vice President for Alumni Affairs and Development, Cornell University, Ithaca, NY

John J. Reilly, Jr., Vice President for College Advancement, Saint Anselm College, Manchester, NH

Peter W. Stanley, President, Pomona College, Claremont, CA

Philip A. Tumminia, Vice President of University Advancement, Rowan University, Glassboro, NJ

Eric Widmer, Headmaster, Deerfield Academy, Deerfield, MA

Donna L. Wiley, Director of Resources and Secretary of the College, Bryn Mawr College, Bryn Mawr, PA

Charles E. Young, Chancellor Emeritus, University of California, Los Angeles, Los Angeles, CA

FOREWORD

by Peter McE. Buchanan

C ASE is privileged to cosponsor this unique handbook on the respective roles and responsibilities of advancement leadership as exercised by the campus chief executive officer, the trustees, and the chief advancement officer. No other book addresses this topic so directly and comprehensively. This book focuses on the critical building blocks of leadership, planning, and execution, and who is responsible for each of these prerequisites for success.

Successful Fund Raising for Higher Education brings together practical advice and challenging ideas drawn from successful case studies at 11 institutions, representing a broad cross-section of what is acknowledged to be one of the country's greatest assets. We believe there is a hue and cry for this kind of information and insight throughout the academy.

CASE is grateful beyond words to Frank Rhodes for his inspiring and tireless efforts in creating and developing this book. Without his commitment and leadership, this compilation of some of the most successful advancement programs would not have been possible. His willingness to do so was greatly encouraged by one of the advancement professionals who helped found CASE in 1974, Richard Ramin. Dick, to whom this book is dedicated, was a close friend, a devoted Cornell alumnus, and the vice president for public affairs at Cornell during Frank Rhodes' presidency.

We thank the authors featured in this book for contributing their timely and valuable insights. By sharing the achievements of each institution's advancement team, we believe the authors have provided their colleagues with models for successful fund raising, and the editor has provided a blueprint for trustees, campus chief executive officers, and advancement officers every-where to help build a stronger foundation for the future of education. Because an ever larger number of American schools, colleges, and universities must develop increased support from private sources, this book is especially timely.

PREFACE

by Frank H.T. Rhodes

The advancement of learning—Francis Bacon's phrase—is the most critical need of our nation. Only learning—and the discovery, skill, knowledge, understanding, insight, enlightenment, and wisdom it embodies—will provide a secure foundation for our well-being and prosperity in the century before us. The health of our people, the strength of our economy, the preservation of our environment, the sustainability of our resources, the defense of our borders, the quality of our daily lives, the civic virtue of our society, the strength of our democracy: all these ultimately depend on the advancement of learning. Of course, they also require other things—wise political leadership, responsible government legislation, prudent financial management, enlightened public policy, a competitive industrial sector, a strong commercial base, and effective military security—but these, too, depend on learning. Without the advancement of learning, we shall flounder; nothing else can support us.

The successful advancement of learning will require new approaches and new partnerships. It will not be enough to leave the task to teachers and professors, to entrust it to state governors or local school boards, or to rely on presidential initiative or national summits. It must become everybody's business, everyone's concern; it will require a nationwide coalition, a social compact, an intergenerational partnership.

This book is about partnership: how to envision it, how to create it, how to nurture it, how to harness it, how to sustain it. This book describes the experiences of leaders in a variety of places of learning—schools, colleges, universities, and community colleges, whether large or small, whether public, private, religious, or secular—in creating partnerships. Much of the emphasis is on fund raising as a particular means of advancing learning. But the partnership that is restricted to fund raising, or so preoccupied with it that other activities are neglected or ignored, is likely to be of limited usefulness. Effective partnership involves not only the contribution of resources, but also the development of trust, the sharing of common goals and creative ideas, and the provision of leadership and oversight. The most effective partnership between education and its allies involves gifts, not only of money, but also of judgment and candor, of understanding and critical review of every aspect of the multitude of learning activities. Some of these tasks are rather mundane, but they are linked in the service of great and worthy ends. Money alone provides no answer to our learning needs, although without it we cannot meet those needs and we shall fail. Beyond money, we need to engage the creative insight, professional talents, managerial skills, critical judgment, and energetic leadership of all our people.

Fund raising is a vital part of this partnership because it facilitates initiative and supports activity, and because it encourages other more active forms of personal engagement and individual leadership. The most urgent challenge before us is how best to link the extraordinary talents of our citizens in service to the common good. On the one hand, there exists an immense untapped reservoir of public concern and personal goodwill towards education. On the other, there is also a widespread and nagging concern that we are falling short of our national hopes and personal aspirations, in part because some of our schools and colleges have failed both to reflect our most cherished ideals and to embrace our most rigorous standards. This concern is the reason for the current spate of criticism of education. The critics condemn the campus, not only because of what they see as rising costs and falling standards, but also because of declining civility and growing separation, increasing professional preoccupation and intellectual abstraction, and decreasing personal concern for student well-being. They suppose that the campus is involved in some larger task than the mere transmission of information, however complex, or instruction in narrow professional skills, however intricate. They suppose that learning involves kindling a flame and passing a torch; that it produces personal enlightenment and individual insight; that it engages the heart, as well as the mind, the affection, as well as the intellect; that it nurtures a generous spirit and a sensitive sympathy, an inner resourcefulness and a steady self-discipline, a sense of personal responsibility and social concern. They believe that learning prizes all these qualities, not instead of, but because of rigorous intellectual requirements and a demanding educational curriculum.

Because money will buy none of these things, fund raising alone will solve nothing. But partnership can elicit them; energetic teamwork, resolute leadership, and sound educational policies can promote them. That is why fund raising is a means, not an end. It is important precisely because it is a means both to the effective pursuit of worthwhile educational goals and an invitation to a larger pattern of partnership that is needed to attain them. Nor is education, for all its benefits, an end in itself; its purpose is to promote the art of life in all its richness, and so contribute to the creation of a just, harmonious, and free society.

I am deeply grateful to all the authors represented in this volume, both for their essays and for their own exemplary leadership. I am grateful, too, to Peter Buchanan, president of CASE, who invited me to prepare a book on fund raising; to Jim Murray of ACE and Ruth Stadius of CASE, who helped in thinking about its contents; to John Wagner, senior editor of Oryx, who edited the essays with discernment and taste; and to Joy Wagner, who helped with the manuscript in countless ways. My greatest debt is to those who, by their devotion, have been champions of learning, and who, by their friendship and example, have been an inspiration.

INTRODUCTION

by Frank H.T. Rhodes

From their earliest days, universities, colleges, and schools have depended on fund raising and the generosity of benefactors, clients, and public bodies who shared their dreams and supported their purposes. The oldest institutions—Bologna, Paris, and Oxford, for example—developed from loose associations of teachers ("masters") who subsisted on the fees paid by students for attendance at their recitations. The growth of these guilds of masters led to their recognition and licensing by the church, which also gave them a measure of financial support. New institutions often reflected the gift or bequest of an individual founder or patron—sometimes a cleric—or the direct establishment of a church-supported institution by a bishop or other senior official. For example, Oxford was winning benefactors and acquiring property by the early thirteenth century. Oxford probably owes its existence to the benefaction of William of Durham, who died in 1249.

In the United States, the earliest colonial colleges were established by the various Protestant denominations. Puritans established Harvard in 1635 with a grant from the General Court of Massachusetts Bay Colony; Episcopalians established William and Mary in Virginia in 1693; and Presbyterians established Princeton in New Jersey in 1746. Individual benefactors also played notable roles in the support of these colonial colleges. John Harvard, for example, donated his library of 1,600 volumes and a bequest of £500 to support the college that would bear his name.

In the second half of the nineteenth century, two new types of institutions came into existence. The Morrill Act of 1862 led to the creation of land grant universities in every state, although a few state universities—Michigan, California, and Virginia among them—were founded before this. These public universities became the nucleus for a steady growth in public institutions—research universities, comprehensive universities, four-year colleges, two-year colleges, community colleges, and professional and vocational schools. Public institutions now enroll some 80 percent of all students. At the same time, a handful of wealthy benefactors founded a group of private institutions—among them Cornell (1865), Johns Hopkins (1876), Chicago (1890), and Stanford (1891)—which collectively formed the prototype for the new American university.

In our own period, the financial distinction between wholly private and wholly public institutions has become less well marked, although the method by which their governing boards are appointed is still a defining characteristic. Private institutions have grown increasingly reliant on public funds (usually federal) for research support and student financial aid; public institutions have increasingly turned to private philanthropy (individuals, corporations, and foundations) as the portion of their budgets provided from public sources has declined, now often to something close to 20 percent of their general purpose budgets. Few, if any, public institutions would now describe themselves as "state-supported"; most are "state-assisted." Some have even described themselves as "state-affiliated" or "state-located." In such circumstances, the need for private support is growing, and all institutions—public as well as private—now rely on private support. Government funding for specific projects—research equipment or facilities, for example—now sometimes requires cost-sharing in the form of matching private funds.

Alongside the nationwide change in public financial support, three other trends in public demand are now conspicuous—the demands for cost containment, improved performance, and public accountability. I do not propose to discuss these trends in detail, but I believe that successful fund raising in the future will depend, to a growing extent, on whether it can satisfy these expectations. No less important than the need to raise funds will be the need to explain and justify the effectiveness of their use.

PRINCIPLES OF EFFECTIVE FUND RAISING

No fund raising will succeed without the development of public trust in the institution and public confidence in the integrity of its leaders and programs. The cultivation of that trust and confidence takes time and effort and presumes the value and coherence of the programs and the integrity of the people involved in them. Fund raising is not a quick fix; it demands careful and systematic preparation and the development of a realistic program. Fund raising, like education itself, is an intensely personal activity; friend raising is the basis for fund raising.

The development of a fund-raising program involves the continuing inter-action and cooperation of four major participants—the president; such campus leaders as the provost, deans, and faculty; the chief professional development officer (typically a vice president); and a committed group of volunteers—alumni, parents, faculty, students, friends, and, especially, trustees. The president must rally and sustain the enthusiasm and support of this diverse group, but can succeed in this only if he or she has a realistic plan that all can support. The development and articulation of this plan and the priorities it embodies form the foundation for successful fund-raising efforts.

No campaign or fund-raising appeal can rise higher than the level of activity it supports. The importance of the mission involved, the quality and effectiveness of the activities represented, the integrity and commitment of the individuals engaged, and the efficiency with which resources are employed will determine the extent to which potential donors are willing to be partners in the enterprise.

FUND RAISING: FROM THEORY TO PRACTICE

On any campus, fund raising is a continuous activity on which the strength of the institution increasingly depends. At most institutions, this involves peri-odic major campaigns—though, in practice, campaigns are never "over." One merges into the next, as phases of a continuing activity. I have described some aspects of the "steady state" fund raising between campaigns in the chapter that follows, but I want here to summarize what seem to me the particular features of a campaign.

Although all institutions devote time and effort to fund raising, a campaign represents the opportunity to consolidate and reinforce individual efforts and to provide a rallying point for wider support. Because no two institutions are alike, each will approach campaign giving in its own distinctive way. But there are, it seems to me, a few general principles and guidelines that can be drawn from the detailed approaches described in this book. Acknowledging that my own experience may not be transferable to other institutions, let me offer the following observations:

A campaign *is not*
- a quick fix for an ailing institution
- a remedy for anemic annual giving
- a booster shot for existing feeble fund drives
- a sure thing, with automatic success guaranteed

A campaign *is*
- an instensely demanding, time-consuming activity
- an institution-building activity

- an affirmation of agreement and confidence in the future
- an effective means of achieving extraordinary one-time gifts
- an effective means of increasing the general level of annual giving

A campaign *requires*
- considerable forethought
- comprehensive analysis of needs, priorities, and costs
- a sound academic justification
- a rigorous, independent feasibility study
- widespread agreement on priorities, goals, timing, responsibilities
- a fully documented, prospective donor-alumni record
- consistent leadership from and participation by the president and Board of Trustees
- seasoned, effective professional staff
- considerable financial support
- persuaded, proactive, informed volunteer leaders
- a substantial "unofficial" prelude
- an effective strategic plan, regularly updated, in light of events
- professional promotion—especially the "kick-off"—and publicity
- regular public reports, with full disclosure
- vigorous, sustained post-campaign activities

A campaign *produces*
- thoughtful strategic planning and choice of priorities
- an infusion of major gifts
- new programs and program support
- a sustainable elevation in annual giving
- institutional commitment, unity, confidence, and pride
- a springboard for post-campaign activity

I do not offer these observations as formulations of natural laws of philanthropy; indeed, I should be surprised if there were not some contradictory experiences elsewhere. Rather, they seem to me to be useful generalizations that will, I hope, discourage naive optimism in the campaign as a cure-all and a half-hearted pursuit of half-baked goals. Fund raising is not for the unenthusiastic or the uncommitted; campaigning is not for the listless or the languid. Conviction, urgency, realism, persuasiveness, hard work, and confidence: these are the attributes needed to assure success. Matching these personal qualities with institutional opportunity and need creates the context for the effective campaign. This "check list" of requirements reflects those attributes in action.

Campaigns are not the means of salvation for ailing institutions—they may exhaust the strength and resources of such places—nor do they offer guaranteed success for the healthy. They require elaborate forethought: needs, priorities, timing, morale, capacity, and feasibility need to be weighed and judged before any campaign is contemplated. To mount a campaign is to state priorities as well as needs, and this, in turn, requires hard-headed review of campus programs and resources. On most campuses, this will arise naturally from regular program review and evaluation, but for others this may be an unusual activity. Because to promote some needs is to deny or defer others, it will also involve division as well as agreement. Nor will it leave the institution unchanged, for "preserving the status quo" is likely to be a rather less effective rallying cry than "changing for the better," or "creating to serve." So a campuswide, broadly participative review of institutional strengths and needs is a vital prerequisite. Only such a review will provide a sound academic justification for the support a campaign seeks to encourage. The translation of this into preliminary campaign goals will involve the president and provost making judgments of institutional balance and interests, capping the ambitions of dean "A," perhaps, and raising the expectations of dean "B."

No campaign will ever develop exactly as planned or progress just as projected. There will be unanticipated failures, unexpected setbacks, undreamt of successes, and a dozen unimaginable surprises, to all of which the campaign must adapt with minimal disruption or distraction. This calls for steadiness, resourcefulness, patience, and confidence by the leaders and the ability to share these characteristics with others.

A campaign is not a sprint or a hurdle race; it is a marathon. Long-term fund raising, like long-distance running, requires stamina and patience. So, month by month, dollar by dollar, objective by objective, the plan will be followed—revised as may be required—and the total will climb, agonizingly slowly at times (especially in the third and fourth years of the campaign), as it seems that donors have become exhausted and donations depleted by the drive for the nucleus fund. But climb it will, and the chief task of the president and vice president for institutional advancement is to set the pace, maintain the momentum, inspire the faint-hearted, encourage the stragglers, and inspire all the runners, pointing always to the finish line and the glorious opportunities that will follow from staying the course and finishing at full stretch.

THE ETHICS OF FUND RAISING

Successful fund raising is built upon a foundation of integrity. I identify nine aspects of the process, each requiring and reflecting this integrity.

Effective fund raising requires

- the integrity of the institution
- the integrity of the program

- the integrity of the proposal
- the integrity of the donor relationship
- the integrity in the negotiation of the gift
- integrity in the acknowledgment of the gift
- integrity in the recognition of the gift
- integrity in the accounting of the gift
- integrity in the use of the gift

The integrity of the institution develops over decades, the product of successive leaders and members, the result of countless individual acts, choices, and decisions. It cannot be suddenly created a year before a campaign, or burnished on demand, or improved by effective PR. It can, however, be reinforced over time by enlightened and responsible leadership. And while it cannot be established quickly, it can be lost or diminished quickly. Its preservation rests in the hands of all members of the university community, but especially those in positions of leadership and those involved in fund raising.

The integrity of the program for which support is sought is also required. A program that indulges in questionable practices or uses borderline standards cannot expect either respect or support. Athletics in some institutions is an area of concern. But the particular proposal, as well as the program it represents, must reflect this same integrity. It must not, for example, exaggerate the stature of the program, or promise what it cannot deliver, or disguise whatever obstacles might exist in implementing changes.

Integrity in the relationship with the donor should require little explanation. The most meaningful gift comes not from a transaction, but from a relationship. This relationship, established on common interests, nurtured by trust, reinforced by time, will mature without pretense into a willingness to respond to a request for support. Solicitation then becomes, not an awkward, one-time visit, but the natural outgrowth of shared values and common goals. These, like the friendship that reflects them, continue long after the gift is made. Nothing is worse than the ardent pursuit of a "prospect" who, having given, perhaps generously, is then dropped and forgotten by those who sought help. Equally objectionable is the lack of integrity that may occasionally emerge during the detailed negotiations for a gift. Tax wangles, questionable business deals and benefits, inflated assessments, and secret self-serving agreements—to allow the donor to select the future incumbent of a chair, for example—discredit both the participants and the institution.

Integrity is needed in the acknowledgement—both personal and public— of the gift. Some donors will choose to remain anonymous; others will choose to receive widespread publicity. The wishes of both must be respected, but the promotion of personal publicity requires sensitive and thoughtful handling. The recognition of the donor is closely related both to the original proposal and to the subsequent acknowledgment. Sometimes this will involve the naming of an endowed chair, program, or facility. Clear understanding on the details of this arrangement should be developed before the gift is concluded, and there should be consultation on how the name is to be used and how its product (appointment, building, and so on) is to be accepted and dedicated. A public dedication ceremony provides an important opportunity to celebrate the generosity of a benefactor and to showcase the appointment, program, or facility involved.

Although the National Association of College and University Business Officers (NACUBO) has established firm accounting rules, accounting practices for recording and reporting campaign gifts vary widely from one institution to another. In the absence of any generally accepted accounting standards, gift reports should state clearly the criteria used in their preparation. Under- or over-reporting of gifts, for whatever purpose, improper use of matching funds, and delayed or accelerated recording of contributions undermine high standards of professional fund raising. The Council for Advancement and Support of Education (CASE), under the leadership of Peter Buchanan, has recently proposed a set of campaign reporting guidelines, that would provide a common accounting standard.

The use of a gift also demands integrity. A gift given with restrictions is restricted, and the restrictions must be honored. An endowment limited to a particular purpose must be used for that purpose. Corner-cutting of donor wishes and improper diversion of funds to other purposes have no place in successful fund raising.

A LARGER MISSION

Let me offer here my single most important conclusion: No fund raising can succeed in support of an institution that lacks integrity, clear purpose, high quality, and dedicated leadership. Fund raising is not a convenient source of extra revenue to be tapped by smart tactics. It is an integral part of the larger mission of the institution. The president's role in fund raising is an integral part of his or her larger educational and support activities. The trustees and other volunteers engaged in a campaign are performing a significant part of their fiduciary responsibilities. The vice president for institutional advancement, devoting time to on-campus college activities and programs, guarantees the first-hand familiarity on which successful development rests.

Fund raising is thus neither an optional extra nor a distraction from the core business of the university. The core business of a university is learning, in its most expansive sense. Fund raising is an exercise in extended learning, an effort to create wider familiarity and a greater support for the most basic activity of our society.

Universities are one of the glories of civilization. They are, as Harold Enarson, president emeritus of Ohio State University, once remarked, as fragile as truth itself, existing by public sufferance, supported by public generosity, yet, "independent, free-standing, openly critical of conventional wisdom, friendly to disputation, enchanted with controversy, and hospitable to those who think otherwise." Yet it is not perversity that persuades donors to support them; it is rather the recognition that this sturdy independence is the essential seedbed for the growth of new knowledge, transforming insight, fresh discovery and creative invention. Within the walls of the university, each generation hands to the next the accumulated wealth of human understanding and wisdom, the habit of inquiry, the skills of professional practice, and the powerful technical, medical, and social capacity they produce. Upon university campuses, age-old questions are engaged, ancient verities are tested, and the achievements of the human spirit are remembered, celebrated, and shared.

To solicit funds is not to go, cap-in-hand, begging support for some marginal activity. It is, instead, to invite a friend to share in the privilege of the greatest partnership of all—the quest for knowledge, on which our present existence and our future well-being depend.

CHAPTER 1

Successful Fund Raising at a Large Private Research University

Cornell University

by Frank H.T. Rhodes and Inge T. Reichenbach

Cornell is an independent university with an enrollment of some 19,500 on its Ithaca campus, including about 13,500 undergraduates, 1,750 professional students, and 4,750 graduate students. Another 620 students are enrolled at Cornell's medical campus in Manhattan. About 5,000 of its undergraduates and some 1,500 of its graduate and professional students are enrolled in its four "statutory colleges," which are assisted by the state of New York.

Founded in 1865, Cornell offers undergraduate instruction and advanced study in all major fields. Its annual operating budget for 1996-97 is $1.4 billion, of which it receives $333 million in tuition and fees, $75 million in investment income, $83 million in current gifts, $320 million in support of sponsored research programs, and $126 million in state appropriations. It also receives some $19 million in federal appropriations, $197 million from its medical faculty practice plan, and $93 million from sales and services, as well as smaller sums from other sources. The university has some 88,000 living "mailable" alumni and has an endowment of close to $2 billion. It has enjoyed strong financial support from alumni, friends, and others.

CORNELL'S ADVANCEMENT PROGRAM

The size and scope of Cornell's advancement program has shown extraordinary growth over the past 20 years. Annual gift totals (cash) increased from

$26 million in 1976 to $220 million in 1996. As the totals increased, so did the importance of private support as a vital component of the university's budget.

Cornell's operating budget actually consists of three separate budgets, each supporting a different segment of the university with somewhat different funding sources. The university's "private" colleges—Arts and Sciences, Engineering, Architecture, Art and Planning—as well as the university's academic and administrative support services—the library system, athletics, the university's museum, admissions, and development, to name a few—are funded by the university's general purpose budget. Tuition, endowment income, federal and state research funds, and private support are the main funding sources of the general purpose budget. Cornell's four statutory colleges form part of SUNY, the State University of New York, and are state-assisted. The Colleges of Agriculture and Life Sciences, Veterinary Medicine, Human Ecology, and Industrial and Labor Relations, which once received two-thirds of their annual support from the state, now draw less than 40 percent of their annual operating budgets from this source, relying more and more on the same funding sources as Cornell's private colleges. Their budget forms the statutory college budget. The budget of the university's medical college, which is located in New York City, draws from all the above-mentioned income sources; the medical college also relies heavily on income generated by its faculty physicians organization. Cornell's Hotel School, Law School, and Johnson Graduate School of Management are enterprise systems responsible for managing their own incomes and expenditures.

While Cornell's enrollment increased by about 10 percent over the past 20 years, its operating budget increased almost fivefold from $224.2 million in 1976 to $1,078.8 million in 1995. During this same period, the growth rate of giving was even greater—a more than sevenfold increase in 20 years. The growth of gifts as a percentage of the institution's operating budget fluctuated significantly during this period, reflecting Cornell's shifting fund-raising priorities. In 1976, $14.1 million of the university's total gift receipts of $26.2 million was for current purposes, representing 6.3 percent of the university's operating budget. Five years later, the portion of gift receipts so used had grown to $25 million or 8.4 percent and continued to increase for the next 10 years. In 1985, current gifts totaled $58.4 million and represented 10.2 percent of the operating budget; in 1990, a total of $108.1 million in current gifts represented 13.7 percent of the budget, the highest percentage ever. The most recent five years were marked by an increase in giving to endowment—a goal of the campaign then under way—and a decrease in current gifts to 8.8 percent of Cornell's operating budget in 1995.

During the mid to late 1980s, Cornell embarked on an ambitious facilities program that was almost entirely funded through gifts. A new $24-million building to house the Department of Theater Arts and provide teaching and performance space for its theater, dance, and film programs was the first in a series of major, privately funded facilities on the Ithaca campus. Campaigns followed for the Hotel School ($30 million), Law School ($20 million), athletics ($25 million), and a Cornell Club building ($40 million) in New York City to provide a significant university presence there. A major new facility to house Cornell's national super-computing center, which had been awarded to the university by the National Science Foundation, was a $34-million fund-raising project. In addition to these major new building projects, renovation projects of a smaller scale, such as residence halls, labs, classrooms, and other teaching facilities, also required gift support.

With the state of New York still providing most of the capital funding for the statutory colleges, Cornell's facilities fund raising during those years was focused on projects in its endowed colleges. Only an addition to the building housing the Department of Nutritional Sciences ($8.4 million) and the interior finishing of a large auditorium in the College of Agriculture and Life Sciences required gift support. Altogether, $200 million was raised between 1980 and 1990 in support of these facilities projects.

During this period, gifts designated for facilities increased as a percentage of Cornell's total gift income from an average of between 10 and 11 percent to an average of about one-fifth of the university's private support. The largest share of facilities-designated gifts was 24 percent in 1989.

Although we continue to be engaged in both large- and small-scale facilities fund raising, the focus of our fund-raising priorities has shifted in the last seven years to strengthening Cornell's endowment. In 1988, when Cornell first began to plan for its most recent campaign, the university's endowment barely exceeded $770 million. With an enrollment of 19,000 and an operating budget of $780 million, Cornell clearly needed a major influx of endowment. Setting a goal to raise $595 million in endowment as part of the university's $1.25 billion campaign, we began to see a steady increase in endowment gifts, from $30 million or 24 percent of gift totals in 1988 to $93 million or 47 percent of gift totals in 1995. These results exceeded the previous 20 to 25 percent endowment averages of the total gift income by a significant margin. The best year ever came three years into the campaign when 51 percent of Cornell's gifts were gifts to the endowment.

Various fund-raising strategies sustained the growth in private support for Cornell over the past 20 years. Cornell followed the launch of its university-wide, comprehensive, five-year capital campaign in 1975 with several smaller, project-focused campaigns, all but one of which were facilities campaigns. This period of smaller, project-oriented fund raising lasted for eight years, and was followed in 1988 by a two-year planning period leading to Cornell's most recent five-year, university-wide, comprehensive capital campaign, which was launched in 1990 with a goal of $1.25 billion and completed in 1995 with a total raised of $1.507 billion.

The spectacular growth of private support for Cornell was entirely due to individual giving; corporate and foundation giving either decreased or held steady. Twenty years ago, during the previous university-wide campaign, corporate giving accounted for 11.5 percent of total giving, while foundation giving represented an average of 25 percent of the total. Although gifts from foundations showed a continuous decline for the next several years, accounting for only 16 percent of the annual total by 1988, corporate support surged to 28 percent of the total by 1988, with a peak of 30 percent of total gifts in 1986. During the most recent campaign, foundation support stabilized at approximately 12 percent of the annual gift totals, while corporate giving showed a steady decline, from 27 percent of total giving in 1988 to 16 percent in the last year of the campaign.

Individuals—alumni, parents, and friends—made the growth in giving possible, providing two-thirds of the support in each of the two major campaigns. From 1976 to 1996, giving by this group of donors increased from $15.9 million to $161.1 million, a more than tenfold increase in 20 years. During the first capital campaign in this time period, individual giving averaged 64 percent of total giving; during the second campaign, which ended in 1995, individual contributions averaged close to 67 percent of total giving.

The most crucial factor in Cornell's development growth has been the university's strategy to focus on major gifts, those of $1 million and more. Given its rapidly growing needs in the face of ongoing budgetary constraints on development and other administrative expenditures, Cornell has followed this overall strategy of emphasizing dollar results over participation rates. The gift table for the most recent campaign called for 166 gifts of $1 million or more for a total of $700 million. The campaign received 275 such gifts, exceeding the original target by $194 million or 28 percent. Although the campaign also more than doubled its annual fund goal of $37 million in unrestricted current gifts, participation rates have remained at the same 20- to 21-percent level they have maintained for the past 20 years.

Another important strategy has evolved over the past several years. The university has actively involved the academic deans and directors of those colleges and units that seek private support in the fund-raising process. Cornell's 1975-80 campaign was conducted exclusively by the president, vice president, and a centrally organized staff and volunteer leadership. The college- and project-focused fund-raising campaigns that followed also provided the deans and directors with the opportunity to act as the primary spokespersons for their projects, to develop and cultivate their own group of donors in addition to the ones identified and cultivated by others in the university. The urgency of getting their project funded focused their attention and energy on the fund-raising process.

When Cornell announced its most recent university-wide capital campaign in 1990, each college and unit, including the statutory colleges, fully participated. Each college or unit had its own campaign subgoal. The deans and directors were the main advocates for their units, representing their needs to prospective donors. College- and unit-specific volunteer committees and college-unit-based professional staff supported the efforts of the deans and directors. This distribution of fund-raising responsibility and the active involvement of the deans and directors provided much of the momentum that led to the successful conclusion of the campaign. Cornell's deans and directors became highly motivated, highly skilled fund-raisers.

THE STRATEGY OF FUND RAISING

Establishing Priorities

Whether an institution is involved in a formal campaign or is in a noncampaign mode in its fund-raising program, having clearly established institutional fund-raising priorities is perhaps the most vital component of any advancement program. Priorities represent the institutional consensus about the future direction of the institution and the endorsement of the vision of the institution's academic leadership. They provide the basis for common action and the core of the message the president, deans, volunteers, and staff give the institution's prospective donors. Effective fund-raising priorities must be broadly defined yet sufficiently specific to generate interest within a wide range of donors, including not only those who can give the institution the major gifts that will define the success of a program, but also those whose giving potential is more limited but whose support, goodwill, and enthusiasm are valuable assets to the university.

The process that leads to the setting of institutional priorities is almost as important as the achievement of those priorities. It involves everyone who will play a leadership role in the campaign, foremost the president, the chief academic officer, and the academic deans; the chief development officer's role is primarily to facilitate the process. The broader the involvement, the firmer the consensus, the more consistent the message, the more successful the fund-raising effort will be.

Both a "bottom up" and a "top down" approach to setting fund-raising priorities can lead to the desired results. Cornell used a 'bottom up" approach to set the priorities for its recently completed campaign. The deans of the colleges and the directors of the participating nonacademic and administrative units identified their own needs and priorities. These needs were then reviewed by the provost and president, who determined the overall priorities by "making judgments of institutional balance," a crucial final step in the process.

The alternative "top down" approach allows more institutional direction and direct influence. Cornell's post-campaign fund-raising priorities have been set in broad categories by the president and the provost, with the deans and directors identifying their needs and priorities within that framework. Most institutions use something of a combination of these two approaches. Whatever the most effective approach for setting fund-raising priorities for an institution, involving those who will actively participate in the effort and the outcome of the process in developing clearly articulated and broadly supported priorities is a vital step in any successful fund-raising program.

Explaining the Needs

Effectively explaining the needs of the institution, the process of creating donor awareness, is the first important step in the fund-raising continuum. A clear communications program, comprising written, oral, and visual elements, is essential. The printed case statement explaining overall campaign needs is still important, although one should examine carefully the benefits of this investment of resources, both in terms of money and time, and the actual return on the investment. At Cornell, we found smaller brochures highlighting the individual needs of each college and unit to be particularly useful and effective. One of our most successful brochures was an informational piece explaining the concept of endowment, especially its importance to the university and its management and performance.

Standard proposals for each of the major priorities that can be readily adapted to an individual donor's interests and needs should be prepared in advance. For example, we found it most effective to be able to mail a personalized proposal for a gift to student aid within a few hours of the original inquiry. Videos, when used judiciously, also have a place in a campaign. They enable prospective donors and volunteers who live in distant areas to participate in the excitement and thrill of a campaign.

As useful and effective as these written and visual communication means may be, they cannot match the exhilaration and deeply motivating spirit of a gathering of people who are profoundly committed to the institution and embrace the opportunity to influence its future in a tangible, transforming way. For Cornell, such an event was a planning retreat several months prior to the announcement of our campaign. The board of trustees, leaders of the various campaign volunteer committees, past campaign leaders, the president, the provost, the entire executive staff, and key development staff assembled in a location away from campus and other frequently used venues to discuss the university's needs, fund-raising strategy, and their own roles in the endeavor.

No printed case statement, no brochure, no video, however professional and impressive, can ever achieve a similar impact.

Whatever the means of communication by which the institution explains its needs, no donor will be motivated to give just to enable the institution to achieve a certain dollar goal. The magnitude of a goal may indeed have an adverse effect on donors whose giving is modest. They may feel that their contribution will not make a difference and may, therefore, not give at all. The effective communications program will be able to illustrate and explain how each gift, large or small, makes a difference and is vital to the overall effort. It will remember that different groups of donors relate to different aspects of the case.

We found that we could most effectively explain institutional needs to donors by leaving the abstract ("the need for student financial aid") and personalizing the appeal by showing how a gift would impact the faculty and the students of the institution. No one can ever forget the emotional impact of a student's testimonial as he addressed a large group of campaign leaders. He talked about what the scholarship he had received meant to him, how it had profoundly changed his life, how "nobody ever makes it on his or her own," and how the scholarship was what he needed to make it. There wasn't a dry eye in the room when he thanked the donor directly, and all who were present will remember their embrace as the most vivid image of the profound impact a campaign can have on human beings.

Encouraging Interest and Involvement

The transition between creating awareness and interest in a prospective donor is often fluid. For some, the mere knowledge of an institutional need and its importance for the university is sufficient to engender interest and personal involvement. For others, more attention and further initiatives are needed. Time and resources are required to advance the cause, and professional judgment is crucial in determining the appropriate investment of time and other resources in each situation.

At Cornell, the most recent campaign had 95,000 donors, including individuals, corporations, and foundations. Fewer than .5 percent of the entire pool, or 275 donors, gave 60 percent or $895 million of the campaign total. Fewer than 2 percent of all donors gave 83 percent or $1.258 billion, and 3,670 donors, 3.8 percent of the total donor pool, gave 90 percent or $1.356 billion of the total amount raised. These figures illustrate the importance of focusing time and attention on the donor groups most vital to the success of a campaign.

The president, vice president, trustees, and campaign leadership focused their efforts on these prospective donor groups. Even before the official announcement of the campaign was made, we involved this group of prospective top donors in extensive discussions of the proposed campaign priorities. A series of privately hosted dinners for 20-40 guests was designed to elicit comments and suggestions on a preliminary draft case statement. Trustees and other key campaign leaders served as hosts for the dinners, with the president attending each dinner and leading the discussion on institutional priorities. The dinners provided vital feedback for the campaign and enabled us to test both the case and the message and make necessary adjustments to both. The dinners also stimulated the interest of this important group in the needs and priorities of the campaign and got many of them involved with the campaign as both volunteers and donors.

Much of the interaction with this important donor group, however, has to be one-on-one and requires the time and involvement of the president and the top campaign leadership. Patience, continuity of initiatives, and sensitivity to the donor's needs and timetable are crucial. Some of these donors made their commitments early in the campaign, after only one or a few meetings. Others made theirs after several years of involvement. For some, the campaign timetable did not match their personal timetable. In all instances, however, the continued involvement of and relationship with the key leadership of the institution remained a vital aspect of their relationship with Cornell.

We also created interest and involvement through a series of training sessions over the first two years of the campaign and through 33 regional campaign kick-off events during its last three years. The training sessions carefully avoided the word "training." Scheduled to occur in interesting venues, such as the newly renovated Madison Square Garden, the sessions aimed to make a broader segment of our volunteers and donors aware of why and how people give and how to ask for a gift. The key to the resounding success of these sessions was the light-hearted, fun approach that did not shy away from using confetti guns and "sneaker phones" to get a point across. The sessions were nonthreatening and nurtured a bond between staff and volunteers/donors that proved vital to the campaign and did much to further the interest and involvement of this important group.

The 33 regional campaign kick-off events that followed these training sessions were designed primarily to interest and involve alumni who had the capacity to make a campaign gift but whose involvement with Cornell had been limited or even nonexistent. The cornerstone of this effort was a multi-media show presented after a dinner event with the president as the keynote speaker. The show had high emotional appeal. It "personalized" the campaign objectives in a way that all viewers could relate to and it made them feel that they could personally make a difference for Cornell and for higher education. The presence of the president and several trustees at each of these events underscored the importance of the endeavor for the entire university. Over 5,500 alumni participated in these successful events, which were in large part responsible for the donation of over 2,000 gifts of $25,000 to $100,000, or over $98 million. Even more important, these events identified and reconnected alumni who had lost touch with the university, as well as many who had never before been involved, but who are now part of an active and financially supportive alumni body.

Although the training and regional campaign kick-off sessions were the most visible and orchestrated efforts to interest and involve a large number of alumni, volunteers and staff had many other ways to heighten the interest of prospective donors. Small breakfasts, lunches, and dinners hosted by volunteers; personal visits; invitations to campus visits with a special focus on a college, program, or project; reunion campaigns; membership on campaign committees or various advisory councils; and large regional events to celebrate Cornell were just some of the ways used to create interest in and involvement with the university.

Enlisting Support

A campaign with a specific dollar goal and clearly defined priorities provides the single most effective solicitation program. At Cornell, we continue to rely on peer solicitations by volunteers and solicitations by the president, vice president, and deans and directors as the most effective approach. The credibility that a million-dollar personal gift provides a volunteer when he or she asks others for a like amount is unrivaled by even the most sophisticated and experienced solicitation by professional staff. The personal involvement of the president or a dean in the solicitation of a commitment to the institution expresses the personal commitment of the institution's leadership to achieving common goals and objectives.

In Cornell's campaign, all major commitments were personally solicited by the president, vice president, campaign leadership, or a dean and director. All of them spent countless hours actively pursuing leads, speaking with prospective donors and soliciting gifts, and serving as powerful role models to everybody involved with the effort.

Cornell was fortunate to have an extensive campaign leadership organization that allowed us to solicit gifts based on many different donor affiliations and interests. The affinity to a college or particular academic program was supported by college- or unit-based volunteer committees. Regional committees involved those who identified most with the Cornell leadership and presence in their geographic area. Separate committees focused on those interested in athletics and those interested in music. Alumni with strong ties to their class were solicited through their class reunion campaigns. Parents had their own committee, as did each graduating senior class. Although face-to-face solicitations were initially important, in the broad-based effort of the campaign, mail and especially phone solicitations also did surprisingly well.

Solicitation activity and success were greatly enhanced at all levels when we were able to offer challenge programs. During the last three years of our campaign, we were fortunate to be able to offer three different programs. All three were designed to stimulate endowment gifts. Two of the challenge programs were targeted toward million-dollar donors by making it attractive to endow academic positions, such as professorships and deanships. The third challenge program matched gifts of $30,000 and more and was directed toward donors contemplating their first "major" gift ever. The program provided challenge funds for scholarships and deans' discretionary funds. All three programs were enormously successful and encouraged new donors to make significant gifts and previous donors to reach for levels of giving they had not contemplated before. For the volunteers, these programs provided the stimulus and the urgency often needed to get the job done.

Ensuring Continuing Friendship and Linkage

For most donors, making a campaign gift involves thoughtful deliberation to balance personal interests with the priorities of the institution and the desire to accomplish the greatest good. In accepting a gift, we, as representatives of the institution, also accept the responsibility of continuing to demonstrate to our donors that they have indeed accomplished their objectives. The patient and competent collaboration with a donor and his or her legal or financial advisors on complex aspects and transactions of his or her gift and the timely acknowledgment of a gift by the president, volunteers, and others are only the first of a series of ongoing interactions. The public celebration of a gift in an appropriate ceremony involving the donor, the donor's family and friends, and university officials indicates to the donor the importance the university attributes to his or her gift and thus reinforces the donor in his or her decision.

At Cornell, we invested a significant portion of the additional campaign resources we received in an expansion of our stewardship activities. Today, we report on an annual basis on the endowment performance of a donor's gift, on the payout of the endowment, and, most importantly, on the use of the funds. We report on the students who receive the donor's scholarship, on the faculty member whose position a gift has endowed, or on a dean's use of the discretionary fund to which the donor has contributed. We encourage students and faculty alike to write personal notes to their donors and to nurture the personal bond between them. At Cornell, one indication of the importance of this interaction between the donor and the beneficiary of the gift is the popularity of a student/donor reception held annually during the October joint meeting of the Board of Trustees and the University Council. What started as a small reception for fewer than 200 students, donors, and staff has now outgrown all meeting spaces on campus except the university's field house. The reception is one of the most uplifting events for donors, students, and staff alike, for it enables a donor to see firsthand the impact his or her gift has had on a specific individual. Seeing how his or her gift has opened doors and afforded opportunities validates the donor's gift decision in the most powerful way.

Cornell's campaign is testimony to the saying, "Your previous donors are your best prospects." The ongoing interaction with many officials and volunteers of the university over many years, the friendships that have been formed and nurtured over long periods, the involvement of donors with the life of the institution have all provided fertile ground for the campaign and contributed to the willingness of many of our nucleus fund donors to make additional gifts at the end of the campaign to help Cornell achieve its unofficial "supergoal."

THE TACTICS OF FUND RAISING: ROLES AND RESPONSIBILITIES OF THE LEADING PARTICIPANTS

The President

The president has the ultimate responsibility for fund raising—for its tone, its priority among other activities, its purposes, and its success. Others play vital roles, such as the trustee leaders and other volunteers, and still others devote more time, such as the vice president for institutional advancement, but the role of the president is unique. The president is the architect, the enabler, the umpire, the spokesperson, the cheerleader, the persuasive advocate, the tireless champion for the campaign. He or she is the face behind the budgets, the person behind the programs, the voice behind the case statement, the spirit behind the effort. The president's role in fund raising demands much in terms of time and personal commitment. It is a part of the larger task of leadership, from which it must not be divided, and the larger responsibilities of office, from which it must not be separated. In fund raising, the president's role as chief educational officer meets his or her role as the guarantor of fiscal responsibility; in fund raising, the president's role as public spokesperson meets his or her role as guardian of the concerns and interests of all members of the campus community and of those who are served by them. This fund-raising responsibility implies an intimate day-to-day working relationship with the vice president for institutional advancement and a close and active relationship with trustees and other volunteer leaders. It also means a personal relationship with all major and prospective major donors—typically 200 to 300 people. Beyond any of these particular functions, it means speaking for the institution, both on the campus—rekindling its vision, interpreting its mission, exemplifying its goals, encouraging its efforts, insuring its standards, nurturing its community, harnessing its resources, raising its aspirations, and challenging its complacency—and beyond the campus—explaining the institution's role, the significance of its activities, the contribution of its members, the needs of its programs, and the effectiveness of its efforts.

Although the president is the chief spokesperson, no fund raising can be successful if he or she is the only spokesperson. The president's relationships with other spokespeople—trustees and other volunteer leaders—are vital. Regular business meetings to review progress are not the only way to ensure effective teamwork; the team is built through frequent contact and consultation—telephone calls, visits, notes, e-mail, joint solicitations, workshops, regional gatherings, video-conferences, and more. To describe this process as "care and feeding" of volunteers is to demean it; it involves far more than touching base or comparing notes. The process involves shared effort between partners, joint commitment between team members, common interaction between friends. The tireless effort, the renewed energy, the unwavering confidence, the spirit of the institution and its campaign will all reflect the effectiveness of the partnership and the mutual confidence and personal trust of its leaders.

The relationship of the president and volunteer leaders to major donors will reflect the same concerns. Because a large proportion of any campaign or fund total will typically come from a small number of major donors, attention to this group is vital. Success in reaching this group lies not in repeated pleas for gifts and support, but in the cultivation of interest, the sharing of concerns, and the development of friendship and trust. Although some regard such efforts as demeaning in their activities or false in their motive, they are neither. Far from demeaning the role of the president or volunteers, these friendships represent the highest privilege—an extraordinary opportunity for exemplifying and sharing the most cherished responsibilities of the institution. These associations often prove to be the most satisfying and rewarding of all relationships. These contacts will be reinforced by every means—by campus visits, by appointments to advisory councils and other groups, by journeys to off-site activities, by special publications, and by frequent contact and greetings.

The Board of Trustees

Two groups of volunteer leaders are vital to effective fund raising. First, the trustees—all of them—must be engaged. They must, of course, approve the fund-raising targets, and they must also support every effort to reach those targets. That means that all trustees will be members of the trustee development committee; that all will be donors themselves, however modest some of their contributions may be; and that all will be actively engaged in fund raising. No alumni body is likely to be persuaded of the urgency of a campaign if the board regards it with indifference. No trustee can solicit another potential donor without himself or herself being a donor. No trustee can encourage a friend's commitment unless he or she is already committed. The vast majority of Cornell's trustees were both committed and involved. Between them, they provided 10 percent ($150 million) of the total funds received. Cornell is blessed with superb alumni leadership. Our board chair, Stephen H. Weiss, our campaign council co-chairs, Samuel C. Johnson, Austin H. Kiplinger, and Patricia C. Stewart, all worked tirelessly on behalf of the university, inspiring others both by their own generosity and their devoted leadership. The vice chair of the board (Harold Tanner) and a senior member (Robert Cowie) served as co-chairs of the campaign executive committee. These leaders deserve great credit for both the spirit and the success of the campaign.

Cornell's Development Committee, whose membership includes virtually all trustees, meets once every quarter, usually at breakfast, during the course of the regular board meetings. Its purpose is to inform, energize, and engage trustees in the many development activities of the university. These activities are endlessly varied, ranging from such obvious tasks as soliciting individual gifts to introducing potential corporate or foundation donors and promoting tax legislation that encourages philanthropy. Every board member has a role to play, and the board, as well as the university, will be the beneficiary of the active participation of its members.

The detailed planning of the campaign was done by a smaller group, the Development Steering Committee, which met about six times a year throughout the campaign.

The Vice President for Institutional Advancement

Much of what has been said here about the role of the president also applies to the role of the vice president for institutional advancement. He or she has long-standing relationships with the institution's significant donors and volunteers. He or she has a strong working relationship with the board of trustees, especially those committees of the board that are directly involved in guiding the planning and implementation of the fund-raising program or the campaign. Aside from the president, the vice president is the other major cheerleader of the campaign, both externally, with the campaign volunteers and the donors and prospective donors, and internally, with the campus community and, most importantly, with the professional staff.

One of the vice president's most significant contributions to the campaign is the judicious and effective use of the involvement of the president and key volunteer leaders in the campaign. They are the most important campaign assets and need to be used accordingly. At Cornell, the president's time had to be carefully scheduled to focus on the most important prospective donors and on the most important stewardship activities. For most of the campaign-related activities, the vice president participated in the president's meetings with prospective donors. Such cooperation requires a close and comfortable working relationship between the president and vice president; the relationship must be anchored in mutual respect and openness and must allow for candid, constructive assessments and discussions.

Most vice presidents of institutional advancement supervise programs other than development. At Cornell, the vice president for alumni affairs and development oversees the offices of Alumni Affairs, Development, the Regional Offices, the Office of Planned Giving, Trusts and Estates, the University Council, Events, Gift and Alumni Records, Communications, and Administrative Support Services. All these programs play a direct or indirect role in the success of Cornell's fund-raising program, and their direct reporting relationships to the vice president of institutional advancement provide programmatic and administrative opportunities for a campaign. A strong regional network of Cornell Clubs, managed by the Office of Alumni Affairs, was in place before the campaign; it provided an important part of the infrastructure of the regional campaign volunteer committees.

The division's 10 regional offices across the country were in a strong position to identify regional volunteers and new prospective donors. They were also indispensable for the success of the regional campaign, its many events, and the solicitation activities of the regional committees.

The staff of the Office of Trusts and Estates provided sophisticated financial and estate planning expertise that was accessible to all staff and campaign volunteers. It proved vital in many of our major gift situations. This office also administers gifts given to the university in trust and as life income agreements. The stewardship, advice, and information the office provides on a regular basis to our donors is consistent with Cornell's overall philosophy of donor recognition and stewardship.

The Communications Office played a major role in the development of the communications program for the campaign. The office's careful and knowledgeable review of the case statement did much to increase its effectiveness. In addition, the office wrote, designed, and produced all the breakout brochures for each of the colleges and units participating in the campaign. One of the most effective communication pieces, a quarterly newsletter, was also produced by the office.

The Division of Alumni Affairs and Development was also supported by the vice president for university relations, whose staff provided and procured effective, timely, and sensitive campaign coverage.

Other Organized Groups

The trustees, whether representing a board of eight or a board of 80, cannot devote all their contributed time to fund-raising activities. Most trustees will have other responsibilities. It is vital to develop a realistic estimate of the time each member can contribute and then to design the optimal way to employ that time, listing activities and solicitations in detail. It is unfair and unreasonable to overburden trustees, especially those who are unwilling to refuse assignments. At Cornell, we have found it useful to employ various existing committees and to create a number of new working committees to accept responsibility for various aspects of the campaign. These committees include the following:

Campaign Advisory Council. This large group of 30-40 members, with co-chairs and co-vice chairs, provides strategic advice and support. Its membership includes the most senior supporters, leaders, and friends of the university, not all of whom have been major benefactors.

University Council. This large body of 440 alumni and associates of the university holds an annual weekend meeting in association with the Board of Trustees. Members are actively engaged in university affairs, and participation is high. The council, which is international in its membership, is engaged in an advisory role in areas ranging from athletics to real estate, from admissions to patenting and licensing, from strategic planning to development.

Major Gifts Committee. This committee of 50 comprises trustees and others. It concerns itself with the identification and solicitation of donors in the $1 million+ category.

Regional Campaign Committees. These committees develop targets, programs, fund-raising events, and solicitation activities in every major region, including metropolitan areas, state and multistate, and international. Membership is generally widely based—typically 20-40—and meeting frequency is geared to local activities.

College and Center Councils. Each college and most of the major activities (athletics, library, campus life, art museum, and so on) enjoy the benefit of an advisory committee or council. These groups develop firsthand familiarity with the many programs involved and the level of organization may extend down to the particular department or subject (e.g., pediatrics, environmental studies, or architecture). Membership is typically 15-30 and often includes one or two trustees, who can provide a university-wide perspective to the discussions; alumni and friends; corporate members; and one or two practitioners in the particular area. In many cases, these groups form smaller campaign committees.

Reunion Committees. These committees play an active role in rekindling interest among many who might otherwise have been inactive in university affairs. Milestone reunions (5th, 10th, 25th, 50th) are powerful catalysts in promoting participation.

Class Officers Committees and a Larger (200-300 Member) Council. These bodies maintain loyalty and interest among alumni and foster personal interaction and friendship. They also provide essential opportunities for training workshops and similar events.

The Parents' Committee. Formed during the campaign, this committee proved to be an energetic and effective group in engaging parents of present and former students in Cornell activities.

We have found the success of these various groups depends on four essential requirements.

- **Regular involvement and participation of senior officers.** In the case of advisory councils, these senior officers will typically be deans, directors, and chairs, with the provost and sometimes the president less intimately involved. In the case of all other groups, these latter officers, as well as the appropriate vice presidents (for finance, planning, research, public affairs, for example) must be actively and regularly engaged. The vice president for institutional advancement, or his or her deputy, is generally involved in all the meetings of all these groups. Communication by university officers with group members outside the formal meetings is an important part of this involvement.

- **Energetic volunteer leadership.** The choice of members, and especially chairs and vice chairs, is crucial to the success of the committees. These leaders need not necessarily be alumni. We have enjoyed superb leadership from many loyal individuals who are not themselves graduates. Membership of these various groups should be seen as an invitation to creative activism, not as a reward for somnolent donation. This means the groups will not be simply decorative. The best groups are likely to be questioning, demanding, exacting; they will challenge the institutional position and advocate the needs of their various units. Although they should never become narrow advocacy groups, they must be knowledgeable about and responsive to the needs of the unit.

  An advisory council should not demand that a certain college or program be the university's highest priority or say, "Yes, this unit is weak, but there is nothing wrong with it that an extra $7 million in the annual budget could not correct." More appropriately, a council should point out to the attention of the administration that an already excellent program is also an area of great potential for industrial interest or that a certain area within the college is ripe for increased student interest and enrollment. To be persuaded of the need is the vital first step to contributing to meeting it.

- **Meeting agenda, timing, and location.** The worst possible outcome of creating committees of interested, energetic people is to have them frustrated by too little knowledge of the units, bored by too much "busy work" or show-and-tell presentations, or indignant that their advice is not heeded or their help not sought. Because advisory committees have as great a possibility of becoming sources of frustration as they have of becoming sources of support, the planning of the agenda and the timing and frequency of meetings are matters of critical concern. Careful planning by the president or dean, in consultation with the volunteer chairs and vice chairs and the responsible professional staff, is vital. What is needed is a balance between background briefings and informational sessions, on the one hand, and hands-on, action-oriented items, on the other. In the first category, we would include budget briefings, officers' reports, faculty presentations, facility tours, site visits, equipment demonstrations, and meetings with campus groups, especially students. In the second category, we would include decisions on institutional goals and strategic plans, budgets, procedures, programs, and so on, and action items on such things as facilities, appointments, and development. There should be feedback, regular updates, progress reports, and candid responses to committee proposals. Responses to, or disagreements over, conclusions or rejection of recommendations should be open, honest, and prompt, and the reasons explained. Each meeting should produce some action items. Minutes should be kept, inquiries and complaints should be followed up by officers and staff, and appropriate roles and responsibilities should be assigned to individual members.

The timing of these meetings must be carefully judged. Meetings once or twice a year may be appropriate for some committees; quarterly meetings may work better for others. Each meeting must have a purpose, a focus, and an outcome. Meetings that have no meaningful business to conduct are destructive.

The location of meetings requires careful thought. Most will probably be on campus, in the university's or college's own facilities. Others may be held in major cities, at an off-site facility, in the state capital, or in Washington. Workshops or retreats may be held in country homes or family estates of committee members. The social component of these meetings is an important means of encouraging teamwork and cooperation. One indirect benefit committee members derive from their service is a strong sense of identity and friendship with others, and this sense is a valuable institutional asset.

- **Superior staffing.** If these advisory committees of able, active, energetic, and engaged individuals are to be effective, they will require superior staff support. Each committee must have an individual staff member assigned to direct its activities: agenda preparation, background studies and analyses, progress reports, minutes, liaison, individual presentations, meeting arrangements, travel plans, accommodation and dining needs, personal contact, and a host of other items. Superior, attentive support work is essential to the harmony and effectiveness of the committees. Responsible staff must be capable of meeting the high expectations of service and support that most committee members demand in their own professional activities.

Interrelationships

The committee structure we have described is elaborate, inclusive, and demanding, both upon its members and upon the administration. It must maintain a high level of interest, enthusiasm, and engagement if personal commitment is not to wither over a five-year campaign. The key to renewal is the vision, confidence, energy, enthusiasm, and personal friendliness of its leaders—both volunteer and professional. Here again, the president, vice president for institutional advancement, and trustee leaders play indispensable roles; they are the prime movers, the champions for the whole effort. They must always be confident, encouraging in periods when gifts trickle in slowly, applauding effort, praising success, celebrating generosity, and maintaining esprit de corps. Nothing can replace this sense of dedication to the task, commitment to the effort, and confidence in the outcome provided by the president, vice president, and trustee leaders.

The other essential need is to keep the volunteer leaders closely in touch with the development of the campaign and to sustain a sense of active partnership and engagement. They need all the information and current news—good and bad—if they are to provide comparable encouragement and support to the members of their various groups.

The most fundamental task of any leader is to inspire confidence in the mission and work of the institution and confidence in the ability of its members to excel in their chosen tasks. Without that confidence, the effort to succeed will never be made; without that effort, no venture will prosper. We have witnessed campaigns in which the turnaround effects of energetic new leadership have been remarkable. In one five-year campaign for $230 million, total annual gifts had declined for two successive years to below pre-campaign levels. Every projection was discouraging. Yet, by the time it concluded two years later, that campaign had raised over $250 million, racing past its original goal. What made the difference? What turned the campaign around? New leadership provided institutional confidence based on the repeated affirmation that the task of the university was vital, that the achievements of the university were praiseworthy, and that, with effort and a committment to one another, its members could succeed in the task.

FROM THEORY TO PRACTICE: MOUNTING A CAMPAIGN

The authors of this chapter have, between them, about 40 years of fund-raising experience. Most of this experience is at Cornell, but some is drawn from two other institutions—a large, public, flagship university (Michigan) and a small, private, selective, liberal arts college (Wesleyan University). We have asked ourselves what are the key ingredients that lead to success in fund-raising activities, and we believe there are three particular requirements.

- Energetic, effective, sustained presidential and professional leadership
- Enthusiastic trustee involvement and volunteer participation
- Deliberate planning, realistic preparation, and continuous, superior staff support

The first two of these requirements we described earlier in this chapter. We now want to discuss the preparation and execution of the campaign.

The first step is the preparation of the list of priorities, winnowed and focussed from the "wish lists" that emerge from program review and assessment. This list, prepared by the president and provost, is reviewed both by the college leaders and the trustees and other advisors.

At this point comes the reality check—the need for a rigorous, independent feasibility study. It must be rigorous because the university must not squander money and energy in an unrealistic effort, for the costs of failure are huge. It must be independent—consultant-driven—because the in-house team members are usually too close to the action—both the planning and the prospects—to develop the necessary objectivity. The consultant must be chosen with great care, seeking references and advice from other institutions. Too many consultants still exemplify the old definition of someone who borrows your watch to tell you what time it is. Confidential meetings with potential donors and careful evaluation of their individual judgment, interest, and capacity are essential. This review will ultimately provide a draft outline of campaign needs and a provisional estimate of the capacity of potential donors to contribute towards the goal. There follows more consultation—both on-campus and with volunteer leaders and groups—regional sounding-boards, group discussions by the president and vice-president, and the gradual refinement and exposition of the goals. This leads, slowly, to the formulation of a case statement: the written justification that forms the most important and widely used document of the campaign. Our experience is that the president will need to write most of the substance of this, although much professional help is likely to be needed in format design and presentation.

Even at this stage, the campaign is not "on"; it is provisional. The case statement is a draft version, xeroxed and simply prepared. There follows 18 months to two years of "hidden preparation," of "secret campaigning," where the "secret" is shared with an increasingly wide audience, a professional staff assembled, the ground prepared, and a "nucleus-fund" amassed. That nucleus fund must be large enough to make ultimate success probable; a quarter to a third of the total goal is typical.

A substantial campaign budget will be needed to support these and future activities. We found it workable to impose a modest "tax" on all units participating in the campaign to provide these extra operating funds. We based taxation not on representation, but on consultation, which, while at times divisive and not always wholeheartedly supported, was generally if reluctantly accepted. Any attempt to run a campaign "on the cheap" is likely to lead to frustration, but there is a delicate line between adequate financial support and lavish and excessive spending. The vice president for institutional advancement must assure a prudent balance here. At Cornell, our cost per dollar raised was 8¢ during the campaign. One essential activity of this "silent" period is the training and preparation of volunteer leaders. This, while it must be effective, and its purpose serious, must also be carried out with a light touch. It is said that angels can fly because they take themselves lightly. That is the style for these workshops.

After a couple of quiet years, all will be ready, the goal determined, the staff in place, the nucleus fund-raised, the strategic plan prepared, volunteers assembled, the preparations in hand. The announcement of the campaign and its initial promotion call for imagination, flare, and taste. Whether the announcement involves a black-tie dinner, a white-tie ball, or a reunion gathering under a huge tent will depend on the tradition and style of the institution. It may involve all these, and more. There are perhaps a couple of guidelines: first, whatever style of event is chosen, whether it involves glitz or grandeur, it should be festive, well-planned, mounted with flare and dash, memorable in its own right. It should make a statement, and a strong one. Second, it should be repeatable. A nationwide campaign—or an international campaign, as ours was—is not likely to be ignited by one event in New York City, however noteworthy. Regional kick-offs will be needed to generate regional enthusiasm. We mounted 33 in various parts of the country, and another four in Asia. And these events must be backed up strongly by appropriate publicity, props, speakers, superb literature (such as an elegant version of the now field-tested case statement), and sustained volunteer solicitation supported by the maximum number of presidential and other staff visits, both personal and group.

The Cornell campaign, based on these extended preparations, "took off," catching the enthusiasm and support of alumni around the world. Leaders—professional and volunteer—worked tirelessly as it developed, until, seven long years later, the goal was in sight, success seemed assured, and time still remained. At this point, a crucial question arose—an open-ended successful finish or a demanding super-goal? The easy choice, of course, would be to coast home and bask in the joys of a successful campaign, of a challenging target comfortably surpassed. To set a super-goal—say $1.5 billion, as opposed to an original goal of $1.25 billion, as we did—is to invite a variety of reactions from weary campaigners, among them dismay and indignation. A third choice, which we used as a step to a super-goal, is to announce a nominal, but unofficial super-goal, which was made all the more potent in our case by regularly stating that it was just a thought, but that our valued friends at the University of Pennsylvania happened to have raised $1.43 billion. "That is a challenge," we mused, to our donors "almost worthy of our annual football contests." This heavy-handed subtlety carried the day. We lost the football battle in the fall of 1995, but we won the campaign war.

Just as the start of a campaign calls for special preparation and planning, so does its conclusion. The announcement of the final result, its celebration, the recognition of its leaders, the dedication of campaign positions, the implementation of new programs—all these require careful planning and preparation. But no campaign is ever "over." Fund raising is never completed; even after a gloriously successful campaign, there can be no close season, no letdown. Two practical concerns arise: What is the most appropriate post-campaign posture? and How can this best be staffed?

First, what post-campaign posture is appropriate? Should the university development activities adopt a low profile, while donors recover their collective breath, or plunge into the next round of fund raising? We favor the first alternative, leavened by intense activism for certain programs and projects and continuing concentration on maintaining the higher plateau of annual giving and on those major donors who, for whatever reason, were unable to participate in the campaign. This message will need to be conveyed in the post-campaign celebration events, activities and publications.

And what of the campaign staff? In most cases, the staff will have grown in numbers in response to the needs of the campaign. What of their fate in the post-campaign period? We believe it to be important in employment interviews for development staff to be realistic about post-campaign needs and candid about the particular individual's prospects of continuation. The secret here is for the institution to plan ahead in providing appropriate resources to maintain a sufficient staff to continue the campaign level of giving after the completion of the campaign. Also, whatever downsizing takes place in the ranks of campaign staff must be done deliberately and humanely.

CONCLUSION

The result of the Cornell campaign has been to leave the university changed and strengthened. 118 new endowed positions, $205 million in student financial aid endowment, $630 million for the endowment, $590 million for program support, and $150 million for facilities: these gifts, and many others like them, tell only part of the story. Great as these benefits are, perhaps the greatest benefits to the institution came from the expanded partnership, greater commitment, and heightened expectations of the university community, and, especially, the alumni body. That partnership, reflected in a host of different areas, and that commitment, exemplified in countless different ways, will continue to contribute to the strength of the university long after the campaign is a distant memory.

CHAPTER

Successful Fund Raising at a Large Public Research University
The University of Michigan

by James J. Duderstadt

O ne of the oldest and most prestigious research universities in the United States, the University of Michigan has led public higher education in garnering private support, with initial gifts dating back to the university's founding in 1817. Over the years, Michigan has recorded a number of "firsts" in the rapidly changing field of public higher education fund-raising.

In 1948, the U-M became the first public university to launch what we now recognize as a modern capital campaign, raising $8.5 million for the Michigan Memorial-Phoenix Project "to explore the ways and means by which . . . atomic energy may become a beneficent influence in the life of man." This campaign was significant because of its size and its appeal to corporations at a time when they were not yet accustomed to making major gifts to higher education. When the Phoenix Campaign successfully concluded in 1953, the U-M became the first public institution to establish a permanent fund-raising unit. A decade later, Michigan became the first public institution to launch a comprehensive campaign.

On 18 September 1992, Michigan launched the five-year, $1-billion Campaign for Michigan, the largest fund-raising effort to date for a public university. Thanks to the generosity of alumni and friends, the U-M exceeded the $1-billion goal 17 months before the official end of the campaign in 1997. The U-M is the first public university in history to raise this amount.

Author's Note: I would like to acknowledge Mary Jo Frank and express my appreciation for the substantial contribution she made to this essay.

Today the U-M leads the nation in yet another facet of development as it focuses on creating a new paradigm, that of the "privately financed" public university. Although committed to retaining its public character and serving the people of the state of Michigan, the U-M operates in some ways like a private university, earning much of its support in the competitive marketplace via tuition, research grants, and gifts. When we include the U-M Hospitals and Medical Center, almost 90 percent of Michigan's support now comes from self-generated revenues. Private fund-raising has become key to the university's ongoing success. In the past, the U-M's goal was to use private giving to provide "the margin of excellence"; today the goal is more basic: To recognize that private giving increasingly will replace—not augment—an eroding base of state financial support. U-M was one of the first public universities to see state appropriations drop to a low fraction of its operating budget, but many other major public universities are now facing a similar privately financed future.

Private giving is the university's only fiscal resource with the potential for significant growth. In 1990, the university started working toward a goal for the end of the decade; by that time, the annual level of private support—the total of private giving and payout on endowment—was to exceed state appropriations. This goal requires increasing private support to more than $300 million per year. As of 1996, private giving is expected to total $232 million, including $160 million in gifts received and $72 million in payout on a $1.6 billion endowment (based on a 4.5 percent payout rate). Aggressive solicitation and management of endowment assets, which have grown from $200 million in 1988 to $1.6 billion in 1996, are keys to this effort. Our ambitious goal for the year 2010 is to build an endowment with a distribution exceeding our annual state appropriation. The continued erosion of state support may bring us to this goal sooner than we expect.

Successful fund raising at Michigan draws upon a number of strengths.

1. A body of more than 400,000 living alumni, often leaders in their fields, who have acquired the resources to give substantial gifts and who do so through the university's annual giving and major gifts programs.
2. Strategic planning involving deans, the president, the vice president for development, and other executive officers.
3. An organizational structure that draws on the strengths of the deans and faculty of the university's 19 schools and colleges.
4. A sequence of university-wide fund-raising campaigns to increase awareness among all alumni of the importance of private support.
5. A central development office that serves university-wide goals and academic objectives at the individual school and college level.
6. Advisory groups of dedicated alumni and friends who work closely with deans, faculty, and staff on fund-raising campaigns.

Considering how each of these strengths contributes to the university's overall development success is an instructive exercise.

MARKETING TO A NATIONAL AUDIENCE

Unlike major private universities that benefit from a small number of large gifts, the U-M receives a large number of more modest gifts. Our approach involves mass marketing nationally and following through with a major gifts program that focuses on highly personalized cultivation. The U-M also benefits from a deep well of goodwill on the part of the people of the state who identify with the university, including many who are not alumni. Academic reputation and a love of Michigan—not the ups and downs of athletic teams—are the wellspring of this support. People donate to institutions of higher education and charitable organizations for a number of reasons: Belief in the mission of the institution and confidence in the administrative leadership, the desire for a balanced budget, personal need and involvement, the example of others, the magic of ideas, and who asks.

Although considerable sums of money had been contributed to the university over the years for buildings, scholarships, research, and special facilities, the Michigan Memorial-Phoenix Project was the first coordinated university-wide effort to raise funds to meet a need. At the close of the Phoenix Campaign in 1953, the Development Council—an organization of about 30 alumni volunteers—was created. The council's day-to-day activities were supported by a small development office paid for with funds raised by the council. Schools and colleges launched an annual solicitation of all U-M alumni and established the Michigan Alumni Fund, an umbrella group to coordinate all annual campaigns undertaken on the U-M campus. These two activities were soon supplemented by special projects to cultivate foundation and corporate support.

In 1961, the Development Council founded the Presidents Club for donors who contributed $10,000; this development marked the beginning of an extensive, multi-leveled donor recognition program designed to attract large private gifts to the university. The program has expanded over the years. Today the Presidential Societies recognize donors who have achieved a cumulative record of outright gifts and pledges to university programs. The five levels of the societies are as follows: Presidents Club, $15,000; Henry P. Tappan Society, $50,000; Harry B. Hutchins Society, $100,000; Alexander G. Ruthven Society, $500,000; and James B. Angell Society, $1 million. The university is in the process of adding two additional recognition levels. The Development Council also developed a program of deferred giving to promote unitrusts, pooled income fund gifts, and bequests, and an office of Corporate and Foundation Relations in the late 1960s. The university's fund-raising strategies have continued to evolve over the years. This willingness to embrace change and break new ground and an ever-growing alumni body have enabled the university to progress steadily and emerge as a leader.

THINKING AND PLANNING STRATEGICALLY

Strategic planning involving the president, vice president for development, other executive officers, and deans has helped spur the university's steady growth in institutional advancement. As the chief executive officer, the president provides both a vision and a strategy for the university. The president also provides the context to mobilize development plans and programs needed to elevate fund-raising efforts to new levels and to ensure critical involvement of all deans by working with these academic leaders to set goals and objectives.

Former President Harold T. Shapiro was one of the first to fully understand the economic challenges public universities would face in the closing decades of the twentieth century. He concluded in the early 1980s that the U-M needed to embark on new levels of high-intensity fund-raising efforts to offset eroding state support. He hired Jon Cosovich, who brought with him from Stanford University highly successful organizational and volunteer recruitment strategies.

The importance of and need for strategic planning became apparent to us during my years as dean of the College of Engineering in the early 1980s. Later, as provost, I encouraged all the university's schools and colleges to plan strategically and to look at private giving as a crucial part of their resource base. When I became president in 1988, I introduced a planning diagram that colleagues characterize as a "four-leg stool" to illustrate the university's four revenue streams: tuition and fees, federal support for research, state support, and endowment and gifts. The stool was lopsided in 1988. The strategic plan calls for making the four legs equal so the university will have a solid, stable base upon which to grow. Endowment and gifts made up only 5 to 6 percent of the university's total revenue eight years ago. Today endowment and gifts comprise more than 13 percent of the U-M's revenue portfolio.

The vice president for development is an executive officer and integral part of the university's strategic planning and management team, carrying on a tradition that began with former Presidents Robben Fleming and Harold Shapiro. Mutual respect has characterized these partnerships, and it describes my relationship with Vice President for Development Tom Kinnear. For example, the gift component is always an integral part of planning new facilities. More than half of our campus buildings have been funded by a private gifts component.

Before TV correspondent and U-M alumnus Mike Wallace publicly announced the five-year, $1-billion Campaign for Michigan in 1992, university leaders established five high-priority program themes for the campaign.

- Undergraduate Education
- Science, Technology, and the Arts
- Cooperative Approaches to World Issues

- The Health Sciences
- The Humanities

We also sought gifts to fund high-priority facility renovation and construction programs. The most ambitious goal was to raise at least $340 million to add to the endowment fund to support faculty positions, student financial aid, and ongoing programs of the institution.

While the president and executive officers play pivotal roles in generating the strategic plan for the university, the vice president for development is in charge of carrying out the advancement program, including mobilizing, leading, and providing the infrastructure and support for the development process.

MOBILIZING STAFF AND RESOURCES

Each vice president for development, like each president, brings to the job certain skills and talents that meet the university's needs for a particular time in history. Vice President Kinnear, the Maynard Phelps Professor of Business Administration and professor of marketing, has encouraged development staff to adopt total quality management techniques—known as "M-Quality" at Michigan—and to be part of TQM teams. Since the early 1990s, these M-Quality teams have worked to enhance customer service and empower employees. M-Quality teams have dealt with such thorny issues as handling matching gifts, programming computers to use the names that donors prefer in a particular situation, and creating a "donor hotline." The hotline, to be activated in 1997, will be a convenient way for donors to register name and address changes, handle pledge statements, and process matching gift designations when they change jobs. The information gathered through the hotline will be used to make better managerial decisions.

Orientation for all new staff working in the development area—whether in central administration or in the schools and colleges—is crucial. New development staff, including all support staff, participate in four orientation sessions, scheduled quarterly. During the course of the year, participants learn the intricacies of the university's development program from a score of speakers who are experts in their fields.

Development staff also have many other opportunities throughout the year to participate in workshops and seminars on campus to learn about such aspects of development as trusts and bequests or working with volunteers. The Office of Development schedules approximately 30 speakers a year from campus and national professional groups.

Central development also maintains a library of materials to keep staff members informed about trends. In addition to current subscriptions to such publications as the *Chronicle of Higher Education* and *Giving USA*, the library has a collection of *CASE Currents* dating back to the 1970s. A monthly publication called the *Development Network Newsletter* goes out electronically to keep staff apprised of the latest news affecting development at the university.

FUND RAISING AS AN ONGOING ACTIVITY

We view fund-raising campaigns not as an end in themselves, but rather as a means to involve more alumni in support of students and faculty. Innovative endowment management has enhanced the value of gifts received. Our endowment now stands at more than $1.7 billion. Through a series of campaigns, we also have developed more sophisticated deferred giving programs and have increased awareness among alumni and friends of the importance of private support.

In 1964, the U-M undertook the three-year campaign, at that time the largest private fund-raising campaign ever attempted by a public university. Raising a total of $72.8 million, the campaign demonstrated the potential for substantial financial support from the private sector.

Many of the academic units developed their own fund-raising programs during the 1960s and 1970s. The Law School Fund was established in 1961. The Medical School, Business Administration, Dentistry, and other units soon followed.

The first comprehensive university-wide campaign—the Campaign for Michigan—was launched in 1983. The objectives of the campaign were to raise $160 million and to achieve a significant improvement in the U-M's fund-raising capacity that would continue beyond the campaign. University leaders spent six months organizing the first National Campaign Committee, which began with 75 volunteers. By the time the campaign officially ended in 1987, the initial goal had been exceeded by more than $18 million. A related two-year program to ask for a gift from all alumni was launched in July 1986. The goal of that program, the Campaign for Michigan Fund, was $20 million. By the time it ended in 1988, the campaign had raised a total of $26 million.

The university has come a long way from the early 1980s, when it was receiving about $5 million a year in gifts and pledges. Today we receive about $150 million annually from approximately 90,000 individuals, 1,600 corporations, 135 foundations, and 700 associations. The current Campaign for Michigan has already surpassed its $1-billion goal.

The Campaign for Michigan has five major components: principal gifts, major gifts, corporations and foundations, trusts and bequests, and annual giving. We have found that measuring progress for each component as well as for the overall campaign gives a valid sense of progress. Throughout a campaign, we also track the number of solicitations required in addition to monetary figures, redirecting our efforts as required.

Principal Gifts

Over the years, the U-M has received several large gifts. Early in the twentieth century, William W. Cook, a Michigan alumnus, gave the university about $16 million to build the magnificent buildings comprising the Law Quadrangle and the Martha Cook Building, which still inspire students and enchant visitors. In 1935, the university received a gift from Horace H. and Mary Rackham, which included funds for the building and site of what is now the Horace H. Rackham School of Graduate Studies and a substantial endowment for carrying on graduate work and research. Other path-breaking gifts have been given by Michigan businessman William Davidson for the Davidson Institute ($30 million), the Dow family and Towsley Foundation ($12 million), and, most recently, a $12-million gift from Ann Lurie for the new Engineering Administration Center and bell tower for North Campus in memory of her husband, Robert H. Lurie.

The university appointed its first director of principal gifts in 1990. The director is responsible for developing a program to secure gifts and pledges of $2.5 million and above from individuals, corporations, and foundations, and for developing a nucleus fund with leadership gifts of $1 million and above. Such gifts account for more than 30 percent of the total Campaign for Michigan goal. Because of the critical importance of this component, the vice president for development personally provides leadership. The vice president for development and the director of principal gifts work closely with the president and the Campaign Steering Committee to plan and carry out discussions at the highest level with potential principal gift donors. Other executive officers, deans, and campaign leaders also play an active role in the principal gifts program. Private visits and events with the president are often key to many of these gift decisions.

Major Gifts

Michigan's major gifts program, gifts ranging from $100,000 to $2.5 million, is the heart of the university's large gift fund-raising, contributing more than 40 percent of the campaign total. Fifteen central staff members are assigned to various geographic regions around the country. Major gifts officers are responsible for cultivating prospects, working with major gift committee members to identify additional prospects in the geographic area, and planning special programs and events that highlight the university.

Our major gifts program has been successful because of the synergy resulting from the collaborative efforts of the major gifts officers in the schools and colleges and staff in the central development office. Together, they plan events and solicit donors for specific programs by geographic region. Volunteer leadership also is essential at the major gifts level. National co-chairs for major gifts serve as members of the Campaign Steering Committee. Michigan's major gift committees are active in 18 metropolitan areas throughout the United States.

Corporations and Foundations

Gifts from corporations and foundations have become increasingly important in the overall fund-raising mix, with gifts from corporations growing from $13.2 million in FY 1985 to $27.5 million in FY 1995-96. Corporations and foundations in Michigan and throughout the state and the world have provided major support. Foundation gifts increased from $14.4 million to $19 million annually over the same period. Nonprofit associations provide an additional $10 million annually. Together, gifts from corporations, foundations, and associations accounted for 38 percent of private support to the university in FY 1995-96.

To better understand and meet the expectations of corporations and foundations, including needs for research and training of graduates, the university has adopted the following strategies:

- Integrate corporate and foundation relations into a comprehensive major gifts program.
- Focus on about 200 corporate and foundation major gifts prospects.
- Develop strategies for working with corporations and foundations that have multiple relationships and interests within the university.
- Work with schools and colleges to identify changing trends in corporate and foundation interests.
- Collaborate with major gifts area directors to more effectively use the skills of individual alumni in key positions in priority corporations.
- Encourage corporate participation in cultivation activities.
- Coordinate teams to work with strategic corporations.
- Enhance relationships with and develop clear institutional strategies for the 13 largest foundation priority prospects through the Foundation Fund-raising Committee.

Trusts and Bequests

Trusts and bequests are important to the future of Michigan and promise to become more so as the nation's baby boomers age. In 1990, the John Monteith Society was established to recognize individuals who intend to include the university in their estate planning. To increase life income and trust gifts, we have expanded the communication and marketing program for trust and bequest gift opportunities to reach all U-M constituents over age 50.

For many individuals, a bequest provides the vehicle for rounding out a lifetime of giving with a lasting legacy to the university. Because of the tax advantages associated with a bequest to a charitable institution, assets from estates that would otherwise go directly to government treasuries can instead be given to the university to meet faculty, student, and program needs. In addition to informing donors about various types of bequests, the Office of Trusts and

Bequests invites them to consider establishing a charitable remainder trust or contributing to the university's Donor Pooled Income Fund.

If donors establish a charitable remainder trust with the Board of Regents as trustee, there are no management fees. To be managed by the university's Treasurer's Office, the trust must be at least $100,000. Some donors select a private or commercial fiduciary as trustee or serve as their own trustee. As of April 1995, the university managed 57 charitable remainder trusts with a market value of $24.1 million.

For donors who would like the tax-savings benefits of a charitable trust, but who also hope to minimize investment risk and investment overhead costs by pooling gifts with those of other donors, the university offers the Donor Pooled Income Fund, a pooled fund of diversified common stocks and bonds. The Donor Pooled Income Fund is ideal for donors who want to make an irrevocable gift to the university, receive the tax benefits of a charitable gift, avoid capital gains taxes, and receive a return on assets in the fund throughout the lifetime of the donor or spouse or another beneficiary over the age of 50. Some donors contribute stocks that have been generating little or no income. By making a gift to the Donor Pooled Income Fund, they assure themselves of a modest return annually for the rest of their lives and that of their spouse or other beneficiary with minimal management fees. Upon the death of all beneficiaries of the donor's portion of the Donor Pooled Income Fund, the money is used by the university as the donor has directed. Currently, about 130 donors participate in the Donor Pooled Income Fund, which has a total market value of approximately $6.5 million.

Annual Giving

For its annual giving programs, Michigan has identified two major objectives: increase the number of annual-giving donors and increase the size of the average annual gift from current donors. In 1995-96, approximately 20 percent of all U-M alumni contributed to an academic unit annual fund. One of the goals of the Campaign for Michigan is to increase the overall participation rate. The average per capita annual fund gift to academic units in 1990 was $139. Our goal is to increase the average gift by at least 10 percent to approximately $153. The university also seeks to retain 70 to 85 percent of donors from year to year.

Other new or intensified efforts to increase annual giving include the following:

- Attract new donors from the nondonor community.
- Identify new nonalumni potential donors.
- Increase market segmentation for all annual-giving solicitation programs.

- Encourage donor average gift increases through giving clubs, second appeals during some years, and promotion of special campaign recognition for five-year participation and growth.
- Initiate a campaign challenge grant for new donors and those who increase the size of their annual fund donations.
- Improve the capacity and effectiveness of the Michigan Telefund program, making it possible to contact all former students annually. The Michigan Telefund phone center, staffed by students, makes 140,000 calls a year. It has become a major vehicle for fund-raising on behalf of the university's schools and colleges.

The Campaign for Michigan structure for annual giving is likely to continue after the campaign ends in 1997 because, as the following figures show, it works:

- Total support has grown from $57 million in FY 1985-86 to $122 million in FY 1995-96.
- Individuals give a total of about $50 million annually. Gifts from individuals who are not alumni have increased from $3 million in FY 1985-86 to more than $7.3 million in FY 1995-96.
- Bequests have grown threefold, now totaling more than $18 million annually.
- Gifts of annuities and life insurance have grown eightfold to almost $6 million during that same period.
- The U-M set a record for the value of cash, securities, and other gifts received in the previous 12-month period—$140 million, surpassing the previous record of $120 million in 1994.

Successfully reaching or exceeding campaign goals comes from planning and hard work in each of the five major components of fund-raising areas. Another key to success is coordination of fund-raising efforts among the university's 18 schools and colleges.

CREATING SYNERGY THROUGH COOPERATION AIDED BY COMPUTERS

Fund-raising at Michigan can be described best as a partnership—a combination of university-wide efforts executed in conjunction and cooperation with deans, faculty, and staff. Each school and college develops the maximum level of volunteer and alumni involvement in promoting gifts to that unit for support of its programs, with special focus on campaign priorities. The objective is to solicit each potential donor for the largest possible gift. Coordination is the responsibility of the central campaign major gifts staff, who adhere to the university's prospect solicitation coordination policies. Central staff members help schools and colleges time their requests.

"Open communication" characterizes the working style and philosophy behind solicitation at Michigan. Contacts with prospects are conducted in an open manner by respecting clearance guidelines and by keeping the university's campaign prospect tracking system up to date; this task is the responsibility of the staff prospect manager. The university's successful prospect tracking system began as a central file of high-end donors and prospects; it was installed in 1987 to store correspondence and other information. Four years later, a new campuswide computer system—the Development and Alumni Constituent (DAC) system—went online. This modern distributed computing system gives deans and staff access to timely donor and alumni information in an easy-to-read format. With the DAC system, we have greatly expanded the volume of information on prospects and donors that we store and track.

The recent adoption of responsibility-centered management throughout the university, including the Development Office, will create new challenges for our development staff. Revenue-producing units will keep the revenues they generate but also must cover the costs of the centrally provided services they use. Schools and colleges will have greater incentives to generate resources and to spend wisely. Responsibility-centered management will provide more incentives for fund-raising, but also will provide new challenges to the central development office because schools and colleges may be reluctant to bear the costs of those central operations.

DRAWING ON THE STRENGTHS OF ADVISORY GROUPS

At Michigan, as at many public universities, the governing Board of Regents is determined by a statewide political process (elections) rather than by the capacity to participate actively in fund-raising. Although the Board of Regents may approve a statement supporting or endorsing advancement efforts, Michigan does not have a board development committee, a chair of development, or a foundation to promote advancement activities. Over the years, some regents have worked individually on development activities, but the board as a whole simply is not selected or structured to play the roles performed by trustees at private institutions.

At Michigan, we have built advisory groups of alumni and friends to help with fund-raising. With each successive campaign, our volunteer network has grown larger and stronger. Today we have about 1,500 development volunteers, 90 percent of whom are alumni; 10 percent are friends, parents, or individuals active in the life of the university in some other way. Most of the volunteers concentrate on a particular program, school, or college in which they have a special interest. Volunteers help identify potential donors, introduce donors to development staff and set up meetings with deans, bring prospective donors for campus visits, help shape case statements, serve on major gifts committees in the schools and colleges, and solicit gifts. Some labor a lifetime to raise funds for Michigan. The 75-member Presidents Advisory Group (PAG) meets twice a year for discussions on long-range planning issues related to the university, including academic initiatives, financial resources, and administrative management. Established in 1989, the PAG is an important source of counsel and guidance. By sharing their expertise and experience, PAG members help develop and implement plans for the future of the institution.

One of the key functions of development officers in the schools and colleges is the promotion of ongoing engagement, which is required if we are to keep 1,500 volunteers motivated and enthusiastic. Campaign programs and field activities are varied and scheduled to inform and involve the largest possible number of alumni, parents, health care consumers, patrons, and other friends of the university. The most successful donor motivational programs at the U-M have been national campaign volunteer workshops in Ann Arbor, working sessions for major gifts committees in large metropolitan areas, receptions and meals with university speakers, weekend university seminars on campus, special on-campus seminars for targeted audiences, leadership gift recognition and appreciation events, presidential dinners and athletic events, and mid-campaign volunteer workshops and progress meetings.

Campaign communications also serve as important motivational tools. Special campaign publications are prepared for volunteers, donors, and potential donors. Videos and slide presentations are produced for individual and group audiences. Campaign information is also incorporated into a variety of existing publications, including *Michigan Today*, a quarterly publication for all U-M graduates. Personalized letters and bulletins are prepared for key audiences. Whatever the event or audience, campaign publications are designed and produced to represent the quality of the university in a tasteful, cost-effective manner.

High-quality publications, such as the award-winning Campaign for Michigan publication *Leaders & Best*, and memorable events produced by central development working in conjunction with the schools and colleges have improved the overall quality of the university's marketing efforts. Fund-raising volunteers help spread the news of Michigan through their personal and professional contacts. Informed alumni who are involved in fund-raising are also some of our best recruiters of outstanding students.

CONCLUSION

When identifying its peers, the university historically has looked to elite private institutions. Using private colleges as a frame of reference has fostered high standards for the university's development activities. A number of renowned professional schools have been part of the fabric of the university for many years, also giving it a leg up with fund raising. Although Michigan is proud to be a public institution, it has never relied solely on state appropriations and tuition and fees for support. We will continue to rely heavily on private fund-raising. Michigan is grateful for the hard work of its deans and faculty members, the striving of its students, the enthusiasm of its 1,500 volunteers, and the dedication of thousands of its alumni and supporters who believe in the university and its mission.

A strong development program has put the U-M in a better position today to live up to the mission and vision statement it drafted in 1992.

> The mission of the University of Michigan is to serve the people of Michigan and the world through preeminence in creating, communicating, preserving and applying knowledge, art, and academic values, and in developing leaders and citizens who will challenge the present and enrich the future.

Fund-raising, the key to fulfilling the university's mission, will not become easier in the years ahead; it will never be a "quick fix." Competition for private dollars is today keener due to increasing efforts by other colleges and universities to tap into foundation and corporate funding. Although increased competition creates awareness of the need for more private fund-raising for higher education—and potentially expands the total pie—competition also requires that development staff work vigorously and that university leaders plan strategically. If we are successful and are able to explain our program to supporters and skeptics, I believe intelligent citizens who are concerned about our nation's future and the welfare of their children and grandchildren will support higher education with their gifts. Whether the institution is a small liberal arts college or a large research university, the basics of fund-raising still apply: We must make a case and ask.

CHAPTER 3

Successful Fund Raising at a Large Public Research University with a Foundation

The University of California, Los Angeles

by Charles E. Young

W hen I became chancellor of UCLA in 1968, I did not imagine that I would one day lead a $300 million capital campaign to be followed eight years later by one for more than $1 billion. Institutionally, we did not think in terms of fund raising as we do today. UCLA had no track record in private philanthropy, and fund raising was not my chief priority. UCLA's entry into institutional development began slowly. Our initial fund-raising efforts were single-focus activities—campaigns for endowed chairs and bricks-and-mortar projects that supported our campuswide enterprise.

The environment today is different from the one that nurtured UCLA's growth from a fledgling institution into one of the world's great research universities. We have had to adjust to an era of constrained resources and increased competition for every dollar. Tension mounts as university administrators across the nation struggle with limited public funding.

The states can no longer carry their educational institutions. In California, state support amounts to just 23 percent of UCLA's operating budget—it is no longer state-supported, but state-assisted. Funds from the federal government are also diminishing, while the cost of education is soaring. Fiscally, we have begun to operate more like a private university to protect the quality and integrity of our academic programs and to shield ourselves from unpredictable political winds. Out of necessity and for greater efficiency, UCLA has cut its budget, restructured its units, and streamlined its operations. During the course of three decades, I have grown to understand that development serves the purposes of the university's highest mission—to support the education of students and further the research of scholars.

As a public institution seeking private funds, designing our first major capital campaign was a new and rigorously challenging exercise for our development staff, faculty, and volunteers. Culminating in 1988, The UCLA Campaign was a landmark six-and-one-half-year drive to raise $300 million for campus academic programs. We reached that goal six months ahead of schedule, ultimately generating more than $370 million in private gifts.

In May 1997, we celebrated the public launch of our second campuswide campaign. Aiming to generate an ambitious $1.2 billion in private funds by 30 June 2002, Campaign UCLA is a bold undertaking that ultimately will engage thousands of members of the university family—alumni and friends, corporations and foundations, faculty and staff. During Campaign UCLA's initial two-year leadership gifts phase, we raised $446.1 million. That figure comprised an impressive 37 percent of the overall campaign goal, but perhaps most significantly, it dwarfed the entire amount raised in the 1980s effort. Clearly, we had come a long way.

Pondering our good fortune, I am humbled by our achievements. Since launching our first campaign, we have gained an institutional perspective that was not possible before. We realized that we must continue to move boldly to find new, larger, and more strategic sources of private support. Having assessed our strengths and weaknesses, we brought to our current development program a more realistic view of what it will take to reach the current campaign goal of $1.2 billion.

We recognized that we must invest significantly to move our annual base level of support from $100 million to the next plateau of $200 million, just as we invested in our previous campaign to move our annual base from $40 million to $100 million. This time, expenditures are budgeted in a much more detailed way. Realistic budgeting affords a clear idea of exactly what we are going to spend; however, we occasionally wonder if seeing these huge dollar amounts on paper will inhibit some of our volunteer fund-raisers.

For university advancement professionals who are interested in UCLA's team approach to fund raising and, specifically, in our internal campaign organization, I offer a frank appraisal of what has and has not worked for us to date. It is our hope that these insights will aid development officers as they design and implement successful fund-raising strategies for their own institutions.

SIZE AND SCOPE OF THE DEVELOPMENT PROGRAM

UCLA's campuswide development program employs 81 development officers and an additional 96 full-time staff (clerical, research, communications, etc.). The development program supports the College of Letters and Science, 11 professional schools, athletics, the UCLA Center for the Health Sciences, and virtually every facet of our enterprise. Through its offices of Principal Gifts, Planned and Major Gifts, Corporate, Foundation and Research Relations, Campaign Operations, and the Annual Fund, UCLA's central development operation serves as a resource for development staff campuswide. The program involves staff in the chancellor's office, finance and information management, university relations, and alumni relations.

Approximately 9 percent of UCLA's $1.9 billion operating budget derives from private gifts and grants. The university allocates an average of $12 million per year to fund the development program. For the past several years, UCLA has raised an average of $170 million, of which $49 million is endowed to provide perpetual funding for faculty research, undergraduate and graduate student aid, instructional programs, and other activities. The remaining $121 million includes gifts-in-kind and current-expenditure funds that may be used for any of these purposes, as well as the enhancement of institutional facilities, construction and maintenance, equipment acquisition, and general campus improvements.

Volunteers involved in development projects on an ongoing basis number approximately 1,200. Their participation in a myriad of boards, committees, alumni programs, and special projects ensures our fund-raising success, for UCLA would not reach its goals without their enthusiasm and dedication.

Overall, the key players in our development operation are comfortable with a team approach to planning and decision making. Once fund raising became one of my chief priorities, I made myself available to meet with development leadership on a regular basis. It is difficult to assess exactly how much time I spent directly engaged in fund-raising activities. Much of the chancellor's role is development-related in the sense that all university affairs impact the ability to raise funds successfully. During our first campaign, I spent an estimated 25 to 33 percent of my time on campaign activities, including solicitation meetings, strategy development, and special events.

DEVELOPMENT OPERATIONS PLANNING AND INSTITUTIONAL NEEDS—DEFINING ROLES AND RESPONSIBILITIES

UCLA's chief development officer holds the title of associate vice chancellor-development. His judgment and guidance were invaluable to me in both internal and external affairs. From the earliest stages of campaign planning, we met regularly to establish realistic goals and set priorities.

Development program requests are usually routed through the chief development officer, but as chancellor I left myself open for the exceptions. It is important to recognize that the total picture of campuswide development has gray areas. A willingness to make exceptions and be flexible only enhances creativity and strength, and, ultimately, the prospects for success.

UCLA's academic leaders—the provosts, deans, and vice chancellors—set fund-raising priorities and determine the overall direction for the institution. Academically driven priority-setting has integrated fund raising into the life of each academic unit and initiated the establishment of a strong volunteer-driven program. Our academic leaders answer the following types of questions: For what purposes do we need to raise money? What is your vision for this institution? How is the money that will be raised central to that vision?

Campaign UCLA was shaped at the heart of our academic enterprise. Early in the planning stages, we asked our faculty, deans, and provosts to articulate their vision for the intellectual life of the campus. We asked them how private philanthropy would transform their departments and programs, and take them to the forefront of teaching and research in the twenty-first century. The result was not merely a "wish list" of funding projects, but a blueprint for the future.

Beyond goal-setting and establishing priorities, the academic leadership helps development staff present their case to prospective donors. For example, during donor solicitation meetings, a dean will discuss why his or her school requires more funding. It is not enough to say that 20 more endowed chairs are needed in the School of Medicine; the provost for medical sciences must be able to explain why that is so, and why five or 10 chairs will not do.

Because all deans have long lists of priority projects, they are asked to carefully scrutinize and prioritize their objectives, for instance, ranking the importance of new construction relative to increasing endowed scholarships. Our development officers advise academic leaders as to which items may be supportable through private philanthropy.

At UCLA, deans are expected to participate in the development process, but running their schools, not fund raising, is their principal responsibility. It is important to understand that some deans are less inclined to personally involve themselves in fund raising and may require guidance from the development staff.

Like any large institution, UCLA has organizational charts that define the relative status of each administrative position; however, many exceptions are made for development operations, where I have been comfortable with a team approach rather than a hierarchical one. When planning a solicitation call, for instance, who does what is determined on a case-by-case basis. Generally, development officers guide and focus the efforts of faculty and volunteers. Here, too, flexibility is essential and, given the particular situation, any one of us could take the lead. Although the volunteer or dean would typically make the introductions or even make the "ask," staff sometimes do so if they are best acquainted with the prospect.

During our first campaign, I had a remarkably gifted team, and the same is true for the current Campaign UCLA. One of their primary jobs is to be sensitive to the unspoken signals that occur during discussions with prospective donors, deans, and volunteers. I trusted their instincts and took their lead. Particularly with major gift solicitations, development staff have made me realize that most people are uncomfortable making commitments to an institution unless they are asked by its CEO. I have always made myself available for those types of discussions.

Prior to a solicitation visit, our chief development officer is responsible for bringing together the best combination of individuals to discuss how to connect the vision and the needs of UCLA with the needs, wishes, and interests of the individual donor. He will convene a strategy session with the appropriate faculty member and volunteer to decide where the meeting should take place, to set the agenda, and to brief the team. He makes certain the solicitation meeting is well orchestrated and everyone is well prepared. Every member of the team recognizes that even the smallest details are critical to the success of our volunteers and academic leaders; little is left to chance. When issues and conflicts arise, staff, faculty, and, in some cases, volunteer leaders meet and debate until a resolution is reached. Depending upon the situation, I would also participate in those meetings.

Before and during UCLA's campaigns, I convened faculty and senior administrators at retreats for the purpose of brainstorming and focusing on where the university was headed with its fund-raising effort. Joining me in those sessions were representatives from development, university relations, finance and information management, and alumni relations, as well as my Executive Committee and Academic Senate leadership. I was a full participant in the creation of each campaign plan, and always a willing partner with regard to meeting key prospects. Because I made fund raising a priority, our own internal bureaucracy worked more efficiently. Expediency and efficiency remain two of our most important internal objectives.

The final months of my chancellorship coincided with the leadership gifts phase of Campaign UCLA and an intensive period of planning for the campaign's public launch. Consequently, fund raising emerged as one of my top three priorities, but, compared to a decade ago, I spent less time brainstorming and planning with senior staff because our team was more experienced. The first campaign had taught us valuable lessons. Everyone now understands his or her role and how to use the chancellor's time most effectively. Our consultants proved to be an invaluable resource, particularly with regard to research, strategy development, and communications and marketing planning. I continued to take part in discussions regarding the solicitation of major gifts, and I would never fail to attend a UCLA Foundation dinner or a Campaign Cabinet meeting. The chancellor's presence at such functions is often critical to creating a sense of teamwork among staff and volunteers.

I also regularly attended meetings with deans and development staff to discuss the priorities they had placed on their fund-raising goals—for instance, finding the right mix of capital versus endowment, or setting the amount of their goal. If I could not be present, the associate vice chancellor-development would attend in my absence, and the primary message would be delivered by an academic leader I had designated—usually a provost or our executive vice chancellor (who, as chief academic officer, oversees all components of the academic enterprise). As in major gift solicitations, attendance at faculty/staff development meetings is decided on a case-by-case basis.

In an effort to remain accessible to our academic leadership, senior development staff, and volunteer leaders, I allotted time each week to discuss campaign issues and overall fund-raising strategies. Every team member must clearly understand his or her role and trust that colleagues will carry out their assignments. Our chief development officer clarifies the roles of everyone involved.

For institutional needs, I took my cues from our academic leadership and senior development officers. As the chief executive of UCLA, I had to be able to share in and articulate our vision, even if the fulfillment of that vision lies many years in the future and well beyond my own career. Even when all the critical elements are present—a large pool of donors, a superior staff, and a strong cadre of volunteers—we must still be ready to justify our academic needs to our local, regional, and global communities.

One of the most basic truths I've learned about fund raising during the past three decades is that one must take a long-term view. Any campaign has two goals: to raise the level of private support, and to do it in a sustainable way. During our first campaign, we nearly tripled our support on an annual basis, moving from $35 million to $104 million in total gifts and pledges per year. Had we slipped back right after the campaign to the $35 million level, the effort would not have been a success.

How does one move from the concept of raising sustainable funds to actually doing so? We addressed this question in part by creating a strong stewardship program that acknowledges donors over a continuum, and by taking a long-term view of all development efforts.

One aspect of taking a long-term view is to collect and analyze data for trends you can use. For instance, our chief development officer recently reviewed the top 50 individual donors in the medical sciences. He looked for correlations in their cumulative giving records, such as the date and size of their first gift and date and size of their largest gift. He found no correlation between size of first gift and size of largest gift. Some donors whose first gifts were $5 are now giving in the multi-million-dollar range. Other donors gave

$1 million the first time and that remained their largest gift. The average length of time between a donor's first gift and largest gift was 13.5 years, but some donors spanned 20 to 35 years between first gift and largest gift. The donors of the largest single gift in UC history to date—$45 million in 1996—started making $50 contributions to UCLA's annual fund in 1978. These numbers illustrate the importance of taking a long-term view because they make us recognize that we are building relationships for an institution that will last much longer than any of us.

VOLUNTEER INVOLVEMENT

I have come to appreciate the critical role that volunteer leadership plays in any fund-raising endeavor. Our former campaign chairman was the first to show us that a relatively few, extremely committed volunteers can make a difference. The current campaign chairman also exemplifies that spirit. One of the greatest benefits of the 1980s campaign was that we reorganized UCLA's volunteer leadership and established a new level of quality and dedication. Although extraordinarily gifted volunteers led our first campaign, we recognized that we still did not have the optimal mix of individuals. To remedy this situation, we stepped outside the extant structures and created new ones. For example, the Campaign Cabinets were formed in response to our institutional need for strong volunteer leadership to carry us through our first and current campaigns. In a similar effort to strengthen The UCLA Foundation, we identified and cultivated specific individuals whom we knew would enliven our fund-raising effort. The UCLA Foundation is a volunteer-driven, non-profit, public benefit corporation that accepts and administers private gifts to UCLA. Gifts are invested, according to the choice of the donor, by the foundation or by the UC Board of Regents.

Volunteer leaders and senior development staff often discuss how to most effectively use a volunteer's time. They must ask themselves how to place the focus on raising money. To address this dilemma, volunteer leaders and senior development officers collaborate to review each of UCLA's board members. They make suggestions regarding who would enjoy serving on certain kinds of committees or who has technical skills. Key volunteers are then assigned to the development officers who know them best. The volunteers are asked, for example, the following: "We realize you can't do everything, but would you serve on the External Relations Committee in addition to being on the School of Engineering and Applied Science Board?" Querying volunteer leaders on how to improve our relations and strategies with other volunteers is an ongoing process.

During the first campaign, development officers and volunteer leaders collaborated on weaving together the new and established groups. Deciding how we could move from a staff-driven fund-raising program to a volunteer/staff team approach was an extremely time-consuming process, yet one that was mandatory to achieving our goals. Our plan worked well, and I am confident UCLA's current fund-raising endeavors will meet with success because we took the time to lay this necessary groundwork.

Currently, our three key volunteer leaders are the chairman and the president of The UCLA Foundation and the chairman of the Campaign Cabinet. I met with them monthly, and several times a month they meet with the associate vice chancellor-development and other senior staff members. These sessions were invaluable as we planned and advanced the current campaign. I relied on volunteers to provide varied perspectives and welcomed their judgment and counsel.

The Campaign Cabinet plays an important role in shaping the campaign and determining its outcome. On a day-to-day basis, Campaign Cabinet members work closely with the vice chancellor for external affairs and our chief development officer. They represent UCLA to the community and identify other volunteers who can provide leadership and make financial contributions. They also review our campaign budget and help develop policy and strategy.

Most of the volunteers who serve on the Campaign Cabinet do double-duty on The UCLA Foundation Board of Governors. The UCLA Foundation has 100 governors, who are drawn from our most active volunteers, and is staffed under the guidance of the associate vice chancellor-development. The current Board of Governors is the result of a recently completed reorganization of the university's volunteer structure—one that more closely aligns our volunteer organizations with our development efforts.

One of the challenges we faced in the past several years was how to increase the involvement of UCLA Foundation volunteers who were not actively engaged with the campus. They had expressed their desire to be more involved, yet, as an institution, we had failed to provide sufficient avenues for their direct participation.

Understanding that there is no quick fix, we decided to take the time to ascertain their concerns and interests through a focus-group study. The foundation's officers and staff, who are also key university development staff, are responsible for volunteer recruitment, organization, and structure. The foundation enlists volunteers with a broad range of interests, skills, and abilities. Because these volunteers represent a tremendous and largely untapped resource, the foundation president aims to engage them more closely with specific UCLA projects and academic units. To do this effectively, he must know as much as possible about his volunteer corps.

Thus, development officers introduced the idea of using focus groups as a means of discovering how volunteer leaders view their role. Foundation trustees (as they were formerly called) were asked the following questions: What do you think you should be doing for UCLA? What do you think the university should be doing for you? What aspects of our operation would you like to see changed and why?

In every focus group, a common theme emerged: Volunteers want to be asked to do more. They want demands made upon them. They want us to request more of them than merely to be present at a board meeting once or twice a year. They ask why we invite them to meetings and then do not give them anything to do. After listening to them carefully, we wondered why we were reluctant to demand more of them.

An appropriate role for volunteers is to identify and provide access to potential donors, to offer support, and, in their own unique way, to present the case for giving to UCLA. From their personal perspective, volunteers can relate why establishing another endowed chair or building a new laboratory is important. They can offer personal testimonials to explain why they helped build a facility, or reveal how their contributions to UCLA have enriched their own lives and have enhanced or even saved the lives of others. Volunteers can provide advice and counsel to faculty and development officers on what messages are likely to be most persuasive. They can test a campaign case statement, or, in individual instances, advise on ideas to which a particular prospective donor might or might not respond.

Among the goals of the foundation's most recent volunteer board restructuring was the strengthening of volunteer leadership campuswide and the reinforcement of ties between campuswide fund-raising efforts and the academic units.

Not every academic unit at UCLA has its own volunteer advisory board, but most do, and many of them need to be strengthened. Such boards focus on their schools' individual fund-raising objectives. Some boards are deeply involved with their school. The School of Dentistry Board of Councilors, for instance, brings creative solutions and suggestions to the table, reviews the budget, and discusses faculty research projects.

Some advisory boards become involved in the reorganization of the faculty or administration. Many deans invite their boards to serve as counselors. These boards are not decision-making bodies in all respects, but the process of offering opinions gives them the power to forge new links between UCLA and the community. This last point is important. The public once perceived UCLA as an island. Today, we continually seek opportunities to integrate ourselves into the community-at-large, and our board members take their roles in this integration process seriously.

Other specialized fund-raising organizations are emerging at UCLA. One of the strongest is Women and Philanthropy at UCLA. Prior to creating this group, our development officers noted several national trends regarding women.

One important trend is that women are controlling an increasing percentage of our nation's wealth. We realized that women had never been well represented on any board at UCLA. To close this gap, we asked women in focus groups to tell us why they were not board members, why they were not donors (separately from their spouses), and what they needed from us to join our cause.

Women and Philanthropy at UCLA was born from the information gleaned from that study. The 30 women on the board, each of whom has pledged at least $25,000 to the university, recognize it as primarily a fund-raising body and know that they will be asking others to give to UCLA.

Our internal publicity efforts have made UCLA's deans, who are mostly men, more aware of the importance of women donors. As a result, the development program has been much more successful in engaging deans to attend events where they can address women directly. For many deans, this new emphasis on women donors demanded a shift in perspective, for they were accustomed to dealing with primarily male audiences and male board members.

INSTITUTIONAL INFRASTRUCTURE FOR FUND-RAISING PROGRAMS

UCLA faces two major challenges today.

- balancing internal expectations with the realities of what is possible from a fund-raising standpoint
- determining the most effective institutional development program infrastructure in which to achieve our goals

Every major educational institution of UCLA's type and size is struggling with these issues.

Based upon my experience at UCLA and upon thoughtful scrutiny of other major research universities nationwide, I initiated a campuswide reorganization designed to shift from a highly centralized development program to a broader-based system. This shift places greater responsibility for fund raising upon individual schools and their deans, many of whom welcome more autonomy in the fund-raising process. The following questions are central to our discussion: How shall we best manage the balance between unit-driven and centrally driven fund-raising efforts? How much, and when, should a dean venture out on his or her own? Who has authority to do what? Who is ultimately responsible for the success or failure of a particular program? Many of these hard decisions cross the chancellor's desk.

If, for example, I proposed $100 million worth of new buildings, our chief development officer would work with me to determine if that was realistic from a fund-raising standpoint. If it was not, we would examine other sources of revenue—state funds or bond issues, for example. This would not necessitate a change in vision, but simply an acknowledgment of what we could realistically accomplish within a limited time frame.

Deans, on the other hand, may be told by a development officer that their vision is not realizable through philanthropy. In that case, they face difficult decisions. Will they risk going against the advice of senior development officers and attempt to do it alone? Will they seek other sources to fund their vision? Will they change their vision? All these responses are appropriate. During a campaign, however, this process could pose problems in terms of realizing campuswide goals and maintaining a unified campus vision. We do not want to fragment our team approach and engender conflict.

Since its first campaign, UCLA has maintained a good strategic balance between campuswide and unit-based development operations. Certain aspects of the central operation are crucial to our success, such as the Prospect Management and Tracking System, a comprehensive management tool that coordinates prospect assignments across campus and assists staff in monitoring and tracking prospect activity for purposes of cultivation, solicitation, and stewardship. PMATS is a unit of the Campaign Operations department in the central development office.

Quality control issues are also important to our campuswide effort. For example, with more than 80 development officers working on a broad range of assignments in every corner of the campus, all UCLA fund-raising proposals should be recognizable as being from the same institution. Written proposals need not be identical, but they should reflect the highest priorities of the university as conveyed in the text and contain certain familiar elements, such as structure and layout.

For development officers, the benefits of a decentralized, unit-based system include working directly with the deans on specific projects or prospects. Never having worked in the School of Engineering and Applied Science, for instance, our chief development officer cannot be expected to know all its needs in minute detail. Only the dean and the development director he or she works with every day know the issues of their school inside-out. They are positioned to move quickly should an opportunity arise.

From the fiscal perspective, unit-based operations provide a more specific accounting of the revenues and expenses for any given program. Given the facts, rather than a hunch, the university can decide whether to support a program or whether it can support itself.

In our own research, we have found that thriving development programs are a hybrid of both centralized and unit-based concepts. Ultimately, we aim to meld the best aspects of each. Our challenge is to make sure we do not lose what is best about centralization. Can we strike a balance that allows deans to have ownership of their programs and the opportunity to be successful?

We expect these changes to affect day-to-day development operations and certain schools more dramatically than others; however, we anticipate that the campuswide development strategies and tactics used in major gift solicitations will remain essentially unchanged. Such strategies rest upon the firm groundwork already laid in the areas of volunteer leadership and development operations.

We understand that there is no single ideal organizational structure within which to raise funds. The design UCLA is moving toward demands—consistent with its own unique culture—a willingness to innovate, take risks, remain flexible, and, most importantly, work together as a team. A necessary part of that dynamic lies in finding solutions to the challenges, tensions, surprises, and conflicts that accompany any worthwhile endeavor. The strength and creativity of our team, coupled with the skill and vision of my successors, will ensure UCLA's prominence well into the next century and beyond.

CHAPTER 4

Successful Fund Raising at a Medium-Sized Public University with a Foundation

Rowan University

by Philip A. Tumminia and Lori D. Marshall

T he short (and perhaps unlikely) description of the role of advancement at Rowan College includes three things: 1) we have had an external fund-raising board since 1983, 2) we have had a senior administrator for advancement since 1984, and 3) the advancement chief's office is a 17-second walk from the president's office. We believe our strange trio of distinguishing factors in successful fund-raising is key for public institutions to survive and thrive. Our short list of fund-raising successes proves the formula works.

- By 1991, we had acquired more than $1.2 million in annual gifts and pledges from private sources, an extraordinary sum for a public college of our size with just seven years invested in private sector fund raising.
- In 1992, we were the recipients of the largest private gift ever made to a public institution, the now historic $100 million pledge by Henry and Betty Rowan.
- Since 1992, we have raised between $5 and $6 million each year.
- In 1996, we expanded on our brief record of private fund raising and on the significant Rowan gift to again make history by offering four-

Editor's Note: Rowan College earned university status in March 1997 from the New Jersey Commission on Higher Education. Although the title of this chapter has been revised to Rowan University, the text retains references to Rowan College

year tuition scholarships to every member of the first engineering class. In just 10 months, we solicited 44 gifts from 36 individuals and corporate partners to make the scholarships part of the recruitment process for these top students from around the country.

All this came about alternately by design and by what we might call fund-raising serendipity. Even with our meticulous plans and many months of donor cultivation, our greatest successes at Rowan have been surprising to us. We are a medium-size, state-supported comprehensive college. Until the early 1980s, significant private fund raising was a remote possibility for us. But Rowan's recent history shows an intentional, systematic shift in institutional commitment to fund raising and a private-public partnership between government and private donors.

Like those at most public institutions our size, our senior staff had traditionally consisted of a president, a senior financial officer, and an academic provost. A board of trustees provided governance. Fund raising—the alumni annual fund, some scholarship endowments and projects for various athletic booster clubs and cultural activities—was not organized. But in 1983 and 1984, we made changes that would chart new territory for the college and initiate a fledgling institutional advancement program.

In 1983, we incorporated an external development board to provide a focal point for fund-raising efforts and actively pursue private donations for specific projects. In 1984, we established the position of chief advancement officer (CAO)—vice president for institutional advancement—consolidating under him all then-current advancement functions and creating new functions.

CREATING THE DEVELOPMENT FUND

The original Development Fund cannot be described without appearing to diminish the already limited charge of the fund board. For a public institution such as Rowan, even the existence of the Development Fund was something of a novelty. In 1983, some observers saw the fund as superfluous because we were part of the state system. But within that comparatively passive, unseasoned Development Fund Board were individuals who would become members of an aggressive, proactive fund-raising and friend-raising team.

The board was formed to acquire and administer private and corporate gifts to the college that had a 501(c)3 status. The board operated quietly. The state's support for its colleges had never been extravagant, but was regarded as adequate and appropriate, given the prevailing perspective on publicly funded higher education. State legislators and institutional administrators assumed that the colleges would remain highly dependent on the state legislature for funding of their education initiatives. A particularly generous state administration might occasionally grant marginal increases in funding to higher education, but static or depressed funding was more likely. The college usually sought only the program growth and physical maintenance that current state support and tuition revenue could make possible.

When the former president initiated the Development Fund in 1983, the idea of creating a private funding arm for a public institution was still relatively new. In 1984, the newly appointed president made fund raising a priority for the institution. With a largely unheralded beginning, the Development Fund acquired small scholarships, grants, and gifts-in-kind. The fund board eventually introduced a gala event to attract public attention to its efforts on behalf of the college and began a scholarship breakfast aimed at exhibiting its interest in opportunities for minority students at the college. The board members, representing many segments of the college community and regional friends, were interested in the college and committed to the board. In most cases, however, they lacked the standing in the financial, social, and political arenas to directly and significantly benefit our efforts or influence those who could. The board's inherently low-key composure produced proportionately low-key results.

APPOINTING THE CHIEF ADVANCEMENT OFFICER

Barely a year after the Development Fund was created, Rowan installed a vice president for institutional advancement. Because our CAO had no predecessor and few public college peers, we took some cues from private institutions' advancement structures. The CAO set about managing the team of professionals already involved in advancement and began to develop other functions as well.

At first, the advancement division consisted of college relations, alumni relations, civic and governmental relations, college publications, and admissions. New positions and offices would ultimately add marketing, records and research, corporate and foundation relations, and the annual fund to the division roster.

Many still see the presence of the undergraduate admissions office in our advancement structure as unusual, but the office has been an essential part of our marketing and development plan. Under the CAO's supervision, admissions, with an already massive responsibility in the academic division, has been able to find institutional support it could not have found otherwise. But, as we will explain later, it's more important that our undergraduate admission program has become an integral part of the marketing strategy for the college and a selling point for cultivating private support.

THE PLAN FOR INSTITUTIONAL ADVANCEMENT

When established, the institutional advancement program had three goals: 1) enhancing the academic profile of new students, 2) establishing a viable private and corporate fund-raising program, and 3) developing a three-year plan to reposition the college in the minds of key business leaders, legislators, and potential students. We needed to create the image of a high-quality academic institution. To do so, we established a marketing approach to all aspects of our advancement program. This new approach allowed us to learn a great deal about what students, faculty, corporate friends, politicians, and those outside our college community thought of us. A realistic and sometimes negative picture began to emerge. Our advancement program began to address the problems we identified.

In announcing the 1992 Rowan gift, the *New York Times* described us as a "meat and potatoes" institution. It was a fair assessment for the most part, especially in drawing a comparison between us and the better-known public institutions in our state and region. Many in the region who knew Rowan as a state school but had no direct knowledge of the college may have described us the same way—substantial but not spectacular. To use the vernacular of many student applicants, we were a "safe" school. But "safe" and "meat and potatoes" did not do justice to the many standout features of the college, primarily several top-drawer faculty members, our nationally ranked academic programs, and a president who had a vision for the institution. In re-crafting the college's image, we aggressively marketed the achievements and awards of our outstanding professors. Cultivating respect for what we offered students and future employers became the business of everyone in advancement. With the support of the institutional advancement committee of the Board of Trustees, the CAO worked with his staff to communicate the distinguishing features of the institution. The administration, the faculty, and anyone working in development were partners in telling the story. The president took the lead in defining the new vision to our external publics.

Each office in the advancement division was charged with certain goals, strategies, and objectives. With each director reporting to the CAO, concerns, ideas, and activities could be handled on an intimate, daily basis. The institutional advancement program increased community and media attention to our fund-raising success and worked its most notable transformation in the undergraduate admissions office. Since beginning our process of assessment and reshaping, SAT scores for incoming freshmen have increased by 280 points. Class rank increased to the top quarter from the top third, and Rowan now admits only 42 percent of the students who apply. This selectivity caused consternation among those applicants who were rejected because of the higher academic standards. After being considered a "safe" school for so many years, Rowan was vilified for raising standards that increased denials to freshmen and transfers. Parents, students, and high school counselors did not always appreciate a more selective admission process, even if it was part of an effort to enhance educational excellence. In 1996, for example, we received 4,688 freshman applications, made offers to far less than half of these applicants, and received deposits from 1,041 accepted students. Breaking with the "safe" school image, an increasing number of deposit-paid students began calling Rowan their first choice.

Clearly, interest in Rowan has become strong and widespread. Although the Rowan gift has developed great momentum for the college since 1992, our advancement efforts at repositioning the college in the mid-1980s were the first steps toward recording these remarkable admissions statistics.

THE FUNCTION OF ADVANCEMENT WITHIN ROWAN'S OVERALL PLAN

The president has reiterated in several forums our intent to thoughtfully and actively shape the college and its future with an emphasis on advancement and fund-raising. Advancement is more than ever at the fore of our institutional planning because we are intent on becoming more self-determining as an organization. Because we know we will need private support in increasing proportions to our state allocations, we must include advancement staff in the development of our institutional goals and strategies. Thus, the president and CAO confer frequently on a spontaneous basis outside regular meetings of the president's cabinet and Board of Trustees. Our sense of the urgent need to keep close contact between the president and the CAO recently determined which senior staff would be relocated on campus. We made sure the advancement offices remained near the president's office, where we felt they had to be.

The developing role of advancement at our public institution is something of an evolutionary hybrid. In scientific theory, the concept of evolution suggests the adaptive, reactive development a species undergoes to survive and flourish in hostile circumstances. To survive and flourish, Rowan College evolved a new fund-raising model, not simply as a reactive, instinctive response to difficulty, but as a contemplated, deliberate move. Our advancement evolution began in the early 1980s, and its development coincided with two institutional planning projects. The first project was primarily an analysis, but the second began to change the college.

Through a year-long process of strategic planning in 1991, we made some difficult decisions to cope with real and projected cuts in state aid. We would alter our approach to funding the business of education at the college. We would focus on satisfying the projected market with our programming and services. Although unpopular at times, our effort at determining priorities and needs demonstrated to observers on and off campus that we were concerned with serving our public well and spending our money wisely, even if it was painful. When fully implemented, the strategic plan accomplished a "leveling out" for the institution that ultimately gave us mid-range stability and the opportunity to plan for long-term development that was less dependent on the vagaries of state appropriations. At the same time, through the Development Fund, we increased our commitment to supplementing the college's resources with private giving.

The progress of the Development Fund was significant, not just for its charge to raise private funds, but for what its very existence said about the college and where it was headed. Our goal was to transform the institution from a respected state college to a regional university of prominence. Our proactive Development Fund Board would be the emerging model for public institution fund raising. This new commitment to garnering private support was about more than money. Certainly the financial benefits were essential. But in addition to the money, the gifts we won would lend credibility to our vision. We had made clear our commitment to spend state aid and tuition revenues wisely. With a newly refocused, stronger institutional infrastructure, our development efforts were not overshadowed by fiscal doom. When the Development Fund asked for private or corporate support, the donor could count on giving to enhance an already viable, visionary organization. We would be a good investment.

We determined that our limiting step would be defined by the energy and commitment of our own advancement effort. We revised our perspective on state support. Rather than being the beginning and end of resources for the college, state support became part of a larger pie. We could not do without it, but neither would we be hemmed in by its fluctuating nature. We would continue to lobby for state aid, but would not spend all our time "talking up" Rowan College solely with New Jersey politicians.

Consequently, our own burden to produce funds increased. By assuming that Rowan College could best determine where our limiting step would lie, we took responsibility for putting the institution over the top in terms of resources. Changeable as it would be, we could always depend on basic funding from the state. But now, instead of being hamstrung if state appropriations dropped when we counted on them to provide for a new program or improved equipment, we could provide on our own for that degree of distinction.

To determine our path and provide the margin of excellence throughout the institution, a shared vision—the big picture—was essential. In 1995-96, this vision was developed cooperatively, articulated formally, and published and distributed under the direct supervision of the president. In the developmental phase of the new fund-raising/positioning efforts, the vision consisted simply of key market-related issues for our institution. We actively discussed these issues and impressed them on the minds of all those who shared our interest in the future of the college.

- We would focus on excellence in academics, purposefully increasing the academic profile of our students to encourage academic prestige and career prospects for our graduates.
- Our institution would become a regional resource for mid-Atlantic higher education instead of being limited to southern New Jersey.
- We would pursue the offering of doctoral degrees.
- We would pursue university status.

Throughout the development of the vision statement, the advancement function was seen as integral to communicating and realizing the big picture.

INTEGRATING ADVANCEMENT INTO ROWAN'S OVERALL PLANNING PROCESS

Rowan's mission statement provides direction for the most fundamental activity and service we provide; it is the foundation for who we are now. Our recently drafted vision statement grows out of that mission and projects the ideals to which we aspire. By bringing external financial and intellectual support to the growth of the college, advancement makes possible the actualization of the vision. And, to a large extent, the vision cannot be conceived unless in the context of the advancement function as its significant source.

For more than 10 years, advancement has played an increasingly prominent role in the life of the college. As the advancement function matures, we plan for the president and Board of Trustees to pay even more attention to advancement. There are two main reasons for this plan.

First, when we created the division of institutional advancement in the early 1980s, the college administration was dealing with notable internal concerns of the established academic and finance divisions. Recent major state cuts had disastrously affected our instructional services and physical plant. The Board of Trustees and president necessarily attended to the most visible needs and far-reaching problems of the school. Everyone, including the advancement staff, was reacting to current circumstances.

It now appears propitious that the advancement division had to work mostly on its own in the beginning. Finding its own way to grow into an integrated institutional advancement structure seems to have been productive. The CAO was able to work with his professionals individually to develop their skills and team-work style. They in turn had the opportunity to research successful models for their new roles and find their way about, recreating service relationships with those on campus in light of the new, comprehensive advancement function.

Second, institutional advancement will clearly be pivotal in the future of the college now that we've "made the turn" in thinking about what our public institution should be and do, and how it can best be funded. The president and board must "think advancement" in the genesis of institutional policy and direction. We don't expect any fiscal windfalls in state support to offset our current needs for private supplements. We are making more links between the administrators, the Board of Trustees, and the foundation Board of Directors. As we encourage interaction, the sense of shared purpose and ownership of the institution increases and we progress with the same agenda. As we plan, we must consider what projects are fundable outside state resources—not just what projects we'd like to do, but what our market wants and what private supporters will consider worthy.

In our recent institutional planning, we did not involve the advancement function early enough or to the optimal extent. We are coping with the consequences of this oversight by spending more time with the foundation board to secure their support. We've learned a costly lesson about planning and integration. We won't make the same mistake again.

We've now embarked on a new planning process. At Rowan, our private funding buzz words have been, "to provide a margin of excellence beyond what state funds can provide." To determine our advancement path and provide the margin of excellence to which we aspire, a shared vision is crucial. The partners in the vision must be not only the administration and faculty, but anyone working in development, whether or not development is part of the job description.

In drafting a development plan of the institution, the shared vision is perhaps even more critical than for a private school, simply because so many traditional assumptions are made about how a public school should be funded. But complying with the assumptions about traditional funding sources is the limiting step for public higher education. If we continue to assume that only state dollars and tuition revenues will be sought for our operating budgets, we will never go farther than the state legislature or our enrollment will allow.

Conversely, if we rewrite the assumptions about the role of public institutions and the need for broader and deeper support than state mandate provides, the limiting step will come from within our own organization. Our shared vision will articulate the future of the college. Our own energy and commitment will determine the extent to which our vision becomes real. Our conviction in sharing the vision with the private sector will compel others to participate.

MOVING FROM DEVELOPMENT FUND BOARD TO ROWAN COLLEGE FOUNDATION

Many insiders and outsiders saw the Development Fund Board at our public college as an anomaly. But given our goals, the Development Fund was an appropriate addition to the college. Prior to 1992, the largest single gift raised by the Development Fund was $100,000 (a charitable remainder trust) in 1991. Ordinary for the fund-raising program of an established private institution, this gift was unusual for a public institution of our size.

To take the next step in cultivating major private support, the Development Fund Board had to evolve. The original 10-member group represented many segments of the college community and regional friends. They were interested in the college and committed to the board, but often lacked the standing in the financial, social, and political arenas to directly benefit our efforts or influence those who could.

Although our senior administration sensed the need to counteract the decreases in state support by expanding the role of the Development Fund, some board members, administrative staff members, faculty members, and peers at sister institutions failed to grasp the same imperative. They were short-sighted or uninitiated at best and lazy or benignly skeptical at worst. But real knowledge was compelling. Our research into private giving and some of our committee members' own affiliations with private institutions' fund-raising efforts provided a veteran first team in what was a new game for us. These internal mentors gave the new plan legitimacy because of their experience with the college and their relationships to key people in the region. They knew what we needed and they knew how to get it. Our CAO summed up the plan: "We have to respond to the changes we anticipate in funding higher education. The way to do that is with private sector monies. We have to move from a primitive development fund to a mature foundation."

To further validate the development plan, the CAO invited a CASE consultant team to campus to review our existing structure and resources. They saw the opportunities and needs for development clearly, and recommended that we seek the assistance of corporations and individuals who could make truly significant gifts to the college.

The necessary philosophical and practical shift in the board would require replacing most of the members and enlarging the group to include more key decision makers. Working with the CAO, the Development Fund executive committee, and the institutional advancement committee of the Board of Trustees, we drew up a plan for propelling the Development Fund into a new era for our public institution.

The agreement and enthusiasm of key people on the existing Development Fund Board helped make for a successful transition. The chair of the Development Fund was also a former vice chair of the Board of Trustees and well-versed in the culture of the college and in higher education in general. She appreciated the potential gravity of state budget cuts in appropriations to the college. She considered our excellent programs "the best-kept secret in South Jersey" and took great pleasure in introducing her friends and colleagues to the school. She had a long-term commitment to the college, especially to our arts programs. She moved in the company of people accustomed to supporting private education and she knew how valuable external support would be to our public college.

We assembled a list of executives from the private and public business sector in our region, and decided that directors had to be vice presidents or presidents of corporations. The idea was to assemble a board of opinion leaders to enhance our image in the external community. By securing participation from key CEOs, the image of the board and our fund-raising fortunes improved considerably.

Are these intrusive measures extraordinary for a public institution? In the early 1980s, they were unusual outside private schools, but are virtually essential now for institutions of our genre to compete and excel in higher education. Cuts in state aid have convinced us that our largely untested, unorthodox plan for funding public higher education was the right one.

Currently, our advancement budget shows an annual average of $4.213 million contributed to the endowment (exclusive of asset gains/losses). The foundation's percentage of the college's budgeted revenues and expenses is 3 percent of the state appropriation and 1.3 percent of the total. Initially, the foundation and college allocated funds by project. The long-term goal is for the foundation to contribute 5 percent of its endowment to the college on an annual basis.

Only recently has the advancement program contributed significantly to the development of the college's facilities and equipment. Notable projects include construction of the engineering building (as stipulated in the Rowan endowment) and installation of a new orchestra shell for the concert hall. The foundation makes a somewhat invisible contribution to the college budget each year in scholarships. More than $1,250,000 in merit-based student aid awards—467 full or partial tuition scholarships—are made each year. The foundation will disburse funds to the college for the purchase of equipment for the new engineering building, as well as strengthening the academic support for engineering, faculty development, and other capital projects.

With the great fortune of the Rowan gift came a great deal of uncertainty about how to re-position the college and about how such a remarkable resource would affect everything we did. We sought professional counsel immediately, investing $200,000 in a study on marketing the college after the Rowan endowment. In the five years since then, we've also invested in image consulting and public relations assistance for the college in general. We're confident that these efforts also affected our activities in student recruitment because 230 points of the previously mentioned 280-point SAT score increase occurred after beginning our advancement program.

THE ROLE OF THE FOUNDATION IN ADVANCEMENT

When Rowan College appointed its Development Fund Board, the lines between its role and the role of the Board of Trustees were clearly drawn. Perhaps because of the fund's originally low-key nature and the well-established governing role of the trustees, many people viewed the Development Fund as insignificant in the scheme of things at the college. That view has changed in the past several years, along with the level and frequency of interaction among the senior staff, the foundation board, and the trustees. Planning for all the advancement efforts has naturally become more integrated.

The foundation's primary purpose is to "raise money and obtain gifts-in-kind and to channel those monies and gifts to assist Rowan College in meeting or surpassing its educational mission." Central to the language in the foundation mission statement is the recognition that public colleges and universities—as has been the case with private institutions—need the support of alumni, faculty and friends of the college, the corporate sector, and foundations to provide the margin of excellence that characterizes outstanding institutions.

The Foundation Board of Directors meets quarterly, with committee meetings preceding the main quarterly sessions. Informal contact among board members happens at events on and off campus. For instance, the annual golf outing offers a day of social interaction with college staff, trustees, foundation board members, alumni, and friends of the college. A guest lecture or cultural event brings together a somewhat different mix of supporters, but the opportunity for shared experience and relationship building is there, too.

The foundation board contains leaders of our regional business community. They bring a network of friends and a wealth of experience to our efforts. As a public institution, Rowan must have people on its fund-raising board who have the stature within the state to project an image of competent, conservative management of donors' gifts. Board members must now have experience handling funds because the fiduciary responsibilities of the board have increased markedly. Also, our success at managing funds has attracted other donors. We need an active board that assists in attracting new gifts, manages the existing endowment, and is recognized for its sound stewardship.

The composition of the board is rather homogenous in a professional sense. All members of the board are successful businesspeople, and no one is below the rank of vice president at his or her respective interest. On the other hand, the board is diverse, with members from privately held companies, public corporations, and a handful who are independently wealthy. The directors hail from throughout the southern New Jersey region and, in a few cases, from greater Philadelphia. One individual is the CEO of one of New Jersey's top five businesses, with $1.3 billion in sales nationwide. Another is a retired banker with a wealth of contacts.

As our advancement functions, foundation activity, and fund-raising approach have evolved, so has our interest in the experience of board members. In our earliest days with the Development Fund, our board members displayed a rather limited range of fund-raising skills and activities. Later, we aggressively sought decision-makers and fund-raising cultivators. Now, with a fully mature foundation and an endowment that has grown exponentially, we do not necessarily look for board members who are fund-raisers. We still rely on the Board of Directors to contribute financially, spend time in leadership of the foundation, and lend credibility to our efforts simply by their commitment. But we now also need individuals who can share their expertise in managing the endowment and handling our investment portfolio. The sheer size of our holdings has challenged a staff that—until the Rowan gift—had only to monitor a traditional interest-bearing account, some mutual funds, and certificates of deposit. Since 1992, our directors' financial savvy has, in some cases, become more valuable than their ability to generate new fund-raising leads.

THE DUTIES OF FOUNDATION DIRECTORS

For three reasons, we have drafted a document formally delineating the duties of foundation directors. First, the description of duties gives prospective board members a clear list of expectations should they accept an invitation to serve on the board. Second, the list emphasizes the distinction between the Foundation Board of Directors and the College Board of Trustees. Third, the description of duties provides a benchmark for judging the performance of each individual. On only two occasions have we needed to refer to the duties list when asking a director to re-evaluate his commitment to the foundation. In each case, the individual conceded that he had not been able to execute his commitment in the specific manner required and agreed to relinquish his position.

In each situation where the director fell short of the benchmark, the financial commitment was not the problem. Writing checks to the foundation is a simple duty for nearly all board members. The sticking point for most of the directors who disappointed us was their commitment to attend meetings and participate in activities. Naturally, seating a quorum for quarterly meetings is crucial (once in 13 years have we failed to seat a quorum). But more distressing to us than the procedural difficulties we might have without a quorum is the morale problem a negligent member causes among members who are faithful to their charge. We try to deliberately engage directors in teamwork that makes them accountable to each other. Committee meetings and conference calls help us maintain contact and be productive throughout the year. But because the full board meets only four times yearly, absences are conspicuous. Repeated absences are intolerable, and the executive director of the foundation must discuss the matter with the individual involved.

Prior to the Rowan gift, the foundation had no notable experience in serving the interests of a major donor or in investing or spending such wealth. Even our most seasoned businesspeople had little expertise in managing endowment funds on this scale. Some on the Board of Trustees envisioned sweeping opportunities for using the capital to meet needs that had long been denied in our college budget. The Foundation Board of Directors was inherently more conservative and cautious. There was little middle ground. Those on one side of the spectrum staggered under frugal fiduciary responsibility, while those on the other side swaggered with the wild expectations of sudden wealth.

Mediation was imperative. The president and CAO addressed both boards to achieve some moderation in their perspectives. In this phase of growing pains, most everyone had a poor grasp of priorities, although many had the best interests of the college at heart. As the CAO says now, "As long as we have the best interest of the institution in mind, there is no conflict. The challenge is knowing what's ultimately best for the institution."

We now see a more frequent meeting of the minds between the Board of Trustees and the Foundation Board of Directors. The fundamental challenge in maintaining the two boards is the relationship between them, rather than their individual relationships to the college or administration. With the president and CAO acting as mediators, the previous misunderstandings over fiduciary duty and governance responsibility have lessened. Building bridges between the boards is everyone's job—president, CAO, and board members— and everyone has risen to the challenge.

ROWAN'S PROFESSIONAL ADVANCEMENT STAFF

Rowan's advancement program includes the external Rowan College Foundation and the internal administrative and support staff. The CAO is also the executive director of the current 28-member foundation. Within the college, the CAO manages a staff that includes the director of corporate and foundation relations, the coordinator of the annual fund, the coordinator of alumni relations, the director of communications, the director of college relations, the director of civic and governmental relations, and the director of admissions. To varying degrees, each office in the advancement division interacts regularly, coordinating strategies for advancement activities from student recruitment to the alumni phonathon.

The advancement team includes three distinct fund-raisers: the vice president as chief advancement officer, the coordinator of the annual fund, and the director of corporate and foundation relations. The vice president must not only advise, inspire, and coordinate fund-raisers, but must also manage them in light of the overall goals of the college as specifically indicated by its market research and strategies.

A glance at some fund-raising numbers indicates our progress.

- $1 million endowment for the School of Business Administration
- $500,000 endowment for the School of Education
- $1 million gift for developing the Institute for Urban and Public Policy

THE ADVANCEMENT TEAM

We believe the mechanics of advancement are much the same at our public institution as they have been for private schools, large and small. The entire advancement team, fund-raising and non-fund-raising, must understand the two primary goals essential for success—improving academic image for admissions and increasing private support from alumni and friends. Each office plays a critical role in this process. For example, we learned that potential donors were paying attention to how we publicized gifts and marketed the college. Behind the scenes, of course, the offices involved—college relations, admissions, and marketing—were not simply related, their interaction was critical to our overall success, and their efforts drew notice.

In fund raising itself, the foundation and the Board of Trustees help identify donors sympathetic to our vision and assist in cultivating a relationship between the donor and the CAO. The CAO works with the trustees to identify potential donors, assess their level of commitment, research the prospects, and develop a script that moves the prospect to commitment. The CAO also manages the rest of his team involved with image-building, marketing, and communication.

As with most public institutions, multiple boards are operating. The Board of Trustees and president have overall responsibility for the college. The Foundation Board of Directors and executive director (or CAO) have overall responsibility for fund raising and foundation management and are vested with the fiduciary responsibility for all assets of the foundation. The Alumni Association Board has responsibility for alumni activities, but is considered part of the foundation for fund-raising purposes.

The Board of Trustees and president have responsibility for allocating the funds acquired and distributed to the college by the foundation. The trustees issue reports to the foundation about their expenditures of foundation contributions. As one would expect in a dynamically evolving situation, there are many "growing pains" in this developing advancement and fund-raising environment. Who is responsible for the money? Which board determines how much is spent and for what purpose? The Rowan College Foundation grew from approximately $500,000 in total assets to $52 million in a relatively short period. Given that situation, minor problems have arisen. To the credit of all concerned, the goal of building Rowan College was always paramount and the minor problems never became major.

The trustees and Foundation Board of Directors have begun to hold joint meetings to further cement the relationship between the two bodies. As these meetings continue, we anticipate new challenges that will in turn develop a stronger, more cohesive team of leaders for the college.

THE PRESIDENT

The president is the most visible representative of the institution. As leader and spokesperson, his presence is telling; what he speaks about, where he goes, and who he associates with all create for the institution and community an "image" for Rowan College. The president must communicate with the Board of Trustees about the advancement activity and affirm to those who can help us that the college is a good investment. He must also determine the value and risk of disseminating policy and fund-raising information and the scope of disclosure to make throughout the process. The president has to be concerned with government relations. He has to be accessible to the press. He has to be concerned with external relations and the future of the college.

A president without a vision is a president who will not be raising private funds. He must have a thorough understanding of the role of advancement in the evolution of his vision for the college because it will become an integral part of what the advancement staff uses in cultivating donors for gifts.

The president is responsible for developing and defining the vision for the institution. The sense of accountability and leadership must reside in one individual, regardless of the number of people who participate in gathering ideas to create the vision. Along the way, ideas develop corporately and consensus builds, but the president must rally the college community to feel a part of the vision, to buy into it. Only after the institution is rallied to participate in developing and supporting the aspirations can the vision be "sold" to anyone else.

The president's vision statement should not be confused with a strategic plan. The strategic plan that we developed and acted on in the early 1990s was a response to particular conditions in our institutional climate. It was primarily internal, indicating how we planned to address our strengths and weaknesses. It is a decision-making process as the word strategy implies, and largely a tactical-heavy plan that we have found most effectively shepherded by the vice president/provost, even when initiated and monitored by the president. Although the strategic plan is an internal operational document that may evoke emotional responses, it should be developed in the most objective environment possible.

Conversely, the vision statement is a dreamer's document. It is about aspirations and ideals that will shape the institution for years to come. It ultimately involves tactical duties, but its genesis is in the mind of an architect unimpeded by prevailing philosophical or fiscal limitations. To intentionally remain free from as much of the tactical and mundane as possible, the desk of the president at Rowan has no personal computer. This omission by design compels interaction instead of e-mail, discussion instead of directives, and dreaming instead of deliberating.

A strategic plan builds confidence in the institution in what may be a response to dire circumstances. A vision document is inherently a positive activity that translates as grand opportunity in private funding discussions. Both documents are the responsibility of the president, whether his hand is visible throughout the development and implementation or not.

THE CAO

On a daily basis, the CAO bears the responsibility for executing the advancement plan. His staff assists in developing the strategies for the plan and ultimately carries out the tactics. The CAO must be a "player" at the institution, and must be privy to the hopes and dreams of the president and Board of Trustees. The CAO must be able to translate these ideas into a successful advancement plan. The various staff members within the office must thoroughly understand their role in the success of advancement and, equally important, must know how the interdependency of their positions contributes to the success of others.

The CAO is the embodiment of the college's fund-raising aspirations. He must set an example both as a fund-raiser and as a leader. The CAO's presence signals the importance of an activity, meeting, luncheon, or other event. He must understand his prospective donor pool as well as his institution so that relationships between each can be built. This understanding is the driving force behind a successful program.

As executive director of the foundation, the CAO provides leadership for the foundation, sets meeting agendas, and works with the membership to accomplish objectives. He seeks volunteers who can be helpful in multiple arenas, provide credibility to the organization, and make a commitment to long-term activity with the board.

What is often more elusive intellectually and more difficult to execute than the mechanics of advancement—specifically in seeking major gifts—is understanding the emotional need of the donor to leave a legacy. This need is perhaps the most novel concept to those of us in institutional advancement for public institutions because we have had little opportunity or need for personal or emotional camaraderie in seeking state assistance from emotionally uninvolved legislators. In private giving, the powerful idea of leaving a legacy often compels an individual or a board to give. Before the fund-raising team makes the ask, the institutional vision and the advancement goals must be clearly articulated. The personal nature of entrusting a legacy requires relationship-building between the advancement officer and the donor.

Sometimes the CAO must provide a "dose of reality" to fund-raising ideas from the trustees, Foundation Board of Directors, administration, or even prospective donors. Occasionally what appears to be a workable fund-raising plan cannot be successful because it has either a high overhead cost or would shift donor assets from a high priority project to one of lesser priority.

Likewise, the difficulty of the task need not be the issue on which a project is judged. For example, our market research indicated that recruiting students to our fledgling engineering program would present certain challenges. We had six enthusiastic, experienced educators with national reputations on the academic team. But with no building, little equipment, and no track record for our curricula, seating a top-notch class of freshmen would be a struggle. We determined that we could not simply recruit students for the first year, but would need to impress upon them our commitment to them through and beyond graduation. Thus, our PRIDE 2000 program was created. PRIDE 2000 would provide a full-tuition scholarship to every freshman in the first engineering class, plus internships throughout the student's education and, in some cases, provisions for employing graduates. The CAO and director of corporate and foundation relations were charged with acquiring the commitments from individuals and corporations to support 60 students from enrollment to graduation.

As one of our watershed fund-raising successes, PRIDE 2000 worked as a superior example of the fund-raising team approach. The mutual commitment to the program of the advancement staff, foundation directors, and college trustees paid off. Forty-four corporate sponsors of the foundation had already committed to the PRIDE 2000 project when we projected that 60 scholarships had to be funded. Working with the director of corporate and foundation relations, the CAO and the foundation signed up the additional partners they needed to meet their goal of underwriting scholarships for the first class of engineering students. Admissions reports show that we received 450 applications, made 155 offers, and received 103 deposits even before the extensive press coverage hit the national markets. When interest in the first-year class exceeded our already optimistic estimates for enrolling 60-75 new engineering students, the CAO, as executive director of the foundation, stepped in to encourage the board to provide the balance of the tuition scholarships to cover all 103 deposit-paid first-year engineers.

Throughout the project, the rest of the advancement division was at work to support the fund-raising and recruiting efforts. Admissions staff members were on the road selling the engineering school to students, parents, teachers, and counselors. They conducted a student search and invited those who matched our profile to on-campus engineering receptions with engineering faculty. We produced brochures and newsletters for students and counselors. College relations pitched engineering news all the way from local to national media. The work paid off handsomely. We are extending PRIDE 2000 on a somewhat smaller scale to the next class of engineering students, and adapting the model to a program for the School of Business.

LOOKING BACKWARD AND LOOKING FORWARD

In the past 13 years, we have learned that our public college cannot flourish without private funding. All the political and financial indicators that we in public higher education watch point to a continuing strain on the funding relationship between the state and its colleges. Private institutions by their nature prove that people are willing, even eager, to support worthy endeavors. Now we know that public institutions can present some of the most persuasive requests for private support.

We have now begun planning to hire more advancement professionals who can extend our reach into private-funding initiatives. Fund-raisers, both on staff and on our boards, will expand our team of institutional advocates. Institutional advancement will assume an even more significant role in planning activities for all we do.

We have worked hard at fund raising and advancement since 1983, but candor compels us to admit we had no reasonable aspirations to achieve what we have. We set specific goals that would require commitment and enthusiasm that was somewhat out of character for who we had been as an institution since 1923. We hired professionals and recruited volunteers who shared our conviction about what was possible. We listened to others, critiqued ourselves, and made difficult choices in response to the self-imposed scrutiny. We continually raised the bar after a successful reach. We did not anticipate the remarkable gifts that we have received from exceptional friends of the college, but that may have been a good thing. When confronted with the largesse of private individuals who consider our college a good place to leave a legacy, we reconsidered what we had to offer and how others perceived us. We have been encouraged about the future of public higher education supported by private individuals who share our vision. We are convinced that the advancement team approach—no matter how unorthodox for public institutions—will continue to make the difference between surviving and thriving in higher education.

CHA5PTER

Successful Fund Raising at a Small Private Liberal Arts College
Pomona College

by Peter W. Stanley

College and university advancement programs are the products of three forces—institutional history, the strengths and weaknesses of major players at critical moments, and the application of management and advancement theory. Certainly these forces have shaped the distinctive character of advancement efforts at Pomona College. Pomona's program has differed from programs at many comparable institutions, principally because of the college's location and because of two notable innovations.

Pomona is younger than any other leading private college in the United States. It was founded less than 110 years ago in a region that was still remote and relatively poor. Few could then have foreseen the dramatic waves of development that would later make southern California one of the country's richest and most dynamic regions. Over the years, however, Pomona benefited from this location in at least two ways. Its lonely beginnings inspired an enduring loyalty, and, in later years, the college shared in the prosperity that increasingly surrounded it. These advantages more than offset the region's lack of deeply rooted philanthropic traditions.

In the 1920s, Pomona decided to foster a closely integrated consortium of institutions of higher education in Claremont instead of growing into a much larger college or a small university itself. This early innovation profoundly affected the environment in which the college sought to advance and develop its resources. The growth of The Claremont Colleges into a consortium of six independent institutions sharing central services and allowing almost unimpeded cross-registration of students created a sense of dynamism, fostered friendly competition, and ultimately drew to Claremont more support than any of these institutions, including Pomona, could have attracted by itself. Without exception, however, each new institution drew some of its support from individuals, families, and foundation or corporate donors once linked principally to Pomona College. For Pomona, the good news in this was that the pie was larger. The bad news was that it had to be shared.

Pomona's greatest innovation in the field of advancement was "The Pomona Plan" for deferred giving. "The Pomona Plan" fit nicely with both the college's location and the effects of its membership in the Claremont consortium. A deferred-giving plan makes especially good sense in a part of the world to which people retire in great numbers. Strategically, it has met Pomona's dual need to be entrepreneurial and at the same time to lock in its donors. Over the years, total gifts to the college through "The Pomona Plan" have amounted to almost $120 million, of which about $60 million have been released.

POMONA'S ADVANCEMENT PROGRAM IN THE 1980s

The modern history of Pomona's advancement program began in the mid-1940s, when a Pomona College vice president, Allen Hawley, and a few trustees conceived the idea of marketing deferred gifts in an aggressive manner. Hawley, having come to his job from the newspaper business, advertised in *The Wall Street Journal* to market "The Pomona Plan." The sustained success of those efforts had lasting effects upon the entire program.

Most of the respondents to the ads were only partly interested in making a charitable gift. They were interested in tax savings, trust management, and investment assistance, in addition to leaving their money to a cause or institution they could value. A nice college like Pomona College, which could ably provide the financial services they sought, would be fine. Many, even most, had not even seen the campus, but given time and involvement many became great partisans for Pomona. Several now have their names on Pomona buildings, and generous scholarship funds are named for others. To some degree, therefore, one could say that the deferred-giving program recruited to the college donors who would not otherwise have known about it.

The success of "The Pomona Plan" gave a distinctive character to the college's development program. There is a substantial difference between seeking major gifts from constituents—alumni, trustees, parents—and seeking deferred gifts from individuals only moderately interested in the college. To some extent, the difference always exists between soliciting deferred gifts and soliciting major gifts. In soliciting a deferred gift, one tries to establish a client-professional relationship in which the donor or client gains enough confidence in the professional or solicitor to reveal what assets and needs he or she has. Only then can the professional really help the client complete his or her financial plan. Little thought is given to the needs of the college, and the professional is committed not to gaining the largest gift possible for the college, but to doing what is in the donor's best interest. In this situation, a volunteer would be in the way because the presence of a third person might inhibit the donor from talking freely.

In soliciting major gifts, volunteers play a key role. Alumni, parents, trustees, and friends are asked to consider the goals and aspirations of the college and to realign their priorities to help the college achieve these ends. Volunteers who are persuaded by the college's arguments and have already made commitments are often the best salespersons. Most frequently the prospects are asked for a predetermined amount, and the donor is left to decide whether and how that amount fits into his or her financial plan.

Over the years, Pomona's development officers tried to balance the college's program and avoid excessive reliance on deferred gifts. The culture of deferred giving usually prevailed, however. As a result of Pomona College's long and successful preoccupation with "The Pomona Plan," the college, as recently as 1980, still found itself with a development program that was staff oriented and that devoted most of its budgetary resources to deferred giving. Neither the president nor the trustees had great involvement in the development program. There were no experienced major gift volunteers. Attempts to enlist a trustee chairperson for the Centennial Campaign a few years later were unsuccessful. Members of the faculty were critical of the development program for devoting too much of its affection to the future and too little to the present.

Whatever the validity of those claims, the answer was not to dismantle a deferred-giving program that was envied by most colleges and universities in the country. What was needed was an annual giving program and a major gifts program that were as effective and distinctive as the deferred-giving program. As a result, a sustained effort was begun to bring all areas of Pomona's advancement program—fund raising, alumni relations, and public affairs—to the level of excellence of the deferred-giving program.

This new energy and excellence would have four bases. One was the generally positive view most alumni had of the college. In the 1980s, as this reorientation of the program began, Pomona differed from many other good colleges in having almost no alienated alumni. Most alumni recalled good experiences and liked the people they had met at the college. The second was the exceptional ability of President and Mrs. David Alexander in cultivating good relationships with alumni and other constituents. The third was a coterie of strong trustees led by a dedicated chairman, H. Russell Smith, who was one of the most respected businessmen in the country. The fourth was an already strong alumni office and alumni association. Early on, steps were taken to increase the effectiveness of the Public Affairs Office so that it could become an additional source of strength. Under the leadership of Donald Pattison, the college's award-winning publications have played a major role in deepening alumni support and introducing Pomona to new constituencies.

When no trustee who was asked would assume leadership of the Centennial Campaign of the 1980s, the campaign proceeded under the leadership of the board chairman, the chair of the development committee of the board, the president, and the vice president for development. Campaign strategy was developed initially by the vice president and vetted by the other three. The vice president met frequently with the board chairman to discuss problems or roadblocks. Most of the solicitations of individuals were done by staff. Trustees did all the solicitations of corporations, however, and they solicited foundations when they had particular leverage. Several trustees with leverage in the Los Angeles corporate community were especially helpful. This informal structure was sufficient to see the campaign through to a successful conclusion, but many who were closely involved believe that even more could have been achieved if a more traditional and theoretically correct organization had been in place.

The campaign was kicked off publicly on Founders Day, 14 October 1982, with a goal of $80 million. It was to end on the same day and month in 1987. Well before the end of the campaign, however, it became clear that the goal would be achieved, and plans were made to raise the goal to $100 million. Then came the unexpected news of a magnificent bequest of perhaps $40 million from the estate of Liliore Green Rains. As a result, the trustees raised the original goal of the campaign by $50 million to $130 million and extended the time to 30 June 1988, the end of the fiscal year. The final total raised was $134.5 million, not counting more than $22 million of regular deferred gifts received in the course of the campaign. New deferred gifts were excluded from campaign totals in response to the long-standing complaint that Pomona's development program was too oriented toward uncertain dates in the future. Pomona wanted its campaign to make a discernible difference in the educational quality of the college's programs—to be *felt* on the campus.

In addition to Mrs. Rains' bequest, three principal reasons accounted for the campaign's success. The most important of these was the giving of Pomona College families, including three unusually generous gifts from trustee families. Thanks to leadership and active solicitation by trustees, gifts from California foundations and corporations played a larger role than might have been expected, given the growing shift in philanthropic priorities away from higher education. The final source of the campaign's success was bequests, most of which were the bounty of the long emphasis on deferred giving.

Although the Centennial Campaign met its dollar goals, and its success gave needed confidence to the campus and, especially, the trustees, its subsidiary goals of involving more volunteers in the college and of identifying more major gifts volunteers were most effectively advanced by the Alumni Fund.

Before the campaign, a task force had been formed to do a self-study of the Alumni Association. This group determined that the number one way the alumni could serve the college was through fund raising. Arriving in 1979, Vice President Ted Gibbens discovered a cadre of able and energetic alumni leaders. These leaders believed that Pomona College deserved a wider reputation and that their energy could help bring greater achievement and recognition to the college. Having just come from Harvard University where much of the fund raising was done through class organizations, Gibbens was pleased when Pomona alumni asked, "Shouldn't we be doing some fund raising by class?" One persistent alumnus insisted that a class agent program be put into place, and a pilot program was attempted using five classes. Because only one person worked in annual giving at that time, the program could not be sustained. What was attempted successfully, however, was a reunion gift program.

Until then, staff members in the Alumni Office had never worked in fund raising. Alumni programs such as reunions, club activities, and alumni college were purposely separate from fund raising. The first year of reunion gifts was the 25th reunion of Lee Harlan, the alumni director, and the 50th reunion of the father of the assistant alumni director. Because of these connections, the alumni staffers were willing to staff those two reunion fund drives. Both were successful, and the 50th reunion fund of the Class of 1930 exceeded expectations. On the strength of that success, the Class of 1931 raised even more money and remarkably achieved 100 percent participation.

From there the program accelerated. Classes wanting to have campaigns exceeded the staff's ability to assist them until the annual giving staff grew from one to four persons. Fifteen years later, all classes have had three reunion gift campaigns. Volunteer committees were formed, prospect-rating sessions were held, and major gift strategies were developed. The knowledge of volunteers and prospects gained from these campaigns is the basis of the major gifts program and the capital campaign of the 1990s.

POMONA'S ADVANCEMENT PROGRAM IN THE 1990s

The success of the Centennial Campaign masked for some the difficulties inherent in Pomona's tradition of staff-driven solicitation of major gifts and the continuing prominence of deferred giving. The work involved in this sort of fund raising is often invisible to faculty, alumni, and even trustees. A fund-raising consultant in the mid-1990s thought it significant, for example, that many Pomona trustees, faculty, and major gift prospects referred to the college's fund-raising success as "miraculous" and its development staff as "miracle workers." As the number of "miracle workers" declined and assignments shifted following the campaign, deferred giving began to reassert its dominance. In the early 1990s, deferred gifts once again comprised half or more of the funds raised. A new president, arriving in 1991, feared that Pomona might underestimate what had been achieved in the recent campaign and take too rosy a view of its future prospects.

Two other challenges faced Pomona as it charted its development agenda for the future. For the first time in the college's history, some potential donors began to say that the college already had its fair share of the world's goods. At the same time, a number of conservative alumni took exception to developments occurring in the academy in general and at Pomona in particular. As new needs continued to appear during the early and mid-1990s, the college realized the need to re-energize its constituency.

Accordingly, the current vice president for development, Gary Dicovitsky, has resolved finally to realize the college's long-term goal of balancing Pomona's development efforts with a full-scale major gifts program. He has reallocated staff to provide more support for major gifts and annual giving and to improve our relations with members of the Pomona family and other friends and donors. Pomona is doing more research and better prospect management than ever before. A critical goal is to sustain the growth in alumni volunteerism that has occurred due to increasingly popular class reunions. Recent Alumni Fund participation rates ranging between 46 and 51 percent are promising, and should increase as national recognition of the quality of Pomona's educational offerings continues to grow. If properly cultivated, the alumni pride generated by the college's national stature will lead to additional gifts in the years ahead.

The most important motivation for balancing the program is the imminence of a comprehensive campaign to address substantial institutional capital needs. The new campaign planned for the late 1990s rises out of two and a half years of broadly based strategic planning involving faculty, students, staff, and alumni, as well as trustees and administrators. It will build upon the achievements of the Centennial Campaign but will be differently organized. The campaign of the 1990s has a more orthodox structure: a chairperson from the Board of Trustees, a steering committee, and a national committee of volunteers. The Board of Trustees has assumed leadership of the campaign in a direct and visible manner, and trustees established the role of volunteers in this campaign by soliciting individuals from the outset. From the beginning, the trustees' campaign planning committee helped to develop long-term strategies and took on short-term project assignments.

The professional staff is being reconfigured to support this more balanced development program. Until 1996, only one staff position, occupied by Associate Vice President R. Kent Warner, was dedicated entirely to major gift prospect identification and solicitation. Recently, two new major gifts officers have been brought on board. These staff members will focus on field activity to recruit and support our volunteers nationally and to continue Pomona's tradition of staff solicitations when necessary. In a related strategy, increased annual giving has been made one of the principal goals of the new campaign. This strategy should have two long-term benefits. It will help Pomona increase its participation rate and build good habits for the future. At the same time, Alumni Fund volunteers will have a stronger motivation to increase gifts and will be more frequently rewarded through recognition of their efforts.

One of Pomona's traditional strengths, alumni relationships, is receiving even greater attention to complement these fund-raising efforts. At Pomona, the success of fund raising has always been directly correlated with the loyalty of the college's alumni. For this reason, alumni relations programming relative to reunions, alumni chapters, and continuing education will be even more carefully coordinated to provide the basis for a revitalized Major Gifts Program. The Office of Public Affairs, with its outstanding publications and communications, is the critical link between the campus and the rest of the Pomona family in setting the tone for positive alumni sentiment.

For all these reasons, Pomona is optimistic about its prospects for strengthening new major gifts initiatives and balancing its development program. The growing emphasis on major outright gifts will not come at the expense of the college's Annuity and Trust Program. More and enhanced donor relationships are expected to stimulate additional interest in Pomona's Deferred Giving Program. The greater visibility that a campaign provides through donor recognition is expected to increase the number of Pomona alumni who participate in the Annuity and Trust Program through life-income plans, as well as through provisions in their wills. If this happens, it will complement the historic role of deferred giving in recruiting donors to the college's other programs. Because much of Pomona's annuity and trust business continues to be with nonalumni, the possibility of significant competition between the Major Gifts and Deferred Giving programs should be minimized.

CONCLUSION

The principal reason for Pomona's success in fund raising is the college itself. Private liberal arts colleges are relatively rare in the western United States. Although Pomona has always had rivals, it has been the best for most of its history. Alumni, parents, and friends felt special pride in the college for this reason; foundation and corporate donors often looked to Pomona as a model. By sponsoring the creation of the Claremont consortium, Pomona divided this natural constituency, perhaps unwittingly. The great innovation of "The Pomona Plan" drew to the college hundreds of new donors and tens of millions of new dollars.

The stunning success of "The Pomona Plan" had its costs, for it led in time to an excessive reliance upon deferred giving. Wisely, each of Pomona's last three vice presidents has worked to strengthen major gifts and annual giving without weakening the flow of deferred gifts. So powerful has been the culture of deferred giving, and so impressive the results, real balance has been difficult to achieve. When the going gets rough, people naturally fall back on what has worked well in the past.

The design and the early successes of Pomona's new campaign in the late 1990s appear significantly different. Alumni giving has risen for four straight years, and alumni participation rates, although never as high as those at eastern colleges, are rising as well. In preparation for the main phase of the new campaign, major gifts are being staffed at a higher level. Meanwhile, the success of "The Pomona Plan" remains undiminished, bringing in new gifts to keep the pipeline full. As the new century approaches, the college is poised to achieve the balanced development program it has so long sought.

CHAPTER

Successful Fund Raising at a Two-Year Community College with a Foundation

Northampton County Area Community College

by Robert J. Kopecek and Susan K. Kubik

Northampton Community College in Bethlehem, Pennsylvania, was founded in 1967 as a two-year, publicly funded comprehensive community college. From an early enrollment of 800 students on one campus in Bethlehem Township, the college has grown to serve more than 6,000 credit and 15,000 noncredit students annually at its main campus, at two additional sites within Northampton County, and at a branch campus in adjoining Monroe County.

Serving a population base of slightly more than 340,000, the college is located in an area rich with higher educational institutions. Within a 30-mile radius of Northampton Community College are six private and four other public colleges and universities, including another community college. The overabundance of institutions of higher education is both an advantage and a disadvantage when raising funds, particularly if you are the new kid on the block.

Northampton has built a reputation as an innovative, aggressive institution that will reach out beyond its geographical base of Northampton County to areas where its services are needed. The college offers university parallel and career curricula, developmental courses, and personal enrichment and continuing education courses. Because the college sees itself as a key part of the economic life of its community, it also responds to the needs of business and industry by developing new programs and customizing training for specific needs. Annually, more than 100 regional companies directly contract with the institution to help meet educational and training needs.

Partnering arrangements have long been a part of the culture of the college, well before they became the way of life for educational institutions in the 1990s. Early cooperative agreements between the college and different segments of its community shaped program development and even led to the founding of the College Foundation in 1969. A recent example of this partnering spirit can be found in the college's Electrotechnology Applications Center, a joint project between Northampton and the Pennsylvania Power and Light Company. The project focuses on industrial coating problems by using an expanding variety of technologies, including infra-red, ultra-violet, radio, and microwave.

The college offers more than 60 career and transfer programs leading to associate degrees, certificates, and diplomas, with a heavy concentration in the allied health and technology fields. As is typical of most community colleges, people of all ages and backgrounds attend Northampton, which has an average student age of 27. The majority of students are the first generation of their families to attend college. Since the college's first commencement, more than 15,800 students have graduated. The college's annual operating budget approaches $30 million.

SPONSORSHIP ARRANGEMENT

By law, Pennsylvania community colleges are sponsored by two parties who share financing responsibility with the students who attend: the commonwealth of Pennsylvania and a local taxing body. The local entity can either be a county, city, school board(s), or consortium made up of any combination of the three. In Northampton's case, eight local school boards "sponsor" the college. Historically, these districts were responsible for funding one-third of the operating costs of the institution, although, in practice, they have never supplied that much. Currently, 17 percent of the college's operating budget comes from this source. In exchange for their financial support, the school districts control the governance of the institution.

The college's 13 trustees are elected by weighted ballot by the members of the sponsoring school district boards. Seven trustees come from the college's two largest sending districts; the remaining six districts are each represented by a single trustee. It is technically possible for the other seven boards to block the appointment of a trustee nominated by the eighth board, but that has never happened in the college's 30-year history.

In the college's early years, trustees were generally leaders within the community, sought out by the local school boards to help guide and shape the direction of this new community resource. Presidents of local companies and members of the different professions commonly served on the college's board. Early Northampton boards mirrored trustee boards at many small, private liberal arts colleges. The first chair of the board was the provost at nearby Lehigh University. The early trustees did not sit on the foundation board and thus were never formally involved in raising private funds. However, many did so informally, in concert with the executive director of the foundation, because of their connections in the community. Several of the "founding" trustees have also become significant donors to the foundation. Within the last decade, as public tax dollars have become increasingly difficult to raise, the school boards have redefined their governance relationship with the college. The have taken a watchdog role and have elected trustees who more readily fit that job description.

The board is still composed of community leaders but their influence tends to be in the political, not the development realm. As is typical in many community colleges, the development responsibility that comes with being a member of a private college or university board of trustees is not viewed as central to the job of a community college trustee. That responsibility falls on the shoulders of members of the board of the Northampton Community College Foundation.

THE NORTHAMPTON COMMUNITY COLLEGE FOUNDATION

The Northampton Community College Foundation had a rather interesting start. It was founded in 1969 by a group of local dentists who were concerned that the college had not planned for the inclusion of a dental laboratory and the subsequent development of a dental hygiene program in the groundwork it was completing for the campus master plan. The dentists approached the college's first president about that possibility. Told that the facilities plans were already coming in over budget and that a dental laboratory could not be financially accommodated, the group, troubled by the lack of trained dental hygienists in the community, lobbied for the laboratory's inclusion. Although the president philosophically supported the need for such a program, he was at a loss for the financial resources necessary to act on the dentists' recommendation.

That situation gave birth to the foundation, whose early board, as might be expected, was dominated by members of the dental and medical professions. The group's first effort was a successful capital campaign to raise the funds necessary to equip a dental hygiene laboratory. That campaign was followed by another, in 1975, to construct a building to house a new statewide funeral service education program on the campus. Both campaigns had well-targeted donors (dentists, funeral directors and their suppliers) with a profound interest in the success of the endeavors. In between the campaigns, the foundation raised enough funds to hire the college's first director of alumni affairs on a one-year, temporary appointment in 1975. In 1976, the college funded the position.

Since its two early project-specific campaigns, the foundation has conducted a modest $1.6 million campaign for endowment with the help of a Title III grant and another $80,000 project-specific campaign among automotive dealers for the local share of the costs of enlarging a facility that serves the college's automotive technology programs. The foundation is currently in the final year of a five-year, $3.5 million comprehensive campaign for scholarships, endowment, and the local share of the construction costs of Technology Hall. With the exception of the current comprehensive campaign, all campaign totals reflect current and not deferred gifts and none include annual fund totals. The foundation's annual fund has generated nearly $300,000 for each of the last three years.

The foundation's endowment is currently approaching $7 million, with nearly half of that amount restricted to scholarships. Disbursements follow a conservative 4 percent spending policy. In a typical year, somewhere between $150,000 and $250,000, depending on the amount of unrestricted income also allocated to this priority, is given in student aid. Another $30,000 to $40,000 is usually allocated to enhance professional staff development opportunities, with about two-thirds of that amount devoted to activities for part-time faculty, on whom, because of funding constraints, the college now heavily relies.

Since 1995, the foundation has also assumed fiscal responsibility for the local share of the college's new technology center. Capital projects for Pennsylvania's community colleges are financed jointly by the commonwealth and a local sponsor. Because funding constraints have limited the amount of support the college's local sponsor is willing to devote to capital projects, the foundation assumed "the local share" of the mortgage for Technology Hall. Unless and until the funding situation in Pennsylvania changes, the foundation may have to continue assuming responsibility for major capital projects on the campus.

Currently, the foundation provides funding support for on-campus housing units and has supported the purchase and renovation of instructional space on a branch campus in an adjoining county. Other activities funded by the foundation fluctuate from year to year, depending on needs. These needs are articulated by the college's faculty and staff and shared with the foundation board, which ultimately makes all disbursement decisions. In the past, support has been provided for the library, for landscaping improvements on campus, for academic program equipment, and for lecture series. The foundation has also assumed increasing responsibility for development-related costs, such as donor research, funds for student phoneathon callers, and partial salary costs for both the executive director and director of special events.

When filled, the director of the annual fund position will also be funded through the foundation. At Northampton, that particular position has become illustrative of the delicate balance to be maintained between the needs and political realities of the college and the vision and strategic thinking of members of the foundation board. The foundation first funded an annual fund position six years ago, in preparation for the reallocation of the executive director's time to the pending capital campaign. Midway through the campaign, the college was involved in a series of budget-cutting measures that included cutting and freezing staff positions. When the director of the annual fund's spouse was transferred, the position was frozen, even though it was funded by the foundation and not through the college's regular funding sources. The position was frozen primarily because faculty, whose ranks were being thinned, lobbied for similar cuts in administrative departments.

Without the position, the annual fund, which had been steadily growing at the rate of about 10 percent a year, stagnated for three years. At a board retreat, the foundation board convinced the president that the position should be restored, regardless of political heat from the faculty. For the foundation to assume more responsibility for the college's funding needs, additional resources were needed in the development office. The position was filled this past year.

That retreat, one of several held about every three years, also pointed out the need to allocate resources for better donor research and better stewardship of donors. Foundation board members also suggested establishing a more consistent method by which they could learn about the strategic thinking of the Board of Trustees and the college staff. An outgrowth of that suggestion is that each of the foundation's quarterly meetings will now allocate a significant percentage of time to interactions with college staff on issues of major importance to the institution.

The communication linkages between members of the foundation board and the college's trustees and staff are critical to the successful integration of the work of the foundation into the lifeblood of the college. Responsibility for those communication linkages falls squarely on the shoulders of the president; vice president for institutional advancement, who also serves as executive director of the foundation; and other senior staff members at the college. These linkages might occur without a senior officer of the institution devoted to advancement, but they certainly would be more difficult to orchestrate.

RECRUITMENT OF FOUNDATION BOARD MEMBERS

Northampton's foundation board currently has 31 members, although its bylaws allow up to 50 people to serve in this capacity. Members are elected to three-year terms, renewable indefinitely, but the average term falls between nine and 12 years. The board has not hesitated to deny renewal to a member who has not been actively involved in its operation. Decisions as to the nomination and retention of members are made by a Board Recruitment and Development Committee, a recent addition to the board's committee structure, which replaced the nominating committee after the most recent board retreat. This committee is led by the past-chair of the board. Northampton's foundation board rotates its chairs every two to four years, although there is no set limit to the number of one-year terms a chair may serve.

The current board membership comes predominately from the Lehigh Valley; that is likely to change in the near future because the college is now offering its services, particularly to business and industry, over a wider geographic region. Prospective members are identified by sitting board members who then cultivate them, in concert with college staff, over a period of time that varies according to the individual's knowledge of the institution. Members tend to be corporate CEOs or COOs, small business owners, or members of professions served by college programs (i.e., medical, dental, legal, funeral).

Prospective members are cultivated as if they were major donors because many eventually become just that. They are given detailed information about and exposure to the college, often at a special event sponsored by the foundation at the invitation of a sitting board member. Those being cultivated receive a foundation board member job description and material on the role of foundation board members before they are asked to serve. That material clearly defines their fund-raising responsibility as central to their service on the board. Candidates are also told that there is a minimum annual level of support expected from board members, making it somewhat easier for the members who work on the Annual Fund to solicit their fellow volunteers later in the year. The formal request to consider joining the board is made by a member of the board, accompanied by the president and the executive director.

Because the area is rich with educational institutions, identifying foundation board prospects who do not have ties to other local colleges and universities is a challenge. The current board chairman, for instance, also sits on the board of another university. However, the uniqueness of the community college mission allows most board members to find ways to support Northampton that do not conflict with the emotional ties and financial commitments they may have with their alma maters. But emotional ties to one's alma mater can be strong. Those ties and the fact that the college is now 30 years old and is beginning to have alumni achieve positions of responsibility have led to recent efforts to add more NCC alumni to the foundation board. Of the 31 sitting members, four are Northampton alums. That number is expected to increase over time.

Once recruited, board members are given a comprehensive orientation to the college. That was not always the case. The foundation board orientation had focused primarily on the foundation and its committees and operations until members themselves asked to know more about the institution. Since many members had prior experience on other community boards, most knew how boards should work. The orientation session was refocused and is now conducted predominately by the president and provost.

Involvement in the life of the foundation occurs primarily through its committees, which, because of the local nature of the membership, are active and meet in between regularly scheduled meetings of the board. Board committees include the following:

- Annual Fund
- Special Events
- Planned and Major Gifts
- Board Recruitment and Development
- Finance
- Capital Campaign (as needed)

The membership of the Executive Committee, which has the power to act on behalf of the foundation between its regularly scheduled meetings, includes the chair, vice chair, president, treasurer, and the chairs of the committees.

In addition to the committee structure and its natural tendency to keep board members active, the president and vice president of institutional advancement work hard to involve members in the life of the college. Because many foundation board members own their own businesses, are company CEOs or COOs, or come from other professions, they tend to have significant clout in the community. Their influence, advice, and counsel, particularly in governmental relations, is often called upon by the president.

To ensure that board members' experiences with the institution match their expectations, the vice president of institutional development began a series of one-on-one meetings with each member of the board this past year to talk solely about that issue. Because of the valuable feedback she received, the practice is likely to continue on an every-other-year basis.

RELATIONSHIPS

Since the Reagan era, community colleges have become increasingly aggressive and increasingly successful in raising private funds to support their efforts.

However, unlike the practice at most independent colleges and universities where funds from donors support some portion of annual operating expenditures, proceeds from philanthropic efforts at community colleges typically are used to support student scholarships, enrichment programs, equipment purchases, and portions of capital projects.

Community colleges have only recently begun to establish endowments to support such ongoing needs as student scholarships, faculty development, or library resources. Because most community colleges are new to fund raising and most individuals involved in establishing new efforts want to quickly demonstrate the benefits of collected funds, the practice of many institutions is still to structure fund-raising activities so that all funds received for a designated purpose are expended within the year the funds are collected. At Northampton, this approach was changed in the mid- 1980s. No commitment for any allocation for any purpose is made unless the funds are in hand. In addition, endowment funds are now actively sought. The practice of expending all collected funds rapidly, and the underlying philosophy and fund-raising and management activities that follow from this approach, along with the regulatory restrictions in some states that hinder colleges from directly engaging in private fund raising, caused community colleges to establish foundations that are legally separate from the college. These conditions have defined a role for community college trustees that is different from the role of their counterparts at private institutions.

Community college trustees are either directly elected by popular vote or appointed by some governmental or educational entity. This method of choosing trustees causes the trustees to assume that, in addition to the other roles usually ascribed to trusteeship, they are to be the guardians of public tax funds. Depending on the state, they either directly levy a local tax or approve a budget that causes some governmental agency to set an annual tax. As elected officials or as representatives of elected boards, community college trustees always feel some elements of a watchdog role.

Although most community college trustees support the private fund-raising efforts of the institution with their own funds, few are financially able to be major or even substantial donors. In most states, it is also prudent to put as much legal distance between the resources of the college and those of the foundation. As a result, only a few trustees are members of foundation boards. Rarely, if ever, at least at Northampton, do trustees provide leadership in fund-raising campaigns. These activities are assumed by members of the foundation board who are community leaders and philanthropists. At Northampton, to foster communication and understanding of the goals and activities of both boards, one active trustee and one or two former members have typically served on the foundation board.

At independent institutions, when the trustees establish annual goals for the college or university, the course is charted for the college and its annual fund-raising activities. How funds received will be used has also been determined. Annual goal-setting for fund raising is less clear at a community college with a separate foundation.

At Northampton, the proceeds of the annual fund drive are used primarily for enrichment activities not covered in the college's annual budget and therefore are not considered by the trustees. The Northampton Community College Foundation Board, its chair, the college president, and the development staff raise the funds, and, to differing degrees, determine how the funds are allocated.

Therefore, how the funds are divided could cause misunderstanding and disagreement between the two boards and their respective leadership. At Northampton, a cooperative and supportive relationship has been maintained since the foundation was established in 1969. The basic understanding is that the foundation should distribute the funds it raises, but the allocations should be guided by institutional goals recommended by the president and established by the trustees. Two factors are key to the relationship between boards: a written policy that establishes the foundation as the official agent for the college for the receipt of private funds, and, more importantly, the existence of mutual trust between the boards, their leadership, and the professional leadership of the college. There is also an equally clear but unspoken acknowledgment that the trustees are ultimately responsible for the operation and well-being of the college. The foundation exists to support and assist the college and not to attempt in any way to dominate its activities.

A few practical examples of how the relationship works might be instructive. Early in the college's history, friends of the institution wished to support students and the recruitment efforts of the institution by contributing to scholarship programs. Such support has been a continuing emphasis endorsed by all without discussion, as has the need to support ongoing faculty and staff development programs, perennial "hot buttons" for local taxing authorities. The methods for administering scholarship programs and for dispensing staff development funds may have become more innovative and complex through the years, but the basic commitment to these programs enjoys overwhelming support.

More interesting has been the mutual support of capital projects that have been undertaken over the years. For a number of reasons, but basically because the college wishes to maintain strong career and technical instructional programs that cannot be economically supported with the student population available in the immediate service area, the president several years ago proposed to both boards the need for on-campus housing. Three residence halls now exist on college property, financed through the foundation and operated by contract for the foundation by the college. Ownership of the facilities will be transferred to the college after the debt is retired.

In 1988, the college was invited to give instruction in an adjoining county. Expansion of the program required the rapid purchase and renovation of a building. Using regular state procedures, the project could not be done in the time frame desired. The foundation board agreed that the project was worthy and initially financed it. When state funding was subsequently obtained, the foundation sold the facility and the surrounding real estate to the college.

The financing of the college's new training and conference center is another example of the relationship between boards. Under state law, the local community, through the college, must contribute 50 percent of the cost of all capital projects. For one building in the center, the foundation pledged to generate sufficient funds to satisfy this obligation and dedicated a portion of its current capital campaign to its financing.

In each of these situations, the president and the administrative staff had to win the active support and endorsement of both boards. Beside the obvious value of these projects to the development of the college and its programs, the lay leadership of both boards, although ultimately committed to the projects, used different lines of inquiry to validate the projects' worth and value. These different perspectives are of significant benefit to the college and its professional leadership.

On a practical level, how to fully use and empower two boards filled with dedicated, hardworking, innovative, and strong-minded individuals can be a daunting question. In a perfect world, this type of organizational structure might not be needed. But the world is imperfect, and the two-board structure, although sometimes cumbersome, has brought significant benefits to the institution.

The members of the two boards can broadly represent the total community. Because most major projects at community colleges that require fund-raising activities will also increasingly require the active support of one or more taxing authorities to be successful, the existence and, more importantly, the cooperative joining of many segments of the community represented by these boards is central. If consensus is achieved between the boards on the value and worth of any specific project or campaign element, the overall fund-raising effort, from public as well as private sources, will be successful.

On the operational level, the president, vice president for institutional advancement, and other senior staff members work to maintain a stream of communication between the two boards, which do not meet together, on major issues. The guidance and counsel of members of both boards is actively sought. When capital projects are being developed, college administrators treat the boards as if they were committees of a larger group, careful to get either formal votes of approval, if required, or informal consensual statements of approval. In ceremonial situations, the leadership of both groups is recognized. However, in mapping fund-raising strategy or in executing any fund-raising activities, the foundation leadership and board members, along with the vice president of institutional advancement and the president, are central. College trustees at Northampton do not involve themselves in these activities.

THE LEADERSHIP TEAM

At Northampton, like all community colleges that have incorporated not-for-profit, 501 (c) 3 foundations as their fund-raising agent, four individuals are central to the relationship between the college and the foundation—the chair of the Board of Trustees, the college president, the chair of the foundation Board of Directors, and the college's vice president of institutional advancement, who also serves as executive director of the foundation at Northampton. Although one might suppose or even wish for a more structural or formal link, the success of the relationship between the leaders of these two organizations is based on tradition and the chemistry that exists between and among these individuals.

The college president, as the chief executive officer of the college and the chief fund-raiser for the foundation, is the linchpin between the two leaders as well as the two organizations. The president must outline and advocate the vision and goals for both groups and work with the leaders of both organizations to ensure that the vision and goals adopted by the trustees are also accepted by the foundation and its board members. The president must ensure that both chairs and their boards are working in tandem as they pursue their particular functions to strengthen the institution.

By law and regulation, authority to set goals for the college and to oversee its administration lies clearly with the trustees, but foundation board members, as influential and knowledgeable representatives of the general community, use informal conversations with the college staff and the president to involve themselves in shaping and molding the development of these goals and specifically in supporting programs and projects that move the college in the agreed-upon direction.

As the executive director of the foundation, the vice president of institutional advancement is on staff to the foundation board and is the foundation's professional development officer. In this role, she is operationally central to ensuring the orderly planning and executing of all aspects of the fund-raising program and carries a particularly heavy burden in working on a personal level with all foundation board members, but especially with the board chair, to facilitate harmonious relationships. Over the years, the personal relationships between the sitting chairs and the president have been close and supportive, in no small measure because of the tact and interpersonal skills of the vice president of institutional advancement.

However, the leadership team for fund-raising purposes has three members—the chair of the foundation board, the president, and the vice president of istitutional advancement. The chair of the trustees does not become involved in recommending or determining the specific fund-raising strategies or activities of the foundation and does not get involved in soliciting funds. Those responsibilities are shared by the others previously mentioned.

For the last 20 years, all the individuals who have served as chairs of both organizations have been dedicated to the rapid development of the college. Although all are individuals of strong convictions tackling potentially divisive issues, each of these leaders worked with unusual selflessness to reach acceptable accords.

ORGANIZATIONAL RELATIONSHIPS

Because fund raising is relatively new to publicly operated community colleges, the specific role of the vice president of institutional advancement with the foundation and its board members and with the college trustees and professional staff is still evolving, and at many institutions is dependent on the personalities of the vice president and president. One aspect of the role may seem unusual to individuals familiar with only the independent sector of higher education. Trustees and professional staff members of community colleges easily understand the need and value of having a senior staff member charged with the responsibility of managing marketing, publications, public and media relations, printing, and even alumni affairs. All these areas are viewed as being traditional and mainstream functions that every community college should staff.

But the establishment and support of a foundation has been viewed differently by some faculty and academic administrators. Establishment costs of foundations in dollars and in human resources are considerable, and the more significant benefits to the ongoing financial well-being of the institution are long range. Immediate gains for the college are mostly symbolic, although a few students are usually given small scholarships that are much needed and appreciated. Therefore, whether on philosophic grounds—public colleges should not have to raise private resources—or on a pragmatic level—the investment in foundation staff does not pay off quickly enough—resource-starved academics often strongly object when a vice president of institutional advancement argues for new positions to support a capital campaign, to intensify donor research, or to manage the annual fund drive.

The vice president of institutional advancement at most community colleges, and certainly at Northampton, to use Joel Barker's term, has had to be a "paradigm pioneer"—a person who has had to change the culture of the college. The vice president has had to convince the president, two boards of control, and her colleagues on the faculty and professional staff that expenditures to support the foundation are essential if the foundation and the college are to compete for donor dollars. Everyone is eager to receive the largess of the foundation, but many are unwilling to agree that investment in the foundation's infrastructure is a necessity.

At Northampton, the process of gaining campuswide acceptance of this need to invest in the foundation began in 1983 and has been led successfully by the vice president of institutional advancement. Today, perhaps because public dollars are proportionately being reduced on our campus, the perceived value of the foundation is high and almost everyone sees the need to employ professional experienced staff for the foundation, although how many and how much they should be paid continues to be debated. This positive change in campus attitude is attributable to the work of the vice president as championed by the president.

The reporting relationships for the vice president, as well as the college president at community colleges that have established 501 (c) 3 not-for-profit foundations is complex. There exists a traditional, clear cut, formal reporting structure, but important informal relationships also exist and must be honored.

Although the foundation at Northampton, among a series of other functions, maintains endowments, owns buildings, borrows money, and pays all or some of the salaries of a number of people who do work for it, it does not directly employ anyone. All individuals who do work for the foundation are employees of the college, abiding by all its personnel policies and regulations.

The vice president of institutional advancement is one of three vice presidents reporting directly to the president who are charged with giving leadership to several college support functions and all its external activities. In this capacity, she is also the executive director of the foundation. Unlike the president, who is reimbursed solely by the college, a portion of the vice president's salary is provided by the foundation and much of her time is dedicated to its operation. In this latter capacity, she must, like the president, be sensitive to the wishes of the foundation board and its members, even though she is directly responsible to and is evaluated by the president.

Because successful fund raising, with its inherent nurturing of volunteers and donors, is a team activity, the president and the vice president of institutional advancement recognize and accept the fact that they are mutually dependent on one another if they wish to be successful. On a practical level, this dependence requires that both individuals strive to achieve bedrock agreement on the broad goals and objectives of the foundation and on strategy and day-to-day tactics. Happily, this agreement exists. A key reason for this is the 20-year history of working together that these two individuals share. A major test of whether these relationships are clearly understood and institutionalized will occur when changes occur in the key professional staff positions.

CHAPTER 7

Successful Fund Raising at a Women's College

Bryn Mawr College

by Mary Patterson McPherson and Donna L. Wiley

B ryn Mawr College is a small liberal arts college with an undergraduate enrollment of 1,150-1,200 women. It is a highly selective institution, with a student-faculty ratio of 9.5:1 that makes it possible for
students at all levels to work closely with senior members of the faculty. The
college was founded in 1885 with graduate programs leading to the Ph.D. in all
departments of the college. In 1997, Bryn Mawr offers coeducational Ph.D.
programs in 13 departments; the college enrolls approximately 500 students in
its Graduate School of Arts and Sciences and its Graduate School of Social
Work and Social Research. The college's endowment stood at over $280
million at the close of 1995-96; the 1996-97 operating budget is $66 million.

Bryn Mawr is included in this study of successful fund raising as a representative of women's colleges. Although some aspects of the fund-raising program
are indeed typical of that group, Bryn Mawr's historical and continuing
commitment to graduate education make it unusual among its peers. At the
same time, many characteristics of the Bryn Mawr program typify the experiences of small colleges, both coeducational and single-sex, that have enjoyed
strong support from their alumni and relied heavily on volunteer networks
over the years.

THE FUND-RAISING PROGRAM AT BRYN MAWR

The objectives of the fund-raising program at Bryn Mawr are to achieve
specific target figures each year for gifts to the operating budget (predeter-

mined annually in consultation with the college's chief financial officer) and gifts to the endowment (to increase the endowment by 2 percent or more of its market value); to fund additional enrichment efforts identified by the president and senior academic officers; and to support specific capital projects. These capital projects may be modest in scale, as for example start-up expenses for new faculty members in the sciences, or major renovations or new construction, such as are possible in the context of a major fund-raising campaign. All private fund-raising for the college is managed by the Resources Office, with the exception of certain faculty research grants from private sources and a volunteer-driven program to secure outright scholarship support through a regional network of used bookstores, benefits, and periodic direct appeals to alumnae and friends. In 1997, the Resources Office included 22 staff members; it grew to a high of 35 during the most recent campaign. Fund-raising costs are low as compared with those of educational institutions nationwide, having averaged 7.9 percent during a five-year period ending in 1995.

The college has received a level of private support that ranks high in relationship to the size of its alumnae body (12,000 undergraduate and 4,500 graduate alumnae) and to its operating budget. Over the last 10 years, private gifts have averaged over $16 million per year. (See Table 7-1.) The college's two most recent campaigns were the Centennial Campaign (1982-85), which achieved $46 million in gifts and pledges, and the Campaign for Bryn Mawr (1991-93), which surpassed its goal of $75 million to reach $92 million. Private gifts support approximately 12-15 percent of the college's annual operating budget, while gifts to the endowment averaged $7 million per year from 1985 to 1995 (for an average increase of 5.7 percent of market value that was well over the 2 percent increase included in financial planning estimates for the institution). In addition to funding a number of laboratory and classroom renovations through private gifts and grants, the Campaign for Bryn Mawr included major objectives for a science library and the department of chemistry, as well as a new library for the college's nationally ranked programs in the history of art and classical and Near Eastern archaeology.

Within this overall record of success, however, a trend has appeared in the pattern of gifts received. This trend has come about, on the one hand, as a result of changes in the fund-raising and financial planning strategies employed by the college, and, on the other hand, as a result of an important shift in the external giving climate. During Bryn Mawr's Centennial Campaign, the major emphasis had been to secure unrestricted gifts, yielding an unusually high level of current support for the operating budget, which continued, in the form of major pledge payments, through the end of the decade. By contrast, the Campaign for Bryn Mawr emphasized gifts for capital projects and the endowment. As a result, although the college's physical plant is much improved and the endowment considerably higher, the level of gifts available for

TABLE 7-1. Bryn Mawr College—10-Year Giving Report

Bryn Mawr College: Ten-Year Giving Report

Sources	1986-87	1987-88	1988-89	1989-90	1990-91	1991-92	1992-93	1993-94	1994-95	1995-96
Alumnae/ Alumnae Fdns	$4,923,709	$2,950,170	$3,101,330	$5,552,919	$6,868,996	$8,339,097	$6,350,710	$8,688,047	$6,545,748	$5,467,874
Parents	184,415	90,626	110,929	136,357	121,073	152,933	208,479	130,853	119,541	124,599
Friends	247,850	241,383	180,023	394,323	190,771	289,391	122,756	298,461	768,102	543,113
Corporations	565,096	321,715	309,564	434,399	346,209	394,481	471,462	593,424	489,295	498,302
Foundations	1,450,473	1,827,256	2,746,926	1,991,794	4,115,823	2,444,980	2,749,924	3,478,976	1,363,293	442,065
Bequests	3,903,453	8,524,136	7,521,883	10,859,581	2,494,024	4,639,174	3,332,561	4,755,661	3,594,751	18,440,451
Total	$11,274,996	$13,955,286	$13,970,655	$19,369,373	$14,136,896	$16,260,056	$13,235,892	$17,945,422	$12,880,730	$25,516,404
Deferred Gifts	1,614,710	1,051,008	601,759	1,055,913	1,589,569	2,214,882	1,818,299	1,121,461	866,802	1,352,360
Grand Total	$12,889,706	$15,006,294	$14,572,414	$20,425,286	$15,726,465	$18,474,938	$15,054,191	$19,054,191	$13,747,532	$26,868,764

the operating budget has not followed an inflation-based trajectory from the levels of the mid-1980s. It has instead fallen to a level sustainable through a combination of steady growth in annual giving and a healthy level of current, restricted gifts for budgeted expenditures. (Bryn Mawr is somewhat unusual among its peer institutions in including a significant level of current restricted gift support in its operating budget assumptions.) At the same time, the availability of major grants from private foundations for core expenses, such as faculty salaries, curricular development, and scholarship assistance, has declined considerably over the last five years. Foundation giving has been central to the fund-raising program at Bryn Mawr for many years. But foundation grants, which accounted for an average of 15 percent of total gifts between 1987 and 1995, dropped to a low of 1.6 percent in 1996, and will make up approximately 10 percent of giving in 1997. The result has been an increasing reliance on gifts from individuals, particularly the alumnae of the college.

Private gifts have, at the same time, enabled substantial endowment growth in recent years. Realized bequests have played an enormous role in this growth, providing $68 million of the total $171.9 million received in private gifts from 1986 to 1996. The history and recent experience of the college's fund-raising program reveals that estate gifts, including deferred gifts and trust agreements as well as outright bequests, are particularly attractive to female donors. Since the 1950s, Bryn Mawr has benefited from a strong volunteer-driven program to urge alumnae to include the college in their wills. Clarissa Wardwell Pell (Class of 1930), the first director of resources at the college (there have been only four), remembers, "I concentrated on developing the program to encourage bequests to the college because this was an area where I knew my way around. By contrast, the corporate arena seemed a bit daunting at the time." The college appointed its first professional staff member in deferred giving in 1984, and the program has grown considerably in breadth and sophistication since that time. The stream of realized deferred gifts, some of which are designated for general support of the college and some for the endowment, has begun to compensate for the fall-off in outright gifts available for the operating budget. Further, the level of gift income from bequests and deferred gifts promises to continue at a high level into the near future, based on an assessment of the total pool of deferred gifts under college management at present and the number of intended bequests of which we are aware. This high level of giving has allowed us to use undesignated funds to support occasional major capital needs rather than adding them automatically to the endowment, a practice established in the 1970s when endowment growth was an overriding objective for the institution.

FUND RAISING FOR A WOMEN'S COLLEGE

The nature and character of fund raising from a largely female constituency is evolving rapidly; such fund raising currently occurs in a complex environment. It encompasses alumnae who graduated in the 1920s and 1930s, many of whom chose profession over family to pursue careers in law, medicine, and academia. The alumnae of the 1940s to the early 1960s were more likely to follow a traditional pattern of family first, followed by full-time volunteer work or late entry into the working world. The graduates of the last 35 years, whose life patterns and choices are much harder to predict, represent a far wider range of ethnic and socio-economic diversity than would have been imagined by their predecessors during their own college years. Although assuming that age alone determines the appropriate fund-raising approach would be insulting to the college's able alumnae, who have been characterized over the years as having in common only their "cussed individualism," certain changes are clearly in process. First, conversations about money and the college's needs, which were elliptical at best in the past, are now clear and forthright. This change was perhaps most dramatically demonstrated by the successful national rating and screening program, called NIP (the National Identification Program), in which 418 alumnae attended 31 sessions of silent review and rating for gift potential of other alumnae. We received through this process single ratings of $10,000 or more on 4,532 alumnae, or over 40 percent of our alumnae body.

In the past, many of Bryn Mawr's donors, particularly the most generous ones, sought anonymity. That is changing. Donor interest in recognition is clearly growing, as is interest in determining the precise impact of the gift made, even at the level of annual giving. (In 1994, Bryn Mawr initiated a new program within the Annual Fund, which pegs the highest donor group at the level of the average undergraduate financial aid award and offers donors a report on the student her gift has supported. This program has been well received.) This change has necessitated a certain readjustment of the institutional culture, which previously tended to avoid overt recognition of major gifts. (The college's Quaker heritage also contributed to this culture.)

We have experienced a rapid and dramatic change in the role of volunteers in the fund-raising program over the last 15-20 years. Through the late 1970s, the program was managed by volunteers on a nearly day-to-day basis (e.g., every foundation proposal was reviewed in draft by a volunteer, with staff members providing support as needed). By contrast, Betsy Havens Watkins (class of 1961), chair of the Campaign for Bryn Mawr, notes that

> One of the most striking changes has been that the professional staff members take on far greater responsibilities, while volunteers do less, both less than the staff and less than volunteers did in the past. This

probably models more closely the structure of predominantly male or coeducational institutions, but it was a change for Bryn Mawr. Most of the volunteers who had key leadership roles were working full-time and we were all less directly involved with the daily operations of the campaign than our predecessors had been. As campaign chair, I enlisted the members of the volunteer Steering Committee, reviewed written materials, discussed policies with staff, attended key campaign events, but it was the staff who developed priorities and objectives, drafted the case statement and supporting materials, prepared the budget, and did all the day-to-day implementation and follow up.

In the 1990s, Bryn Mawr alumnae have less time available to undertake volunteer jobs for the college, even when those jobs are closely defined. Recruitment for campaign volunteers was much more difficult than in the past, even though we offered them an extraordinarily high level of staff support. Volunteers in the regional campaigns, which target gifts between $10,000 and $50,000, were asked only to attend a training session and to make three follow-up calls; the proposal letters were mailed from the college. Still, as many as one-third did not complete their three calls. This failure to finish was particularly true in the major metropolitan areas, including New York and Los Angeles, where the atmosphere of competing demands and over-commitment seemed sometimes to take on a life of its own. This instructive experience has caused us to restructure other volunteer fund-raising jobs, specifically those in support of the Annual Fund.

THE ROLE OF DEVELOPMENT WITHIN THE INSTITUTION

The reporting structure for fund raising at Bryn Mawr is an unusual one; the college has no coordinated institutional advancement program. Rather, the development office (called the Resources Office) and public information offices report directly to the president. Alumnae programming, including publication of the *Bryn Mawr Alumnae Bulletin*, is managed by the independently incorporated and tax-exempt Alumnae Association, which has no reporting relationship to the college administration. The association is overseen by a self-governed and self-selected volunteer executive board. The Alumnae Association has a small endowment of its own and more access to unbudgeted outside income than would be the case for departments within the college (e.g., via voluntary contributions made in connection with alumnae travel programs). Its operating budget, however, is provided almost entirely by the college and is subject to the same scrutiny and review that prevails within the college's overall budget process. This unusual situation demands particular attention to information-sharing and cooperation, especially between Resources and the Alumnae Association. It also yields a certain amount of inevitable duplication of effort (e.g., in terms of record keeping and atten-dance at meetings), which may not represent the best use of institutional resources.

This model was prevalent in private colleges and universities, particularly the Ivies and Seven Sisters, earlier in the century, but has been modified to varying degrees by many institutions and eliminated entirely in favor of a consolidated program by others. In Bryn Mawr's case, the decision to unify the fund-raising program within the Resources Office in 1985, replacing the earlier system whereby the Alumnae Association managed alumni annual giving and the college's Resources Office handled "other" fund raising, was made at the recommendation of a committee of trustees and key Alumnae Association volunteers. This wise decision allowed the development program to build organically from grass-roots to major gifts fund raising and allowed the development staff to work closely with volunteers and donors at all levels, thereby developing relationships of trust with various constituents. At the same time, the Alumnae Office can concentrate productively on outreach programming for the entire alumnae community.

The role of development in overall college planning is integral. The Re-sources Office takes as part of its central responsibilities the need to be aware of the overall financial needs and programmatic directions of the institution and to advise colleagues in the academic administration on the fund-raising marketability and strategic development of new initiatives. Because the direc-tor of the Resources Office has been on the college staff since 1978, and the associate director (director of grants and stewardship) since 1984, this process is easier. Although neither is an alumna of the college, both have advanced academic degrees and take an active interest in the academic programs of the college, a clear advantage in an institution like Bryn Mawr. Beginning in 1994, the chief development officer began to join regularly scheduled meetings of the president and the chief academic and financial officers; this measure has helped build a fuller understanding of the complex interaction of funding and program development for the institution.

One example of the successful integration of development operations into overall college planning is the way in which the drafting of the table of needs for the Campaign for Bryn Mawr in 1988 became, in effect, a major planning effort for the college. It followed closely on the heels of the institution's re-accreditation study and a comprehensive review of Bryn Mawr's finances undertaken in response to a study by the firm of Cambridge Associates. In preparation for the development of the campaign program, the associate director of resources met with many groups and sub-groups on campus: academic programs and faculty development (provost and three deans); technical support (director of computing, library automation coordinator, provost, assistant treasurer); library needs (three senior librarians); campus needs (treasurer, director of student services, director of physical plans, dean of the undergraduate college); faculty and staff salaries (director of personnel, provost, personnel manager); financial aid (director of financial aid, two graduate deans, director of admissions); and operating support during the campaign (treasurer and director of resources). The associate director of resources had to make clear throughout the process that her role was not to set priorities or funding levels, but rather to interview and to collect and collate information. The result was a compilation of desired objectives with a total cost that far exceeded the institution's potential for fund raising over a period of several years. Draft documents were then vetted in sequence by the Executive and Development Committees of the Board of Trustees, the faculty Academic Planning and Curriculum Committees, the college's Administrative Office Heads, and the Bryn Mawr Council (which includes faculty, staff, and student representatives). Although the campaign plan produced by this lengthy process may not have differed greatly from the plan that could have been developed by a few senior administrators early on, the process itself was valuable in terms of educating the campus community and minimizing concern about the campaign's major objectives.

THE KEY PLAYERS: PRESIDENT, TRUSTEES AND VOLUNTEERS, AND CHIEF DEVELOPMENT OFFICER

As with all human relationships, the interaction among the volunteer and paid leaders of Bryn Mawr College's fund-raising program is complex and multifaceted. It is professional and reasonably well defined in terms of areas of responsibility, yet at the same time personal. The ease with which cooperative planning takes place and decisions are made is facilitated or encouraged by key players in the administration and volunteer ranks who have been in their roles for a long time and have, each in her own way, "grown up" within the institution and helped to shape its fund-raising culture. President Mary Patterson McPherson (Ph.D. 1969), has led the institution since 1978, and was a graduate student, assistant dean, and dean of the undergraduate college before that. Ruth Kaiser Nelson (class of 1958), chief fund-raising volunteer of the college, has chaired the Trustee Development Committee since 1991, and has volunteered for the college in admissions, in regional alumnae work, and as chair of the Major Gifts Committee from 1985 to 1990. Betsy Watkins (class of 1961) had been executive director of the Alumnae Association from 1976 to 1981, chaired the Alumnae Association's Nominating Committee from 1984 to 1987, and became a trustee of the college following the close of the Campaign for Bryn Mawr in 1993. Donna L. Wiley joined the Resources Office staff in a junior position in 1978, has served as director of resources since 1985, and became secretary of the college as well in 1995, further underscoring the central role of development for the institution and the Board of Trustees. Because they have known one another and worked together successfully for a long time, the distinctions among their various roles are perhaps not as clear as they might be in a more hierarchical organization or one in which change at the top level has occurred more frequently. Nonetheless, we must be able to describe these differences; change will occur in the future, and the roles of each must be both clear and flexible enough to work successfully with others in the same roles.

The role that President McPherson has played in the fund-raising program is probably the best illustration of how an intensely personal approach to institutional advancement can mask the appearance of a carefully planned set of strategic approaches. Her relationship with the alumnae body as a whole, as well as with potential donors, spans the full range of informality to formality. Many donors and volunteers have enjoyed a comfortable relationship with the president over the years, such that worries about "fit" and working relationship are rare. Her genuine enjoyment of people, particularly of Bryn Mawr's students, and her ability to rise above the setbacks one inevitably encounters in the cultivation and solicitation of major gifts is a great advantage and sets an example for junior colleagues. At the same time, her extensive experience as a board member for foundations, corporations, and other educational institutions contributes to her stature in the field, and the opportunity for an inspirational "time with Pat" is an important factor in planning alumnae gatherings at the college or afield. However, having so many constituents who believe themselves to have a close relationship with the president can prove a disadvantage; such a widespread belief makes it more difficult to structure a hierarchical approach to fund raising with the introduction of the president as solicitor at the final stage of a series of events leading to a truly major gift. In a constituency as small as Bryn Mawr's, the potential donor is likely to have known this president for a long time. Especially at such a small college, this situation allows and encourages a highly individualized solicitation program. For example, salutations and solicitation amounts for all prospective donors at the $10,000 to $50,000 level within the regional campaigns were reviewed by both the president and the campaign chair, whose signatures were on the letters. In most cases, prospective donors were known personally by one or both of the signers.

Within the institution, the president carries the functional responsibility to support and underscore the centrality of the fund-raising operation in her dealings with administration and faculty alike, to support appropriate and reasonable budget and staffing requests, and to ensure that senior development staff members have access to the information they need to represent the institution accurately and successfully. According to President McPherson,

A president's role is key to the success of any fund-raising program. Not only must the president understand institutional needs in detail, but she must be able to match these creatively with what she knows of donor interests. The president also has the ability to influence the spirits of the fund-raising staff and the volunteers as it helps the effort enormously if both groups enjoy the challenges provided by a campaign and have some fun working together. Fortunately, at Bryn Mawr this last is never a problem.

The role of the key volunteer in fund raising is a distinctly different one. It is, first of all, to set an example as a donor and a supporter of the institution and its administration. Beyond that, she should have her ear to the ground regarding trustee, volunteer, and donor responses to a range of issues and concerns—whether the treatment of a controversial subject in a college publication, the reception accorded a new dean or visiting faculty member by the local alumnae group, or the quality, accuracy, and potential appeal of the materials produced by the development office to support the fund-raising effort. She must balance the need to be supportive and encouraging of the staff with the need to be absolutely honest and clear about misdirections, ineffective or inappropriate behavior by staff members, or any facet of the development operation likely to impede the fund-raising effort. Such constructive criticism is vital to the shaping and reworking of the program, and the president and chief development officer must make clear to the volunteers that they welcome well-intended advice and the swift voicing of concerns. (In situations where the chief development officer is relatively new to the institution, communication about the need for improvement is likely to take place between the top volunteers and the president; however, honest conversation between volunteers and development officers is essential to achieve a successful working relationship.) Finally, the top volunteers must provide leadership for the crucial network of volunteer-to-volunteer contacts that must undergird a successful fund-raising effort—true to varying extents for all nonprofit organizations, but especially so for an educational institution able to draw on the immediately available constituency of its graduates. Trustee Ruth Nelson notes, "Bryn Mawr is an extraordinarily close-knit community. This encourages good and productive relationships across geographical and age lines, as well as between volunteers and college staff members. In fact, real friendships develop at all levels."

As manager, the role of the chief development officer is to provide the invisible underpinnings for the whole operation, including accurate and timely information and materials, well-trained staff members, and discreet encouragement of the volunteer ranks; as lead fund-raiser, she must be prepared to function as the voice of the college in the absence of the president, a top trustee, or volunteer figure. The development officer's role shifts as needed between a transparent role—in effect, the potential donor should "look through" the fund-raiser to see the institution represented—to a more substantial role, in which the relationship between donor and staff member is significant to a successful solicitation. For this reason, the chief development officer must herself understand the complexity of these relationships, and must also be able to teach staff members the fundamental truth that gifts are given not to the person who solicits them, but to the charitable organization.

The responsibility of the chief development officer also includes being aware of the comprehensive financial picture of the college, assessing the relative attractiveness to potential donors of various areas of need, and working closely with the financial officer to achieve a clear, shared understanding of the potential for gift support for various areas of need. This last area generated some tension within the college administration in the 1980s, but careful attention to defining the precise meaning of fund-raising objectives and announced achievements and to improving the nature of consultation and discussion between the Treasurer's and Resources offices has resulted in a much more productive and cooperative working relationship. For example, although clear fund-raising reasons exist to "credit" donors of trusts and deferred gifts on the basis of the gifts' original market values, the financial officer is more concerned with the current and projected flow of income from realized gifts. Both are important indicators, but they serve different purposes.

Bryn Mawr's Campaign Steering Committee was typical for institutions like Bryn Mawr, which operate on the basis of collegiality across organizational divisions and which are founded on a history of volunteer management of the fund-raising program. As such, it included key volunteers from the Alumnae Association and ongoing fund-raising programs (Annual Fund, Bequests, and Deferred Giving), volunteers recruited specifically for the campaign, and the president and chief academic, financial, and development officers. It also included four graduates of the 1970s and 1980s, appointed by the campaign chair as "members-at-large" to achieve some age balance among the membership. (The Bryn Mawr alumnae body is a relatively young one; in 1996, half of living alumnae had graduated in 1976 or later.) It did not include a representative of the faculty. This omission could have resulted in a failure of communication about the effort and its achievements, but this problem was overcome by paying close attention to the need to keep the faculty informed and to answer their questions directly. Faculty members received the campaign newsletter, which was produced quarterly over the four years of planning and implementation of the effort. Also, the chief development officer, who does not attend faculty meetings, reported in detail on campaign progress and results annually to the faculty throughout this period.

The question of conflict resolution among the top leadership of the Bryn Mawr Campaign is difficult to answer because none of its members can cite an instance when they disagreed among themselves. However, two instances exemplified the spirit of cooperative decision-making that characterized the campaign and the key role of the Campaign Steering Committee in planning the overall effort. In one case, the process resulted in significant savings of both time and money; in the other, a change in strategy may have served a particular set of interests well, but turned out to be ill-advised in terms of the overall fund-raising effort.

The comprehensive budget for the campaign, which had been developed by the chief development officer early in the planning process, included significant funding for the production of a film or video. However, the volunteer steering committee spoke out unanimously against an expensive visual production of any kind, and in favor of presentations by various members of the college community. According to Campaign Chair Betsy Watkins,

> This decision was probably determined, or at least informed, by institutional style. Bryn Mawr alumnae are typically very verbal and comfortable with well-articulated descriptions of institutional needs (both oral and written) and less receptive to (perhaps even suspicious of) multimedia presentations. For many, they signify trendy or less tangible means of communication than the written or spoken word. This may, of course, be a generational issue, and we will need to consult with recent graduates whenever making this kind of decision, which has to do with the constituency as a whole.

The choice to forego a visual presentation meant, of course, that we had to devote more effort to recruiting speakers for various events from members of the faculty and administration and, in some cases, alumnae whose expertise complemented the featured event or exhibition held in conjunction with regional campaign dinners. It was a good example, however, of the need to tailor campaign plans to the needs of the institution at the time; Bryn Mawr had successfully used a slide presentation with taped narration in the Centennial Campaign in the early 1980s, and the volunteers worried that an updated version of canned visuals, coupled with a speech by President McPherson, would not be different enough from the previous round of events to draw in a large audience.

The other instance in which volunteer reaction resulted in a shift in the original plans for the campaign had to do with our overall solicitation strategy. We had planned a tri-partite solicitation: top prospects, at the level of $50,000 and up, were to be solicited individually, each on a timetable appropriate to the particular circumstances, by the president, a trustee or Major Gifts Committee member, or a senior development staff member. Regional campaigns were organized in 14 major metropolitan areas, with volunteer solicitors recruited to solicit gifts in the $10,000-$50,000 range. All other alumnae were to be solicited for increased Annual Fund gifts; our plan was to feature annual giving as a primary objective of the campaign. However, the Campaign Steering Committee insisted that the entire alumnae body be solicited for the campaign, believing the Bryn Mawr constituency too cohesive to tolerate a transparently two-tier system. As a result, we organized a student phonathon program through which this third segment of the alumnae body (about 70 percent of the whole) was telephoned for campaign gifts. Although this procedure was useful in many regards (and helped us meet the conditions of a major challenge grant from the Kresge Foundation ahead of the deadline), we believe in retrospect that a three-year plateau in Annual Fund totals during the active years of the campaign is directly attributable to this shift of strategy. Further, it proved frustrating for annual giving volunteers and staff who were working hard to bolster that program during the campaign to be competing directly against the campaign solicitations, especially at the level of smaller gifts and in terms of achieving higher levels of participation. In the final year of the campaign (1992-93), we stopped telephoning alumnae 10 years out and less for the campaign and simply asked for their Annual Fund gifts. (The Annual Fund has now regained its momentum entirely, in large part as a result of a major initiative of the college's trustees, described below.)

A third example illustrates well the way in which Bryn Mawr's administration and top volunteers worked together successfully to develop a strategy to make the most of a potentially difficult and highly complex situation. The two major building projects included in the campaign were approached sequentially, both in terms of fund raising and construction timetables. The second of these, a new library for the collections in art and archaeology, underwent several major changes in scope and cost during the early years of the campaign. Although the total project cost had been estimated at $6 million in 1990, and then raised to $8 million in 1991 when campaign materials were produced, it had risen to nearly $13 million by the fall of 1992. At that point, although we had over $4 million in early major gifts and pledges for the project, the trustees decided to step back and reconsider the project. We had already scheduled a special weekend program for prospective major donors to the project later that fall, and decided, after much consultation, to proceed as planned. Despite the lack of specific information about the building project, the program was a success, and led to a number of significant gifts. We focused explicitly throughout on the faculty members and students who would benefit from the improved facilities and were honest with the 48 guests in attendance about the state of planning.

An ad hoc committee of administrators, faculty members, and librarians had been appointed by the president to redefine the scope of the project (expanding it to include seven major teaching spaces, in addition to the library space per se). At the same time, the project architect was charged with the development of a new and more economical design. By the fall of 1993, with a new plan approved by the board, we launched a targeted appeal for the project that would go beyond the official campaign end date of December 1993. First, we wrote to 125 donors and potential donors and 450 campaign volunteers to describe the change in design. We also described the revised plans and new timetable in *Money Matters*, the campaign newsletter mailed quarterly to the entire constituency. We identified a pool of prospective donors, many of whom would be solicited for second gifts to the campaign, and proceeded with a fund-raising program. This program resulted in approximately $8.7 million in total gifts for the project by the close of the campaign; we had secured $11.6 million by the end of the 1994 fiscal year. In retrospect, our decision to be frank about the setbacks experienced and to share progress at each stage with the constituents was clearly a wise one.

One final example may serve to illustrate the extent to which the college relies upon a highly personalized approach to fund raising. The handwritten note, which currently characterizes the Bryn Mawr process, may shortly be replaced by the spontaneous electronic mail message, but the same principle holds: Personal relationships based on trust and familiarity achieve successful fund raising. As one example of Bryn Mawr's reworking of conventional fund-raising tactics, the college has never conducted a prototypical feasibility study, in which outside, "objective" consultants interview important prospective donors and volunteers to gauge the level of support and interest in a major capital campaign. We felt instead that Bryn Mawr donors would respond honestly to the leaders of the institution, and shaped a program intended to have positive cultivation outcomes and provide useful information. A series of 14 presidential consultation dinners were held around the country in 1989-90. In each case, a small group of individuals were invited to help assess the potential appeal of the proposed campaign plan to potential donors. Each event took place in the home of a trustee or prominent supporter (by contrast with other institutions, which might choose a public setting instead). The sessions were small, varying in size from 12 to 40 individuals. Each was attended by the president and chief development officer; the chair of the Trustee Development Committee or other trustees were often present as well. Guests were sent a 20-page document to review in advance; this document laid out in careful detail the college's financial and programmatic positions and the proposed campaign objectives. Although the document contradicted all advice about readers' level of tolerance for lengthy prose, it was well received by this particular subset of the Bryn Mawr constituency. These were serious, structured events, during which the president spoke directly to the document and guests were encouraged to voice their concerns and questions. The dinners were, on the whole, highly successful, and we believe that the ensuing success with the solicitation of major gifts for the campaign, which proceeded more quickly than we had expected, followed at least in part from the strengthened relationship with the institution developed through the consultation dinners.

THE ROLE OF BRYN MAWR TRUSTEES IN THE FUND-RAISING PROGRAM

The explicit involvement of Bryn Mawr trustees in the fund-raising program is a relatively new phenomenon. The Trustee Development Committee was established in the late 1970s, and not until the Centennial Campaign were trustees solicited personally by one another for gifts to the college. (Previous solicitations had been undertaken in the form of personal notes.) In fact, trustees were not solicited for specific gift amounts until 1989, when they were asked for their commitments to the Campaign for Bryn Mawr. At that time, a small group, consisting of the chair of the board, the president, the chair of the Trustee Development Committee, the campaign chair, and the director of resources, met to review a proposed list of solicitors and solicitation amounts. A group of trustee solicitors was recruited, and the method of solicitation was left in the hands of individual solicitors. Since that time, trustees have been solicited each year for their Annual Fund gifts; in general, each receives a letter from the chair of the Development Committee naming a fellow trustee who will follow up with phone call. This system has proven successful and also seems a useful method to more personally include those trustees who do not serve on the Development Committee in the fund-raising enterprise.

With the exception of key trustee volunteers, the Bryn Mawr Board does not, as a rule, involve itself with the details of the ongoing fund-raising program. This seems to be an expression of their confidence in the strategies employed and the results achieved. However, trustee voices were instrumental in the 1989 decision to set the campaign goal not at $60 million, as campaign counsel and the professional staff were advising, but at $75 million. During a special meeting to review the campaign plan and formalize its objectives, the review process initiated on the campus and continued through several small groups of trustees in its early stages was extended to include the entire board. According to Development Committee Chair Ruth Nelson,

> The involvement of the trustees in the determination of the goal strengthened significantly their own commitment as individuals to providing and to helping to secure leadership gifts. Our conversation, serious and, at times, agonizing, grew beyond those most directly involved with campaign planning to draw in members of the board generally concerned with other areas of the college. It was an important process for the Bryn Mawr trustees.

As the Campaign for Bryn Mawr drew to a close and we examined closely its results, the trustees expressed concern about the leveling off of Annual Fund gifts. We needed a dramatic way to express to the constituency as a whole the critical nature of the Annual Fund to the college's fiscal health. The result, which was spearheaded by Ruth Nelson, was the Trustees Challenge for annual giving, in which the trustees agreed to double their own gifts overall to the Annual Fund in 1993-94 if annual giving reached specific levels of total gifts and participation from undergraduate alumnae. This effort, undertaken immediately on the heels of the Campaign for Bryn Mawr, was enormously successful, yielding over 2,700 increased gifts and a 31 percent increase in annual giving overall. Further, it demonstrates the ongoing evolution of the Trustee Development Committee in terms of its leadership of and responsibility for all college fund raising from the time preceding the integration of the Annual Fund into the college program, when annual fund raising was seldom, if ever, discussed by the Bryn Mawr trustees. This commitment has also been demonstrated through a recent decision by the trustees to invite the volunteer leaders of three important fund-raising committees (Annual Fund, Bequests and Deferred Giving, and Major Gifts) to meet with the trustees once each year and report on the work of their committees.

CONCLUSION

Some of the trends highlighted in this report—the growing professionalization of the Bryn Mawr fund-raising effort, the challenge of defining volunteer roles that make best use of alumnae abilities and contacts yet are manageable for women who lead extraordinarily complex lives—will continue. Whether and how we will be able to maintain the intensely personal character of the program is an important concern, because this character is clearly crucial to the demonstrated pattern of success. President McPherson concludes, "Our good results in fund raising are directly attributable to the fact that we have had fun in the doing. Visiting old friends and making new ones on behalf of an institution about which we all care deeply can hardly be called difficult work. We have in common a genuine enjoyment of and affection for the Bryn Mawr community, in all its diversity and complexity. This work is never boring."

CHAPTER

Successful Fund Raising at a University Serving Hispanics
The University of Texas-Pan American

by Miguel A. Nevárez

T hroughout its 69-year history as Edinburg College, Edinburg Junior College, Edinburg Regional College, Pan American College, and Pan American University, the institution that is now The University of Texas-Pan American has been the primary source of higher education for a large portion of the vast Rio Grande Valley of Texas. Strategically located in Edinburg, Texas, within a few miles of the United States/Mexico border, UT Pan American is the 10th largest of the state's 35 public senior institutions of higher education, with 95 percent of its predominantly Hispanic enrollment coming from a four-county area that also constitutes one of the fastest growing areas of the state and nation.

The population of UT Pan American's service area is an interesting and ecclectic mix that includes a growing number of upwardly mobile first-generation college graduates, many migrant farmworkers, and thousands of "Winter Texans" who for several months in the year make the Valley their retirement home. This operating environment has for many years provided some unique challenges and opportunities for UT Pan American, a component of The University of Texas System since 1989, a charter member of the Hispanic Association of Colleges and Universities, and one of the nation's largest Hispanic Serving Institutions (HSI).

Developing an institutional advancement program to take advantage of these unique opportunities and to meet the many challenges of a minority-serving institution was a top priority for me when I was named president of Pan American University in 1981. From the beginning, I stressed the fact that the institution could not attain the level of excellence for which it strived without funds from the private sector. That message was important then, and is even more important today.

THE FINANCIAL REALITY

A decade or so ago, state universities in Texas generally considered private gifts and grants to be "margin of excellence" funds that could help us take advantage of opportunities not supported by state funds. In recent years, however, the financial situation has been changing. While state appropriations supported about 94 percent of the operating budget at our university in the mid-1980s, that percentage has dwindled to a little less than 74 percent today, a number that would be much less if we were not receiving some special line item funding as part of a state initiative to improve educational opportunities for residents of South Texas.

The prevailing attitude now is that the student should shoulder more of the responsibility for his or her education; thus, colleges and universities should be able to make up the difference in state appropriations through higher tuition and fees. This attitude presents a difficult problem for institutions such as UT Pan American, where 77 percent of our students receive some form of financial aid and many would not be able to attend school at all without the extra help.

These realities give new importance to those "margin of excellence" funds and certainly give new importance to the university endowment, the Annual Fund, restricted and unrestricted gifts, and the donation of equipment by corporate friends—and, in essense, magnify the importance of our fund-raising activities at UT Pan American.

In the early years, the fund-raising "team" consisted mainly of T. Edward Mercer, vice president for institutional advancement, with me stepping in as needed. In 1985, we added a development officer to coordinate the Annual Fund, and in 1987 a director for our first capital campaign. When the campaign was over in 1990 (we went $5 million over our $4.6 million goal), the campaign director decided to move on, and we used his salary to establish two new positions—a director of development and alumni relations and another development officer.

Today, the vice president for institutional advancement, while remaining the chief fund-raising officer, supervises a professional fund-raising staff that includes an administrative assistant in his office, an accountant for the foundation, the director of development, and two development officers—one for the Annual Fund and the other for the computer information system. As we face the challenge of increasing private gifts to offset dwindling state appropriations, we also must address the need for additional professional staff so that we can broaden our cultivation efforts with corporations, foundations, and individual prospective donors throughout the country.

Although our institutional advancement program is young by most standards, we feel we have made considerable progress in our first 15 years. For example, the endowment (including planned gifts) has grown from $52,414 in the 1981 fiscal year to $9.65 million in FY 1991 and almost $17 million today.

In that same period, unrestricted donations increased from $21,776 in FY 1981 to $114,179 in FY 1991 and $280,408 in FY 1995. Although no restricted donations were recorded in FY 1981, the university and the UT Pan American Foundation received restricted gifts totaling $462,438 in FY 1991 and $1.425 million in FY 1995.

Capital equipment also has been an important fund-raising objective for us in recent years, especially as we continue to develop our high-tech programs, such as computer science and electrical, manufacturing, and mechanical engineering. Over the years, UT Pan American has received several million dollars' worth of equipment from a variety of corporate partners.

THE FUND-RAISING BUDGET

The operating budget for the fund-raising effort at the university is divided between the Office of the Vice President for Institutional Advancement and the Office of Development and Alumni Relations, which is responsible for most of the stewardship activities. Also, since its creation in 1982, the university foundation has been generous in underwriting some operational activities and in supplementing such areas as staff travel when appropriate and necessary. That support has been extremely important because the institutional appropriation we have been able to dedicate to the fund-raising effort, as a percentage of the institution's operating budget, has fluctuated from a low of .49 percent in FY 1990 ($134,477) to a high of .95 percent in FY 1991 ($273,859), with an 11-year average of .72 percent. The FY 1997 budget for the two offices totals $345,355, or .81 percent of the total institutional appropriation.

In addition to the vice president's office and the Office of Development and Alumni Relations, the Division of Institutional Advancement includes the Office of University Relations and the Office of Placement, Testing and Cooperative Education. When I became president in 1981, I placed the Office of Placement, Testing and Cooperative Education in the Division of Institutional Advancement. Although an unusual move at the time, and perhaps still today, it was a good idea because it has helped us maximize our corporate contacts. For instance, when a corporation recruits on our campus during "career days," our chief advancement officer has easy access to the corporation's representatives because his division is sponsoring the event. When our fund-raisers make corporate calls, they also promote the idea of that company recruiting on our campus. We think the benefits to our students are multiplied.

The UT Pan American Division of Institutional Advancement is built on a traditional philosophy of service that includes fostering public interest, promoting a positive image, enhancing the financial base, and promoting student success through career planning and placement. The division is guided by the vice president for institutional advancement, whose responsibilities are to "plan and administer a program of public support for the University, giving general supervision to improving relationships with its many publics and developing financial support through alumni, private and corporate donors, private foundations and other sources."

The division's Mission Statement, which is reproduced below, was adopted in 1995.

> The Division of Institutional Advancement supports the educational mission of The University of Texas-Pan American by cultivating, sustaining and maximizing links between the University students, faculty and staff and all of the institution's internal and external constituencies.

The Division seeks to accomplish this general purpose by

- fostering the public interest by encouraging and facilitating involvement of external constituencies with the University;

- promoting University development by initiating and coordinating institutional efforts to acquire private contributions and ensuring responsible stewardship and administration of all gifts;

- increasing awareness of and support for the institution through public relations programs, public information services and special events;

- fostering relationships with employers and assisting students with career entry by providing cooperative education programs, career planning, placement and testing services; and

- promoting continued support of the University from graduates and other former students through an organized program of activities and communiqués and by developing and advocating an active, effective and supportive Alumni Association.

> In fulfilling its mission, the Division of Institutional Advancement adheres to the Rules and Regulations of the Board of Regents of The University of Texas System and the University's *Handbook of Operating*

Procedures and, as appropriate, abides by the policies and procedures of the UT Pan American Foundation and the UT Pan American Alumni Association. The Division also subscribes to the principles of institutional advancement established by the Council for Advancement and Support of Education (CASE).

The goals, objectives, and strategies to support this mission statement are outlined in a written strategic planning document that was prepared in 1995 to address the critical concerns of the university and to serve as a framework for a team approach that will help maximize our institutional advancement efforts at UT Pan American.

The *Strategic Plan 1995-2000*, the result of a two-day planning retreat with the university's director of institutional research and planning and months of preparation by the staff, is of special importance because of the changing educational landscape in South Texas. For many years, Pan American was an "open admission" institution because it provided the only access to higher education for thousands of students in the Rio Grande Valley. With the creation in 1993 of a new community college in our primary service area, UT Pan American is now able to develop as a comprehensive university within The University of Texas System. As noted in the university's *Agency Strategic Plan for the 1995-1999 Period,*

> Having STCC (South Texas Community College) as an ally in the higher education endeavor will permit UT Pan American to review its institutional mission, its admissions standards and its resource allocation as it concentrates more attention on high-end baccalaureate programs and master's and doctoral programs and places greater emphasis on the concomitant research and public service efforts associated with a comprehensive university.

This new emphasis on upper-division and graduate education as UT Pan American develops as a comprehensive university, the tightening of admissions standards at the undergraduate level, and the growing need to recruit better-prepared students, with its accompanying need for a much-enhanced scholarship program, are combining to create a different operating environment for the institution as we approach the twenty-first century. To be successful in this new environment, we must strengthen our institutional advancement program so the university can continue to address its mission of providing educational opportunity to a predominantly Hispanic population.

One of the most significant steps we have taken to address some of the new challenges, especially the loss of enrollment to the community college and the increase in admission standards, was the convening in March 1994 of an

Enrollment Management Task Force, which I asked our director of university relations to chair.

As a result of that study, we are placing much greater emphasis on market-ing the university and its programs to a broader public, and we will be counting on the Division of Institutional Advancement to play a major role in the process. Specifically, the Office of University Relations will be involved because it has responsibility for developing public relations and publications programs to enhance the image of the institution, and the Office of Develop-ment and Alumni Relations will be asked to increase its efforts to raise scholarship funds to aid in student recruitment and retention.

BUILDING AN INSTITUTIONAL ADVANCEMENT PROGRAM: A PRESIDENT'S PERSPECTIVE

I first arrived on the Pan American University campus in 1971 as associate dean of men. With a developing interest in grant writing, I began encouraging the university leadership to allow us to seek funding from the numerous federal programs spawned by President Lyndon Johnson's "Great Society." As was the case at many public colleges and universities in that era, the attitude at Pan American was that accepting support from the federal government, or private sources for that matter, meant opening the door to outsiders who would try to tell us how to run the university. Most gifts and grants, it was felt, came with too many strings attached. Also, the Texas economy was booming in the 1970s, and the state legislature was able, as one member later recalled, "to play Santa Claus" to higher education. In those days, there was no pressing need for external funding. Because of those conditions and attitudes, just getting approval to start an alumni association was a real challenge. The president did not agree to the need for an alumni association until our self-study and accreditation process in the mid-1970s forced us to ask questions about how active the alumni were and if we did follow-ups on our graduates.

To jump-start the process, we created teams up and down the Rio Grande Valley and challenged ourselves to sell 500 memberships at $100 each. We eventually signed up some 600 charter members, and their names are listed on a plaque kept in the University Library to remind us of how important that group was in broadening our advancement effort.

By the time the Alumni Association was formed, we had already begun submitting proposals to federal agencies and were writing about the institu-tion, its mission, and the role it played in the community. After a few rounds of successful proposals, we realized that our institution, serving a predominantly minority student population, had a good case that should also appeal to private foundations and corporations. After this realization, I began attending meet-ings of the Council for Advancement and Support of Education (CASE) to learn how to do fund raising. (It may seem strange now that a vice president for student affairs, which I had become by then, was taking a lead role in this arena, but at the time we had no development officers and I had a real interest in finding external funds for scholarships and other programs that would directly benefit our students.)

Although we felt we had a good case to make to foundations and corporations, we had a lot to learn about how to approach them. How do you know what their interests are? If you want to go to Foundation X, how do you know that they will be interested in a particular project?

When we first approached foundations, they would always ask about the size of the alumni association, how many active members we had, and how much money the alumni collected. They were also especially interested to know if we had the support of our local community.

By 1978, I was spending a lot more time actually doing fund raising, both in the private arena and with the federal government, and we were being fairly successful in our efforts. My title then expanded from vice president for student affairs to vice president for student affairs and university relations, and I was given the go-ahead to work with the university's schools and departments on fund-raising projects.

With the addition of a dean of students to the staff, I was able, as vice president, to spend more time seeking external resources for the university and less time in student affairs. When I was named president of Pan American in 1981, we were well positioned for an administrative reorganization that allowed us to dissolve my old vice presidency and create the position of vice president for institutional advancement and our first formal advancement program.

I had always been convinced that we had a good case that would appeal to the private sector. We used the "value added" approach. We would say, for example, "Here's where the kids are when they come to us; here's where their parents are (educationally and economically); here's what we can do for the students after four or five years. Look at the enhancement." In a vice president for institutional advancement, we were looking for someone who knew how to take that powerful message to the right people, someone who had more fund-raising know-how than I had, someone with experience in approaching foundations and corporations. But we were also looking for more.

By 1981, I had been to a number of CASE conferences and had discovered that private fund raising was a lot more than I had thought it was—a whole package needed to be developed. We needed a vice president who could guide us through setting up a total advancement program, including fund raising, alumni, and publications—all the pieces of the advancement puzzle that then constituted the different interest area tracks at CASE conferences.

In the second edition of the *Handbook of Institutional Advancement*, G.T. Smith, president of Chapman College in California, noted: "We are only as good as the people we work with. Get the best, and they make us better too." I most certainly agree with that observation, especially when Smith added: "This is probably nowhere more evident than when attracting a chief advancement officer and staff."

From its beginning, the institutional advancement program at Pan American has been synonymous with the name of T. Edward Mercer. I like to think we were insightful, but maybe we were just lucky when we chose him as our first advancement vice president in 1981. He is an experienced professional who brought with him not only a sound knowledge of his craft and an impeccable reputation as a fund-raiser, but also a corporate and foundation contact base that provided immediate benefits to the university.

After Ed joined Pan American on 1 January 1982, I asked him to visit several other state-supported schools throughout Texas to see how they were developing their advancement programs. This assignment was especially important because Ed's background was in private institutions, and I knew that doing fund raising for a public university would be different for him. We certainly were not pioneering the idea of a public institution advancement program, so we wanted to find out what was working for other schools and apply some of those successful methods.

Although we were depending on the new vice president for institutional advancement to develop the organizational structure and operating guidelines, I knew that the president had to provide the leadership for the overall effort—both on and off campus. That role has not really changed over the years. Although the chief advancement officer and other members of the development staff are certainly key to the cultivation process and work hard to develop relationships with foundations, corporations, and individuals, the president of the university is expected to be there when it is time to share the mission and vision of the institution and to show support for the individual projects.

Prospective donors, whether multinational corporations, local small businesses, or alumni, want to see commitment to the cause. They want to know that the project will be supported by the institution, and they want that assurance first-hand from the president—and, in the case of academic projects, from the dean, who will make it happen day to day. In essence, they want to see where the university is heading and they want to be reassured that the program to be funded is in synch with the university as a whole.

We also found out early on that donors are not interested in funding projects that will require support indefinitely. When you talk to corporations and foundations, they are willing to give you seed money to get you started, but they want to see institutional and local support that will keep the project going. They want to know that the university will eventually consider the program valuable enough to pick it up—to institutionalize it—and the CEO is probably the only one who can make that commitment.

We recognized from the beginning that fund raising had to start at home and that we needed to have several successful local campaigns before we could begin asking foundations and corporations outside our area for help. We started with scholarship fund raising through some of our local businesses, hoping that it would translate into other support, and we followed the same procedure some years later when we wanted to find out how strongly the local community felt about an engineering school. We decided then to try to raise $200,000 locally before we got involved in a major capital campaign for engineering. Our young engineering program, which graduated its first mechanical, manufacturing, and electrical engineers in 1995, has attracted excellent financial support from major corporations and foundations as a result of the Campaign for Engineering. In addition, we received $23 million to construct a new Engineering Building through the South Texas/Border Initiative, a special legislative effort to improve educational opportunities in an underserved, predominantly minority area of the state.

As evidenced by the South Texas/Border Initiative, HSIs have begun to receive more attention from state and federal governments, private foundations, and Corporate America, and Pan American has been one of the leaders as well as one of the beneficiaries of the effort. A major advance for HSIs came a little more than 10 years ago when a number of institutions, including our own, joined together to form the Hispanic Association of Colleges and Universities (HACU). The charter members knew they had a good case for support, and also felt there could be strength in numbers (a concept so successfully illustrated by the Historically Black Colleges and Universities). In the last decade, we have developed a number of partnerships with various departments of the federal government that have resulted in summer internships for students, research projects, and other collaborative efforts; we have been successful in obtaining a $12 million set-aside for HSIs in the federal budget; and HACU member institutions have had much more visibility with Corporate America.

I was recently asked if being an HSI has been an asset or a liability to The University of Texas-Pan American in its advancement effort; I did not hesitate to answer that I think we have definitely benefited from our status as a minority-serving institution. People recognize that the Hispanic population in this country is growing, is relatively young, and is the future workforce. The widely accepted need for a well-educated workforce will keep Corporate America interested in institutions serving the fast-growing Hispanic population.

UT Pan American also has benefited from its strategic location on the U.S./ Mexico border. The North American Free Trade Agreement (NAFTA) has caused U.S. companies to try to form trading blocks not only with Mexico but also throughout Central and South America, and these companies need employees who understand the Hispanic culture and language. The fact that our bilingual graduates are well prepared to fill that role is a story that our institutional advancement staff tells often throughout Corporate America.

While we are explaining to corporations and foundations outside our region how some project fits into the mission of the university, we also talk about how it relates to the needs of the area we service—and how those needs are changing. For example, although Pan American began as a teacher training institution, our College of Business Administration took on new importance when the Rio Grande Valley's economy began expanding more into the retail and service areas. Manufacturing and health care now are booming parts of the regional economy, and we are adjusting our academic and service programs to meet those needs and opportunities.

To help spread the word about all that is happening at UT Pan American and in the Rio Grande Valley and to help position the institution as uniquely deserving of private support, we depend on an important group of volunteers who serve on our foundation Board of Trustees and on advisory boards to various academic areas, such as engineering and business administration.

How we established the Pan American University Foundation in 1982 and our strategy for developing its governing board is an important part of the institutional advancement story at UT Pan American, because the foundation trustees have played a key role in the fund-raising process at the institution.

Although Ed Mercer's contacts helped position us to bring state and national representation to the board early on, we felt it was essential first to identify local and regional trustees who already knew about the university and who could tell Pan American's story from a community perspective. Local civic leader Margaret McAllen, who later was named to the Pan American University Board of Regents by Texas Governor Mark White, was one of the three original trustees who signed the incorporation papers establishing the university foundation. Recalling those early days, she says that she viewed the role of the first foundation trustees as one of helping the chief advancement officer make contacts with possible contributors and helping to develop the strategy and the direction for the university's fund-raising efforts—a focus that remains today for foundation board members.

We next began looking at corporations with some presence—a plant, a store, or a distributorship—in the Rio Grande Valley to help us develop an outreach for the cultivation of gifts because we considered board members to be extensions of the university in their own communities, whether New York, San Francisco, or Houston. This development was important because most corporations and foundations had never heard of Pan American University, and they wanted to know who they could call to find out more about us. Because establishing credibility for the institution was the first step in the cultivation process, it was helpful when our chief advancement officer could refer someone in New York to a vice president at AT&T who was serving on our board. In essence, we have an anchor in every city where we have a board member.

Today, The University of Texas-Pan American Foundation Board of Trustees includes representatives from AT&T, Intel, Wal-Mart, Haggar Apparel, Southwestern Bell Communications, Texaco, and the Southland Corporation. Not only do our trustees provide access to their own corporations, but also, through the foundation's Corporate Partners program, they help open doors for us at other companies with which their employers do business. A Corporate Partners packet, designed and written by our Office of University Relations, includes an invitation letter to the prospective partner, a description of the various ways a company might become involved with UT Pan American, and a listing of the benefits to be derived by the company through either a formal or informal partnership with the university. Also included are testimonials from university foundation trustees describing what a partnership with us has meant for their own corporations.

To assist with other facets of our fund-raising program—especially planned and annual giving—several attorneys, a financial planner, and area businesspeople also serve as trustees to provide important guidance and expertise and help represent us within our own community.

In his first days on campus, Ed Mercer sold us on the importance of an estate planning program; he also was careful to make us understand that the rewards from planned gifts would be slow in coming. At the time, we already had a little experience with such gifts, since a former regent had included the university in his will and a Winter Texan from Illinois, whom we had never met, had left us half of her estate simply because she believed in the university's mission. (Her other beneficiary was the University of Chicago.) Despite these gifts, we knew little about the planned giving process until we began our institutional advancement program and Ed initiated, as a free public service, the first estate planning seminars ever to be offered in the Rio Grande Valley—a project that is still going after some 15 years.

Although the gift from the Winter Texan was not a large sum, Ed has always considered it one of the four most important gifts this university has ever received because it was an excellent early example of how someone could give to the university. He includes the other three gifts for the same reason. They are an unrestricted gift of $75,000 from the Haggar Foundation, which resulted from an established friendship Ed had with a member of the Haggar family before coming to Pan American; the deferred gift of their home in

Austin by former Governor Allan and Marialice Shary Shivers (Mrs. Shivers once served as chair of the university's Board of Regents); and a $400,000 gift to support the business administration program from Gulf Oil Corporation, which became the university's first major corporate donor. Larger and extremely important gifts have followed, but those four helped give us confidence in our ability to raise funds for the university and also provided us with some early successes that we could share with other corporations, foundations, and prospective individual donors.

For years, Ed Mercer has identified major corporations and foundations that already have an interest in helping minorities and minority-serving institutions by participating in the conventions of such organizations as the NAACP, LULAC, and La Raza. What he has done so skillfully is to get the corporations who participate in those organizations also involved in some way with the university, even if it is nothing more than an invitation to come visit and recruit on campus. Later, if we are talking with Corporation X and we can say, "Your recruiter was just down for a visit," we have an automatic tie to the company. People don't normally give to you the first time you ask; you need some kind of involvement with the corporation. Ed's presence at all those meetings throughout the year, my work with HACU, and all those small contacts give us that involvement.

Over the years, our advancement team—and I include myself here—has worked hard to develop relationships with various corporations and foundations that have allowed us the opportunity to tell our story to an ever broadening external public. Throughout the process, we have also worked hard to ensure that the advancement staff maintains an active role in the ongoing affairs of the institution.

For planning purposes, the chief advancement officer must be involved in the university's daily life. Our vice president for institutional advancement, for example, is an active member of the President's Council, its Executive Committee, and the Campus Facilities Planning Council. As such, he is an integral part of the institutional strategic planning process through which we not only prepare our legislative requests but also identify needs that cannot be met with state funding and for which we will need to appeal to other sources. As our chief fund-raiser, he is not simply given a "shopping list"; he is very much a part of the decision-making team. In my mind, nothing can substitute for the president and chief advancement officer sitting down together, discussing where the needs are and how to communicate those needs to others, and channeling gifts in the proper direction.

As the institutional advancement team has grown, Ed and I have found it increasingly difficult to balance the need for him to be involved on campus with the need for him to be in the field making contacts, cultivating relationships, and presenting the university's case to potential donors, something he does so well on behalf of UT Pan American.

Now, after 15 years with the university and more than 25 years in institutional advancement, our first and only chief advancement officer is beginning to plan for retirement. He and I recognize that we will need to make a decision about the future direction of the institutional advancement program at UT Pan American. Will we want someone to head institutional advancement who is a day-to-day administrator or will we continue to need someone like Ed—an effective fund-raiser for the university? It was easy when we hired him as our first advancement vice president because he was the whole show back then. But as the staff has grown, it has become more difficult for Ed to continue his almost constant travel while also providing administrative leadership to his division. Considering the special attributes required of a good fund-raiser like Ed Mercer, I know that it will be difficult to replace him when he retires.

When we have developed a really productive relationship with someone at a corporation or foundation, we find that the focus can shift when that person leaves the organization. The door may remain open, but the relationship has to be developed anew with an entirely different person. When the chief advancement officer leaves a university, that problem is greatly multiplied because every relationship at every foundation and corporation is affected.

I am also looking ahead to retirement in a few years, but I feel strongly that the president and the chief advancement officer should not leave at the same time. Ed and I must develop some sort of "phase in, phase out" process that will allow for as smooth a transition as possible to a new chief advancement officer. Otherwise, the new person may knock on a door that has been open to us for many years only to find it not open quite as wide.

What all this proves to me is how important institutional advancement is and how much fund raising is a person-to-person activity. Sure, you have to have a good cause, a real need—that's essential. But that's not enough; there are so many good causes, so much real need. You need to develop a relationship that allows a corporation or foundation to say, "Look, these are the things we are interested in; this is what we need to develop, and this institution and this person are good conduits to get this done." With all else being equal, the institution that has developed the best relationship is the one that is going to be successful.

The best way to develop that type of relationship is through the efforts of a fund-raising team such as we have at The University of Texas-Pan American—a team that believes strongly in the mission and uniqueness of the institution and one in which the chief executive officer and the chief advancement officer understand the importance of fulfilling their respective roles and accepting their respective responsibilities. Our institutional advancement program is a vital, energetic, and dynamic part of UT Pan American, and we look forward to an exciting future as one of the country's leading Hispanic Serving Institutions.

CHAPTER 9

Successful Fund Raising at a Religious-Based College

Saint Anselm College

*by Rev. Jonathan DeFelice, O.S.B., John J. Reilly, Jr.,
and Paul A. Dowd*

S aint Anselm College is a Roman Catholic college founded by monks of the Order of Saint Benedict in 1889. The college, which is located on a spacious campus just outside Manchester, New Hampshire, continues under Benedictine governance today. Saint Anselm is a four-year liberal arts college with no graduate programs. By far the major portion of its graduates earn bachelor of arts degrees, although a significant number are awarded bachelor of science in nursing degrees The student population of approximately 1,900 is drawn mostly from New England, New York, and New Jersey. Like most regional colleges, Saint Anselm is making an effort to widen the area from which it regularly draws students. Its alumni population, although somewhat more widespread, reflects this same geographical pattern. Saint Anselm boasts a strong academic reputation. For example, for the past eight consecutive years it has been ranked among the best regional liberal arts colleges in the north region in the annual *U.S. News & World Report* ratings of the best colleges in the United States.

For the purposes of this discussion, the history of the college may be divided into two eras, roughly pre- and post-1960. We will concentrate on the post-1960 era. At that time, the college organized its first Board of Trustees (an advisory board consisting of laypeople) and embarked upon its first major fund-raising campaign. In approximately four years, the college conducted a successful $3 million capital campaign, constructed six new buildings, and doubled the size of its enrollment to 1,200 students. Upon this base, the college built its continuing advancement and its fund-raising program.

One common misconception about the funding of Catholic colleges and universities should be cleared up at the outset. Like most Catholic colleges and universities, Saint Anselm receives no financial support from the Catholic Church. However, practices vary among non-Catholic churches with affiliated colleges. Some colleges conducted under the auspices of religious denominations do receive support from their local, regional, or national church organization.

BRIEF HISTORY OF SAINT ANSELM FUND-RAISING CAMPAIGNS

In 1958, the $3 Million Building Fund Campaign raised $3.5 million to build six buildings and double the size of the college. The campaign exployed professional fund-raising counsel. In 1963, the $1 million targeted Capital Fund Drive focused on raising funds to build a college church. The campaign was successfully completed without outside fund-raising counsel. It concentrated mostly upon major gifts and undertook only limited general solicitation. In 1967, the Annual Fund was established. In 1980, the $3 million Building Fund Campaign, a capital campaign to build a theater/humanities center and an activities/sports center, raised $3.2 million. The Annual Fund was suspended for the period of the campaign, which employed professional fund-raising counsel.

The college launched its $12.5 Million Centennial Campaign in 1989 to coincide with its centennial celebration. This campaign had three components: 1) endowment, 2) faculty development, and 3) expansion and renovation of the college library. Professional fund-raising counsel was employed. For the first time at Saint Anselm, campaign goals included projects other than specifically bricks and mortar. Also for the first time, deferred giving was included as a component of the campaign goal. Annual Fund solicitation was continued as a distinct fund-raising effort throughout the campaign, which eventually reached $14.5 million.

In 1995, the college launched the $1.5 million targeted Science Center Campaign, which was designed to assist with renovation of the college's science center. The campaign employed no professional fund-raising counsel and concentrated on major gifts and foundations. Successfully completed in 1996, the campaign included no general solicitation and did not interrupt the Annual Fund.

For the future, the planning and cultivation phase is underway for a campaign for endowment, which is due to launch in 2000. The goal for the campaign is still to be announced.

SIZE AND ORGANIZATION OF THE ADVANCEMENT TEAM

Stripped down to essentials, college and university fund raising has only two overlapping modes: pre-capital campaign and campaign. Before the current capital campaign concludes, preliminary plans for the next campaign are being sketched. The important time between campaigns can be characterized as pre-campaign planning and cultivation of leadership and major donors. Of course, pre-campaign has a succession of stages defined by increasing intensity. No longer do college advancement staffs have the luxury they once had of relatively extended post-campaign and between-campaign periods. This is not to suggest that the vital components of what formerly was considered post-campaign activity can be neglected. The importance of campaign follow-through and stewardship is greater than ever. The point here is simply that today's college is constantly in "campaign" mode.

At this writing, Saint Anselm College is nearing the latter stages of pre-campaign preparation. This stage includes building staff in anticipation of the campaign. The fund-raising operation of the college is organized under the vice president for college advancement (VPCA). The departments of public relations, alumni, and development report to the VPCA, who is the chief advancement officer and an extension of the office of the president. The VPCA's role is to help shape and implement the advancement policies of the college. This role includes orchestration and coordination of the efforts of the departments within the college advancement division.

The Alumni Office, which operates with a director and a secretary, plays a traditional supporting role and avoids direct involvement in fund raising. Saint Anselm has about 12,500 alumni. The college is blessed with a supportive and reasonably tight-knit alumni body, which is considered the principal source of financial support for the college. Because the alumni population is young, 50 percent having graduated since 1979, the growth potential for alumni giving is excellent.

The Public Relations Department plays an active role in support of the college's fund-raising programs. Besides the usual mission of "cultivating the soil" and "preparing the environment," the public relations director has, in past capital campaigns, conceived and produced the case statement and supporting publications, served as a member of the campaign strategy team, participated in direct cultivation, and assisted with organizing regional kick-off events. The Public Relations Department has two full-time professional staff members plus a part-time editor and a technical/clerical assistant.

The key department is the Development Office, which is organized under the director of development. The department also employs a major gifts officer; an annual fund officer; a grant writing specialist, who also concentrates on corporate relations; an entry-level development assistant, who concentrates on anniversary class giving and assists in other areas; a senior clerical staff employee, who is responsible for the gift recording and accounting program and also manages the parents program and organizes telethons; a research assistant, who is also responsible for database management; one full-time clerical staff member, who is responsible for gift acknowledgment, correspondence, and other secretarial duties; and one part-time clerical person.

The major gifts officer fills a newly created position in anticipation of the upcoming capital campaign. Initially, this officer's role will be to increase the number of major gifts for the Annual Fund. This is one of the strategies being employed to rapidly advance the Annual Fund to a million dollars per year.

The development office is charged with all direct fund-raising operations, including capital campaigns, Annual Fund, corporate and foundation relations, anniversary class giving program, senior class gift program, and parents organization.

In addition to the departments reporting to the VPCA, a vice president for endowment (VPE) operates independently of, but in concert with, all the departments in the college advancement area. The separate Office of Endowment was created following the college's highly successful centennial campaign when the potential for deferred giving was fully explored for the first time. Previously, the vice president for development had been handling deferred giving opportunities "as they came along." During the centennial campaign, the college began to recognize enormous potential in the area of deferred giving and estate gifts. The vice president for development then accepted the challenge of concentrating full-time on deferred giving as a means to build the college's endowment. This initiative is considered so successful that the college soon will have to consider assignment of an additional part-time officer to handle the increasing case load. The VPE will groom a sufficiently experienced individual for an eventual smooth transition of this sensitive position, in which long-time personal cultivation is the key to success.

The level of development staffing described above is relatively new for Saint Anselm. Traditionally, the college operated with a vice president for development as the sole fund-raising officer. In anticipation of the centennial campaign, the college added a director of development and a research assistant. At the conclusion of the centennial campaign, the college established the Office of Endowment (as described above) and initiated a plan to increase the Annual Fund to $1 million over an eight-year period, beginning with approximately $550,000 in 1992. Accordingly, a full-time Annual Fund officer joined the staff. This investment in staff reflects the increased emphasis the college places on fund raising in its overall financial plan and recognizes capital campaigns, as well as a growing Annual Fund, as regular and necessary features of that plan.

IMPACT OF FUND RAISING ON OPERATING BUDGET AND FACILITIES

Since the initial building fund campaign of 1958, capital fund raising has been used to build necessary facilities. Providing excellent facilities located on a beautifully developed campus has been one of the keys to attracting quality students and expanding the college's reputation.

The initial 1958 building fund drive provided the means to build a library, science center, student union, gymnasium, and two dormitories. The 1963 drive built a church, which is central to most of the activities taking place on a Catholic college campus that has a Benedictine monastic community in residence. In addition to the college community, many people from surrounding communities worship regularly at this church, and some of these people have become significant contributors to the college. Because the church is considered one of the most beautiful buildings in New Hampshire, it attracts many visitors to the campus. The 1980 capital campaign provided a performing arts/humanities center and a recreation/sports complex. The 1989 centennial campaign produced a modern, state-of-the-art library twice the size of its predecessor.

These building initiatives, which were supported by fund-raising efforts, enriched the learning environment and kept the college competitive in attracting quality students. Although the recent long downward slide in the number of college-age students was particularly acute in the Northeast, Saint Anselm was able to maintain the size of its applicant pool, steadily improve the academic profile of its enrolled students, and maintain full enrollment throughout.

Fund raising further contributed to the college's ability to improve its position in the higher education marketplace by raising endowment for student aid during the centennial campaign. Numerous endowed scholarships were added during the campaign, allowing Saint Anselm to be highly competitive in offering financial aid to top quality students with demonstrated financial need.

Saint Anselm College is a tuition-driven institution and the budget relief afforded by the Annual Fund is an important factor in the college's economic health. The college's annual budget averaged almost $34 million per annum over the past five years. During that same five-year period the fund-raising effort produced an average of almost $2.5 million annually, about 7 percent of the annual budget. For the 1995-96 fiscal year, the overall development program produced $2.98 million, including an Annual Fund total of $750,000.

The Office of Endowment also reports that estate and deferred gifts were the principal source of an increase of approximately $3 million per year in the college's endowment over the past four years. Of course, the annual amounts derived from estate instruments can vary enormously from year to year, dependent as they are upon unpredictable events.

The endowment was less than $4 million before the beginning of the 1989 centennial capital campaign, which included a deferred giving component for endowment. The endowment has now reached approximately $30 million. Despite this dramatic progress, the college realizes that the endowment is far from adequate. Hence, one major fund-raising goal is to double the endowment by the turn of the century.

GOALS OF THE ADVANCEMENT PROGRAM

The college and the advancement division have set three objectives to be achieved by the end of the decade.

1. Increase the annual fund to $1 million per year.
2. Double the college's endowment to $60 million.
3. Mount a capital campaign to raise $25 to $50 million to address endowment and other needs.

To achieve these ambitious objectives, the president of the college and the chair of the Board of Trustees must match the commitment of the VPCA and the college advancement staff. The model the college will use to achieve these objectives is the one employed with success during the college's centennial capital campaign.

TRUSTEE COMMITMENT IS THE KEY TO SUCCESS

The *sine qua non* of successful fund raising for a small church-related college is the commitment of the board of trustees. Saint Anselm College learned this lesson early when the members of its first Board of Trustees grasped a vision of the future of the college as articulated by the president and became determined as a group to make the vision a reality. The resulting $3 million capital campaign was board driven, and the board, in turn, was driven by its chair, who was in constant contact with the president and the chief development officer. Each successive campaign has been built upon the same successful model. The campaign mantra is "The trustees must own the campaign."

Of course, the trustees will not own the campaign without the concerted efforts of the college advancement team, particularly in the persons of the president and the chief advancement officer. The experience of Saint Anselm College bears out a fund-raising principle articulated by many fund-raising experts—the successful campaign absolutely depends upon the effective collaboration of the president with the chair of the board to mobilize the trustees. The chair and the president rely heavily upon the expertise of the chief fund-raising officer and his or her staff. Saint Anselm College illustrated the importance of this collaboration by planning and executing a $12.5 million centennial capital campaign.

THE ROLE OF LEADERSHIP IN THE CAPITAL CAMPAIGN

Leadership is a critical element in a capital campaign. Without strong leadership in the persons of the president, the chair of the board, and the chief advancement officer, a capital campaign is in deep trouble. But having three strong leaders in pivotal fund-raising roles can create tensions, so the roles must complement one another. The VPCA must be able to choreograph the dance in such a way that the volunteer leadership occupies center stage but all necessary movements are completed in their proper order.

This coordination is particularly true for a church-related college such as Saint Anselm, which has an unusual governance structure. The legal entity that conducts Saint Anselm College is the Order of Saint Benedict of New Hampshire, Inc., i.e., the community of Benedictine monks of Saint Anselm Abbey.

The college also has an advisory Board of Trustees made up of laymen and laywomen. For almost 40 years, the Board of Trustees has worked closely with the Governing Board. The deliberations and decisions of the Board of Trustees are regarded as much more than advisory in nature. The Board of Trustees meets twice each year. The members of the Governing Board meet with the trustees at these general meetings, as well as at all executive and committee sessions. The trustees and their chair are volunteers in the pure sense of that term, and all the rules pertaining to the "care and keeping" of volunteers apply here. Thus, engineering trustee ownership of a campaign becomes markedly more difficult and requires superior communication and motivational skills.

THE MAKINGS OF A CAPITAL CAMPAIGN

Long before the 100th anniversary of Saint Anselm College approached, the college's vice president for development suggested that the centennial would be an ideal time for a capital campaign. The college certainly had a long list of needs that a campaign could address.

The college president, a member of the Benedictine community, consulted with the college's senior leadership and enthusiastically embraced the idea of a centennial campaign. He began informal discussions of the prospect of a capital campaign with the chair of the Board of Trustees. After a series of discussions, which soon included the vice president for development, the chair endorsed the idea of planning a campaign. The chair, who had participated in a previous Saint Anselm drive and who had considerable experience as a leader of capital drives, agreed to serve as general chair of the centennial campaign. This decision was a result of good communication between the president and the chair and went a long way toward securing the enthusiastic involvement and support of the Board of Trustees.

The college developed a list of high-priority needs and the public relations director wrote a preliminary case statement incorporating those needs. Meanwhile, a committee whose makeup included major representation from the Board of Trustees interviewed potential fund-raising consulting firms. The first task of the selected counsel would be to test market the case and make a preliminary assessment of the college's readiness for a major capital campaign. The college advised fund-raising counsel that it hoped to raise in excess of $10 million to address multiple needs.

The preliminary assessment of prospective major donors by fund-raising counsel set the college back on its heels. At first reading, the report was not encouraging. It pointed out some weaknesses in the college's development approach and forced the creative collaboration of chair, president, and chief advancement officer to face its first crucial test.

Based upon his firm's assessment, counsel suggested the college had two choices. It could move forward with its planned capital campaign, but could expect to raise no more than $5 million, approximately half of what the administration had hoped to raise. Or, it could postpone the campaign for a year or a year and a half and use that time to cultivate major prospects and convey the urgency of the college's needs. Counsel predicted that after a period of intense cultivation, the college would be in a position to successfully raise about $12 million. Counsel's preliminary assessment revealed exceptional interest in the college and much loyalty and willingness to assist the college to achieve its goals. However, counsel also discovered that the college had done an inadequate job of conveying its needs to its constituencies and of creating a sense of urgency about the need for assistance.

The chair, the president, and the vice president for development faced the disappointing news and made the difficult and courageous decision to delay the campaign and to engage in an intensive period of identification and cultivation of major gifts prospects. At the same time, the college launched a public relations offensive to communicate the urgency of its needs, presenting a preliminary case to its alumni and friends for library expansion, faculty development, and endowment. The trustees were kept fully informed of these developments and were involved in the decision. As it turned out, these events provided an extended period of concentrated education in capital fund raising for the trustees that proved valuable in the long run. When the time was ripe to begin the campaign, the trustees were primed.

The apparent setback turned out to be a blessing in disguise. For one thing, it sharpened the focus of the entire advancement staff, making the team more effective. It also cemented the working relationship among the three leaders. The chair and the president worked as a team to make cultivation calls upon major prospects. The chair, with a small, carefully selected core group of trustees, called upon the members of the board for their commitments. Board members were asked to make larger commitments by far to the college than had ever been requested before. Because of the strong leadership of the president and the chair, the board responded magnificently. Board members assumed leadership roles on the steering committee and on the major gifts solicitation committee. Their involvement proved to be the key. During the planning for the campaign, and throughout most of the early stages, the chair of the board met weekly with the president and the vice president for development—sometimes they were joined by fund-raising counsel, sometimes by other members of the team. This close working relationship focused the core team on the task, and ultimately led to the campaign exceeding its $12.5 million goal by more than $2 million. Delaying the start of the campaign to use the time for preparation and cultivation proved to be the right decision, and that decision reflected the collective wisdom of the three leaders. Such team leadership, based upon good research and expert advice from professional fund-raising counsel, appears to be a winning formula.

RESPECTIVE ROLES OF THE THREE LEADERS

The governance structure at Saint Anselm was once prevalent at Catholic colleges and universities; a similar approach was, perhaps, typical at other church-related institutions as well. This approach, which vests governance in the religious community that sponsors the college, not in the board of trustees, survives at a few colleges. Such a governance system must influence the role relationships among the president, chair of the board, and chief advancement officer.

Throughout the history of Saint Anselm College, the president of the college has always been a member of the Benedictine community of Saint Anselm Abbey. The president is appointed by the chancellor of the college. (The chancellor, the highest ranking official of the college, has always been the abbot, i.e., the religious superior of the Benedictine community.) The president reports to the chancellor and the members of the Governing Board.

The chair of the advisory Board of Trustees is also appointed by the chancellor of the college. Because the president is not subordinate to the chair of the board, the relationship between the chair and the president is defined in terms of cooperation and coordination rather than authority. In essence, the chair becomes the college's number one volunteer. The chair assumes a most visible public relations role on behalf of the college with respect to the external community, and is the chief organizer and motivator of board activities. The chair and the board do not set the college's goals nor oversee the president's efforts to achieve those goals.

In this scheme, the president's role, in relation to the board, is enlarged. The president must be the chief "dreamer of dreams" and must be the chief motivator of the campus community and the trustees in achieving the dreams. Without the president's complete and unrelenting commitment of time and attention to fund raising, all such efforts will be severely handicapped. The president must be the chief and constant cultivator of major gifts prospects. The president must spark the enthusiasm and commitment of the chair of the board so that, together, they can motivate the members of the board. The chair has an invaluable role to play as advisor and counsel to the president. These two develop vision and strategy together.

Although the president must commit himself without reserve to the fund-raising goals of the college, he also has many other relationships to manage, including with the on-campus community. The president must work with the faculty and staff to determine the goals of the institution and the fund-raising activities needed to achieve those goals. If the president fails to win the understanding and support of the on-campus community, his efforts in fund raising will be undermined. For example, if the faculty has a role in defining needed capital projects and understands the necessity of raising the money to accomplish such projects, it is much more likely to understand and support the outlay of funds needed to build the development staff and meet other campaign costs. On the other hand, if the faculty is not intimately involved in goal setting and planning of fund raising to achieve those goals, a move by the president to build fund-raising staff may be opposed by the faculty as one more attempt to expand the administration at the expense of the academic program. Clearly, the president has the never-ending challenge of communicating with and persuading a whole range of constituencies.

In this area, the college's chief advancement officer, who must have demonstrated public relations as well as fund-raising expertise, can play a major supporting role to the president. The VPCA must have input into the vision and goals of the institution. For example, at this writing, Saint Anselm College is in the process of developing a new long-range plan. The chief advancement officer is one of a half-dozen people on the steering committee that is assisting the president in developing this plan.

Beyond that, the advancement team provides the specific fund-raising strategies to achieve the college's goals. If the president is to be an effective fund-raiser and the successful leader of the capital campaign, the chief advancement officer must school the president and the chair of the board in the art and science of fund raising. (This need for instruction is particularly great at an institution such as Saint Anselm, where the president is appointed from the membership of the Benedictine community of Saint Anselm Abbey and is unlikely to have had any previous fund-raising knowledge or experience.)

As a practical matter, the advancement staff also schedules the president's fund-raising activities, arranging meetings with key prospects, developing and following through with cultivation strategy, and providing background research. The interaction between the chief advancement officer and the president is constant and takes place almost daily in both formal and informal exchanges. The relationship is mutually respectful and candid. The relationship also has an informality and ease that encourages creativity and initiative but nonetheless recognizes the need for professionalism and meeting deadlines and goals.

The chief advancement officer is also encouraged to be in frequent touch with the chair of the board. This relationship is also characterized by a certain informal intimacy that allows for candor and ease of response.

During the planning and execution of a capital campaign, these three meet constantly to develop strategy and review progress. This relationship requires teamwork.

RESOLUTION OF CONFLICTS

In fund raising at Saint Anselm, the president is like the head coach of a team. The chair and the chief advancement officer are like members of the coaching staff. Obviously, the staff members must be compatible with the coach and follow the coach's lead. If there is a personality clash or if the coach and the staff are on a different "wave length," the head coach must somehow resolve that issue or, in serious cases, replace staff members until he has a staff that works well together.

If the president and his staff have the essential synergy, most conflicts will arise over particulars in strategy, tactics, and timing. In these conflicts, the professional expertise of the chief advancement officer should be given the most weight, but the chief advancement officer also needs to be most persuasive at these times. The chair and the president will not necessarily see the situation as the professional fund-raiser sees it. The professional must bring expertise to bear and should not be too quick to simply bow to the ideas of the chair or the president. Candor and an established relationship of trust and confidence are most important at these times. The chief advancement officer must be in a position to vigorously defend an approach or a strategy, but also must be open to the (generally) broader perspective of the president and the chair. Conflicts need to be worked through and eventually resolved by consensus rather than by presidential fiat. Such consensus requires flexibility and self-confidence on the part of all concerned. With a spirit of teamwork, conflicts can be creative and lead to positive results. Without it, results will be disappointing, both in the bottom line and in the satisfaction of those engaged in the process. A lack of professional satisfaction can lead to further problems all along the line.

TRUSTEE RECRUITMENT AND INVOLVEMENT

Members of the Board of Trustees and of the college faculty and administration are encouraged to be conscious of people who could potentially make a positive contribution to the college as trustees. They are asked to submit the names of such people for consideration. A committee of the board considers such recommendations and confidentially follows up on the most promising suggestions. After a period of information gathering and discussion, the committee may recommend to the chair that an individual should be invited to join the board. If the board chair and the president think well of the recommendation, they submit the prospect's name to the Governing Board for tentative approval.

If the Governing Board approves, the president, the chair, the chief advancement officer, and the person with the closest relationship to the prospective trustee develop a strategy for making the approach—a process not dissimilar to developing the strategy to cultivate a major gifts prospect. Ultimately, if all goes well, the college president, sometimes accompanied by the chair of the board, will visit the prospect and present the invitation to join the board. Most prospective trustees are identified by current members of the board.

When approached, each prospective trustee is made aware that the college community and the Board of Trustees has the following expectations of its members:

1. A trustee will give of her or his talent, time, and expertise to assist in the decision making of the college.
2. A trustee must be willing to support the fund-raising activities of the college within her or his financial ability to do so.
3. The trustee must provide leadership for the fund-raising endeavors of the college.

Trustee involvement in a campaign is achieved primarily by encouraging the board to determine the need for the campaign and to help plan the campaign and set its goals. Trustees are actively involved in all campaign committees. A major communication strategy of the campaign is to keep up a high level of two-way communication with the trustees throughout. At every opportunity, and by all means available, the campaign leadership team constantly reminds the trustees of their ownership of the campaign and encourages their efforts. Saint Anselm has found that professional fund-raising counsel can be particularly effective in addressing the trustees. Sometimes the outside professional can say things to board members that might not sit as well coming from their chair or from members of the college's staff.

Solicitation of the trustees is done after "screening" and evaluation of their potential. Similar to all other major gifts prospects, a strategy is developed for each solicitation. Generally, the president solicits the gift of the chair of the board and the campaign chair. The chair of the board and the president select a small committee to solicit other board members. The chair asks these trustees for their gifts and recruits them for the committee. These members, in turn, approach the other members of the board.

Saint Anselm College has learned that the old fund-raising axiom, "If you don't ask, you won't get a gift," applies to trustees as well as to others. The college proceeded for some time on the assumption that the need for a trustee to give to the college was obvious, and that regularly soliciting members of the board was somehow inappropriate. This passive stance yielded disappointing results. The strategy has since been altered to what one development officer jokingly refers to as a more scripturally based approach: "Ask and you shall receive."

CLOSING OBSERVATIONS

Institutions of higher learning contribute so much to society that they certainly can make a compelling case for philanthropic support. Yet, many who generously support church-related colleges see themselves as doing more than furthering higher education—they believe they are promoting the salvific work of the church. Such religious motivation on the part of many donors may present additional fund-raising opportunities for church-related colleges, but also imposes special obligations. Church-related institutions such as Saint Anselm must be especially diligent to ensure that the added measure of trust that motivates such donors is merited by our teaching and our example.

With respect to their religious identity, some church-related colleges retain the tradition that the president of the college is a minister of the sponsoring church. Others successfully carry on their church-related mission under lay leadership. Each college adopts the approach that best serves its own circumstances and advancement needs.

Saint Anselm College considers itself fortunate that the president of the college is an ordained priest and a monk of the Order of Saint Benedict. The college believes that this image is rich symbolically, speaking powerfully to its Catholic, Benedictine tradition. The fact that our president is a priest influences the way he communicates about the college's mission, both internally and externally and, to a certain extent, his fund-raising style. The priest-president may have some unique advantages but also carries an extra burden, and the dual role may often be difficult to balance.

Minister of the church or not, the president of the church-related college must match the president of other colleges stride for stride in every aspect of the job, including fund raising. As Saint Anselm College has learned, the church-related college cannot expect its church affiliation alone to attract philanthropic support. It must adopt an aggressive and professional approach to fund raising. It must hire a dedicated, talented, and professionally trained development staff. It must set fund-raising goals. Like all institutions, it must forever be the good steward.

CHAPTER 10

Successful Fund Raising at a Historically Black University

Hampton University

by William R. Harvey

ampton University is located on 204 acres of Virginia's Peninsula. It is a privately endowed, co-educational, nonsectarian institution of higher education, with an enrollment of approximately 83 percent African-American students, 15 percent Caucasian students, and 2 percent international students.

The institution was founded in 1868 for the purpose of educating free Blacks and recently freed slaves. In 1878, Hampton pioneered Native American (Indian) education, and by the turn of the century, its enrollment was about evenly divided between Black and Native American students. Indeed, between 1878 and 1923, more than 1,300 Native Americans from 65 different tribes were educated at Hampton.

The university is accredited by the Southern Association of Colleges and Schools and by the Department of Education of the Commonwealth of Virginia. It holds membership in the Council of Graduate Schools, the Council of Independent Colleges in Virginia, and the American Council on Education. Its programs in chemical and electrical engineering, nursing, music, architecture, communicative sciences and disorders, computer science, mass media arts, teacher education, and chemistry are accredited by their respective principal accrediting boards.

In 1997, the university had an enrollment of 5,549 students, drawn from 61 states, territories, and foreign countries. Its multi-ethnic student population includes a talented mix of third-, fourth-, and fifth-generation Hampton graduates. The university's academic distinction derives from its excellence in professional and technical emphases, undergirded with a strong liberal arts background and integrated with new technologies that facilitate the teaching/learning process.

The university's 389 faculty members take seriously their roles as guardians of the university's curricula integrity and prime facilitators of the teaching/learning process. With an appropriate balance of teaching/research initiatives, faculty members have consistently distinguished themselves in their ability to develop innovative teaching strategies, to enhance instruction through research, and to advance their disciplines through active participation in professional organizations.

The university is organized into three colleges: Hampton Institute, the undergraduate college; the Graduate College; and the College of Continuing Education. Hampton Institute houses five schools: Business, Engineering and Technology, Liberal Arts and Education, Nursing, and Science. Within these schools, bachelor's degrees (B.A., B.S., or B.Arch) are offered in 50 academic areas. The Graduate College offers doctoral degrees (Ph.D in physics and Pharm.D in pharmacy) and master's degrees (M.A., M.S., M.B.A.) in 14 fields, including biology, chemistry, applied mathematics, environmental science, communicative sciences and disorders, nursing, museum studies, counseling, computer science, and business administration. The College of Continuing Education offers programs leading to degrees in aviation maintenance technology, fire administration, emergency medical systems, paralegal studies, systems organization and management, business management, and general studies.

UNIVERSITY HISTORY

From 1868 to 1930, Hampton University was named Hampton Normal and Agricultural Institute; from 1930 to 1984, the university was known as Hampton Institute. From its inception, the university served as a distinct model in higher education. In an excerpt from the 25 March 1869 edition of the *New York Tribune*, the editor described the Normal and Industrial School of the American Missionary Association as an educational venture "which promises better help to the freedmen than any other institution of which we have knowledge."

The American Missionary Association had an enormous impact on the university's early progress. Using Hampton as a sterling model of southern educational pursuits in behalf of Blacks, this Association garnered for the institution substantial financial support from wealthy northern benefactors.

The university's first building, Academic Hall, was designed in 1869 by the distinguished New York architect, Richard Morris Hunt. With bricks made by Hampton students, this now historic landmark has served for over 128 years as a classroom building, a dormitory, an art center, and, more recently, a museum. The university's first domicile for students, Virginia Cleveland Hall, was dedicated in 1873. Financed with funds raised from appearances by the Hampton Singers, this building is also an historic landmark.

General Samuel Chapman Armstrong, the institution's founder, believed that Hampton's physical facilities should be designed to facilitate maximum learning. Through the years, Hampton's leadership has fully subscribed to Armstrong's notion; the university now has 118 buildings, all of which help to create a comprehensive living/learning environment.

Throughout its history, Hampton has gained the support of influential Americans, from corporate giants to United States presidents. John D. Rockefeller of Standard Oil, Coleman Dupont of E.I. duPont de Nemours and Company, and George Eastman of Eastman Kodak have all served on Hampton's Board of Trustees. Indeed, from 1870 to 1876, future President James Garfield served as a tustee. From 1914 to 1930, former President William Howard Taft, then sitting as chief justice of the United States Supreme Court, served as president of the Board of Trustees. More recently, Bill Ellinghaus, president of AT&T; John Dorrance, chairperson of Campbell Soup; Ernest Drew, chairperson of Hoechst Celanese; and Roger Enrico, current chairperson of Pepsi-Cola, Inc. have served as Hampton trustees. In 1991, President George Bush was keynote speaker for Hampton's commencement.

During the late 1800s and early 1900s, the institution was a self-contained industrial and educational village. Faculty and students made the bricks and built the buildings, grew the vegetables, and developed large poultry, pig, and dairy farms. These and other endeavors provided practical "classroom" experiences for students enrolled in the brickmasonry, tinsmithing, tailoring, printing, and farming trades.

In the early 1920s, Hampton began offering college-level courses in its Schools of Agriculture, Business, Education, Home Economics, Library Science, and Trade. Through the years, the institution has perpetuated Armstrong's vision of an "Education for Life." Guided by this motto, the university today remains committed to using education as a mechanism by which students learn both how to make a living and how to live productively and harmoniously in a diverse and ever-changing community.

FUND-RAISING HISTORY

From its earliest days, Hampton has attracted loyal supporters. During the 1870s, General Armstrong gained entree to families of wealth and social position in New England. Many of the persons who supported the institution were the sons and daughters of New Englanders who had contributed to the abolitionist cause and who then extended their support to newly freed Blacks. These contacts and interactions developed into a fund-raising pattern that prevailed for many years. New Englanders sponsored special fund-raising events in Boston homes and churches, with General Armstrong and the Hampton Singers in attendance. During the summers, New Englanders sponsored musical programs in Maine and New Hampshire, where they spent their vacations.

Another important factor influencing early fund raising for Hampton was its physical location on the Virginia coast. With its campus surrounded on three sides by water and located halfway between the North and the South, Hampton became a popular stop on long trips by water or rail. Many of Hampton's early contributors first became interested in the institution when they accepted General Armstrong's invitation to visit the campus. Their yachts put into Hampton, where students and faculty provided music and other forms of entertainment for their guests along the shores of the Hampton River. These visits resulted primarily in scholarship donations (the first scholarships date back to 1875) and in several large gifts for building construction.

In 1925, Hampton, in cooperation with Tuskegee University, launched its first endowment fund campaign. Fueled by a few large gifts, Hampton and Tuskegee raised $10 million in this joint undertaking. During the 1920s and 1930s, Hampton received several other large legacies.

In 1943, Hampton University became a charter member of the United Negro College Fund (UNCF). With the transfer of its list of donors to the UNCF, Hampton, for all practical purposes, lost its established supporters.

In 1963, with Dr. Jerome H. Holland as president and in conjunction with its upcoming centennial in 1968, the university initiated a capital campaign with a goal of $18 million. The campaign generated more than $21 million— a feat that had never before been accomplished by a predominantly Black college.

In 1969, Hampton began its second century. In the late 1970s, during a period of unprecedented growth, the institution distinguished itself as a special educational resource in our nation, particularly in the areas of teaching, academic programs, research, and fund raising. Hampton accelerated its efforts toward addressing specific financial priorities, and continuously raised funds for major ongoing needs, endowment growth, unrestricted operating support, research funds, and a multitude of other special projects.

Overall, Hampton's fund-raising efforts were characterized by aggressiveness, persistence, and boldness. At the same time, donors and others responded to the university's leadership with gifts and other support that gave Hampton a firm financial foundation. During this period, one published survey of college and university endowments ranked Hampton's endowment 96th among all those surveyed.

In 1982, the institution conducted a major fund-raising campaign that had a goal of $30 million. The purpose of the campaign was to provide a firm foundation for the future advancement of the university, for the development of innovative programs to meet student and societal needs, for the provision of scholarships for needy and deserving students, for the payment of adequate salaries to obtain and retain able faculty and staff, and for the construction of buildings to provide first-class facilities for efficient quality instruction.

The $30-million campaign generated $46.4 million. This campaign, the largest fund-raising effort in the university's history, was completed in less than three years and exceeded its goal by more than 50 percent. During the campaign, the university received its largest gift ever from a foundation—a gift of $7.5 million—and its largest federal grant—an award of $2.25 million. Other seven-figure gifts included one for $4 million and another for $1.25 million. The successful completion of the campaign raised Hampton's endowment to $70 million.

The campaign's unprecedented success is documented in a number of tangible developments during the early 1980s. A marine science center, the Hattie McGrew Towers and Conference Center, a science and technology building, the Olin Engineering Building, and a storage/warehouse building were erected. The University Book Store, dormitories, classrooms, and faculty offices were renovated. Twenty-four new degree-granting programs were initiated. Twenty university-endowed professorships and several endowed student scholarships were established.

During the early to mid-1980s, Hampton's fund-raising enterprise was characterized by challenge and progress. Overall, the university greatly increased its share in the philanthropic market. Contributions from all the university's constituencies also grew sharply. Private gifts consistently reflected dramatic increases in the amount of funds generated. Foundation gifts rose by more than 1,400 percent, and corporate gifts increased by more than 400 percent.

FUND-RAISING STRATEGIES AT HAMPTON

Although its enrollment is a relatively modest 5,500 students, Hampton has, of necessity, developed an extensive fund-raising program. Its fund-raising model is structured around an annual alumni fund campaign, a local annual fund campaign, corporate and foundation relations, federal relations, a capital campaign, and planned giving.

Alumni Giving

The alumni annual fund is organized in a manner that takes full advantage of the 95 alumni chapters spread throughout the nation. These chapters are subsumed under seven geographical regions: Northeast Region, Mid-Atlantic Region, North Carolina Region, Southeast Region, Southwest Region, Midwest Region, and Far West Region.

Each alumni chapter has a fund-raising chairperson who, with the assistance of the university's alumni office staff and the national alumni fund chairperson, organizes and recruits a volunteer organization to raise funds at the chapter level. The alumni chapter fund-raising chairpersons fall under the auspices of their respective regional fund-raising chairpersons who, in turn, are responsible to the national fund-raising chairperson. In this organizational structure, the responsibility for fund raising is not vested with the alumni chapter president, but is the direct responsibility of the chapter fund-raising chairperson. Vesting fund raising with a particular person at the chapter level ensures greater attention to this single responsibility. Annually, a national fund raising goal is agreed to by the National Hampton Alumni Association, Inc. and Hampton University. Through prospect rating and alumni giving in the particular regions during the previous year, each region of the alumni association is assigned a portion of the overall national goal.

The national fund chairperson, the regional fund chairpersons, and university staff conduct fund-raising training sessions for alumni volunteers in the seven regions to ensure that the volunteers are familiar with the campaign case, organization, role of volunteers, reporting procedures, etc.

With the assistance of key alumni and alumni trustees, special events are held in key cities around the country so that the university's president can share with alumni the university's programs and plans and present Hampton's case for support. Some special events are planned around art exhibitions with works from Hampton's University Museum on display.

National and international traveling art exhibitions also occasionally include works of art from Hampton's collection. In such cases, special events are planned as adjuncts to facilitate alumni fund-raising activities. As an example, at a recent nationwide retrospective on the world-renowned artist Henry O. Tanner, Hampton University loaned six of his paintings for the exhibitions. The show traveled to the Philadelphia Museum of Art, the High Museum in Atlanta, the Detroit Institute of Art, and the DeYoung Museum in San Francisco. A fund-raising gathering was held in each of the cities in which these exhibitions appeared. In some instances, a corporate CEO agreeed to host a luncheon where other CEOs were invited to hear the Hampton story. In other instances, a prominent alumnus or alumna hosted the special event at his or her home or club where other alumni and friends had gathered to hear the Hampton story.

The solicitation efforts for the chapters and regions are the responsibility of the alumni and development staff in conjunction with alumni volunteers in various cities throughout the United States. The university's primary objective is to mobilize a nationwide volunteer solicitation effort and to ensure that the alumni fund will reach its goal. Through these widely visible efforts in major areas, alumni become familiar with the university's goals and plans and have an opportunity to participate in campaign-related activities in their respective areas.

Hampton alumni who are capable of making major gifts are identified for personal solicitation, and cultivation and solicitation strategies are designed to solicit their contributions. The overall management of cultivation/solicitation efforts is coordinated from a central perspective by alumni and development staff so that resources and volunteers are used in an effective and efficient manner.

The alumni fund-raising effort also involves a class leader/class agent program. Each reunion class has a class leader who is responsible for galvanizing class interest and class participation during Alumni Reunion Weekend and Commencement in May. During the fall Homecoming Weekend, class leaders meet with the alumni office staff on campus to initiate plans and strategies for garnering broad support from the reunion classes. During non-reunion years, class leaders continue to serve as the catalysts in sustaining class interest in supporting the university.

Through Hampton's fund-raising efforts, alumni are endowing named scholarships to expand the scholarship endowment pool. An alumnus/alumna can endow a named scholarship with a minimum contribution of $10,000. Scholarships are attractive gift opportunities that allow the donor to witness first-hand the impact of his or her gift on a currently enrolled student. At Hampton, named, endowed scholarships provide an excellent way of ensuring that future generations of deserving students have the same magnificent Hampton experience and education that contemporary alumni had. In addition, a named, endowed scholarship is an excellent means of etching one's name or the name of a loved one in the annals of Hampton's history.

During the Annual Alumni Reunion Weekend and Commencement, thousands of alumni return to the campus for a weekend of planned activities. The Alumni Reunion Banquet culminates the competitive fund-raising activities of the reunion classes. The reunion class leaders report the total contributions given by their respective classes, and a special award is given to the class that contributes the largest amount of money to the university. An additional award is given to the class with the largest number of class members returning to the campus for each annual reunion.

Local Fund

Hampton conducts a local fund campaign in the Hampton Roads area. This campaign is designed to involve the local business community and friends in giving to the university. The local fund campaign is conducted through a volunteer organization that is responsibile for calling personally on each prospective donor. Every effort is made to simplify the personal solicitations and to use the volunteers for a minimum time period. The chronological sequence used in the organization and solicitation is as follows:

1. Volunteer organization
   a) Recruitment of the local fund chairperson
   b) Recruitment of division chairpersons
   c) Recruitment of division team members
2. Organizational meeting
3. Kick-off event
4. Periodic report meetings

Following the recruitment of the local fund chairperson, the development staff, in consultation with the chairperson, identifies division chairpersons. Once the division chairperson and division team members are recruited, a meeting is held at the convenience of all parties to discuss the campaign, delineate roles and responsibilities, plan for soliciting leadership gifts, and identify prospective donors. Prior to the kick-off event, volunteers solicit lead gifts.

Most of the prospective contributors and volunteers are invited to the kick-off event. The event is aimed at galvanizing interest and enthusiasm for Hampton and for its local fund campaign. At the kick-off event, key individuals are introduced, and the local fund chairperson gives introductory remarks and champions the case. The president gives a speech on Hampton, its case for support, and its importance to the local area. The local fund chairperson presents a brief overview of the local campaign. The volunteer organization is supported by development staff. The public relations staff handles the publicity for the campaign.

The local campaign has a religious committee division that comprises clergy in the community. This committee solicits named, endowed scholarships from the churches and synagogues in the area. The plan calls for each church or synagogue to donate $10,000 to Hampton's scholarship fund. The money is placed into the endowment. The interest generated from the $10,000 (or $1,000) is available each year to a student from that church or synagogue who is admitted to Hampton University for a course of study.

In organizing this committee, the president invited a number of key clergy to a meeting on the campus to explore the feasibility of organizing such an effort under the local campaign. The concept was well received and suggestions were offered as to the organizational structure of such an effort, clergy that should be invited to participate, and means of selling the concept to a broader group. Subsequently, the president held a breakfast meeting at his home and invited the ministers from the local area. At this meeting, the group discussed Hampton's program, its plans for the future, the endowed scholarship program for churches and synagogues, and the advantage of the program for members of each congregation. The program was unanimously and enthusiastically endorsed by the group.

Corporations and Foundations

Our corporate fund-raising initiatives emphasize the development of close reciprocal relationships with corporations/foundations. The corporations/foundations that employ Hampton's graduates and those offering products and services are consonant with Hampton's educational programs and research capabilities form our top prospect pool. These corporations/foundations, along with those that have given previously to the university, are targeted consistently for broader relationships. Additionally, corporations/foundations for which our trustees serve as directors or CEOs, and companies in which Hampton alumni are members of senior management constitute another priority group. Corporations/foundations that have operating facilities in our area form a third group of prospects.

The strategy for corporate/foundation solicitation involves a three-pronged or three-level process.

1. First, the use of trustee/corporate and foundation linkages
2. Second, the exploitation of campus marketability
3. Third, the involvement of school deans and faculty in direct corporate/foundation fund raising and grantsmanship

Impeccable research is conducted to determine the direct or interlocking board ties that our trustees have with the corporations/foundations and directors. Our trustees have important relationships with CEOs or with directors serving on foundation boards of trustees or on the contributions committees of corporations. Where relationships exist between Hampton's trustees and corporate/foundation CEOs and directors, a strategy is designed to benefit from these associations. For example, the trustee and the president will call on the CEO to solicit a major corporate/foundation gift. The trustee facilitates the appointment with the CEO, and discusses Hampton's case and proposal with the corporate/foundation directors who serve on the contributions committee. While these interactions are occurring, a member of the development staff calls on the corporate/foundation contributions officer. This strategy does not bypass the corporate/foundation officer who has direct responsibility for corporate/foundation giving.

Corporate and foundation fund-raising strategies include fully exploiting the marketability of the campus. Hampton has one of the most beautiful and picturesque campuses in the United States. Therefore, campus visits are an integral part of the university's overall cultivation/solicitation program. Campus visits by prospective corporate/foundation donors are important steps in personalizing donor cultivation. Such visits are intended to make the potential donor feel that he or she is part of an inner constituency.

At Hampton, schools and academic programs provide opportunities to have potential corporate/foundation donors sit on advisory councils and committees and serve as guest speakers. In the School of Engineering and the School of Business, advisory councils facilitate the schools' achievement of their missions, provide technical assistance in the further development of curricula, ensure that program offerings are consonant with the needs of the workplace and graduate school education, and assist in raising funds. Each advisory council is chaired by a member of the Board of Trustees. The trustee and the president, along with the dean and the chief development officer, identify individuals to recruit for membership on the advisory council. In addition to the trustee's stewardship, participation on the advisory council provides him or her with a challenging and meaningful role in the university's advancement.

The advisory council for the School of Engineering was chaired initially by Ernest Drew, chairman and CEO of Hoechst Celanese. Invitations to join the advisory council were extended to energy, technology, space, and chemical companies, and to the academic community. With the assistance of the advisory council, our newly initiated four-year engineering program, after only five years of operation, was accredited by the Accreditation Board of Engineering and Technology. The F.W. Olin Foundation, Inc. provided the funds for construction of the engineering building.

The advisory council for the School of Business functions in a similar manner. This council is headed by trustee William Nelson, CEO of HARRIS DATA. The advisory council is assisting the School of Business with its plan to attain accreditation from the American Assembly of Collegiate Schools of Business and to raise $15 million for endowed professorial chairs, endowed scholarships, and technological enhancements.

In the university's capital campaign, the Schools of Engineering and Business have a funding goal of $15 million each. This fund-raising effort seeks to establish named professorships and to improve faculty salaries, to endow special scholarships and generate more regular scholarships, and to equip teaching and research laboratories with state-of-the-art equipment.

Capital campaign staff members are being added to the Schools of Engineering and Business to assist with their fund-raising programs. The campaign staff members are responsible to the University Development Office, but execute the fund-raising effort in concert with the dean and faculty of the school. The dean and the associate campaign director are responsible for achieving the $15-million goal for each of the schools. They are focused on generating substantial gifts for the school's needs from individuals, corporations, and foundations.

School deans are ordinarily responsible for raising one-third of their annual operating budgets. Over the years, the fund-raising efforts of deans and faculty have been institutionalized and regularized through systematic training and nurturing. Faculty members play a direct role in corporate fund-raising and grantsmanship. Indeed, their fund-raising efforts are assessed as a part of their annual evaluations. Inasmuch as the faculty and dean are best able to articulate the specific needs of their programs, their fund-raising initiatives are conducted independently.

Federal Grantsmanship

The director of sponsored programs coordinates all federal programs and sponsored grants at Hampton. The director reviews all proposals, following their review by academic administrators, to ensure that all commitments meet the university's policies and standards.

Acting as a resource person to faculty and administrators, the director stimulates proposal activity, assists faculty in drafting proposals for educational programs and research projects, holds proposal writing workshops for faculty, and operates an information service on federal programs for administrators and faculty. The vice president for research plays an advocacy role for Hampton at the federal level, articulating the needs and capabilities of the institution. These efforts have resulted in major federal grants to support academic programs, to establish scientific centers of excellence, and to fuel broad research efforts.

$200-Million Capital Campaign

The organizational structure and fund-raising strategies described above have served Hampton exceedingly well. As a direct result of successful fund raising, we have been able to balance the budget with a small surplus every year for the past 19 years. The student body has increased from approximately 2,700 to 5,500. The SAT scores of entering freshmen have risen over 300 points. The number of faculty has increased from 190 to 389. Twelve new buildings have been added to our campus facilities, and 33 new degree-granting programs have been implemented. These programs include several progressive and innovative curricula, such as undergraduate programs in electrical and chemical engineering, physical therapy, and criminal justice; master's degree programs in business administration and museum studies; and a doctoral program (Ph.D) in physics. Additionally, a College of Pharmacy and an Honors College have been initiated.

The university's endowment has increased from $29 million in 1978 to $125 million in 1997. Although the Hampton community is enormously proud of its extraordinary progress, present and emerging needs dictate implementation of even more intense fund-raising initiatives. As a consequence, the university, buoyed by its history of successful fund raising, is embarking upon a $200-million capital campaign. The goal of this campaign far exceeds that of any other Historically Black College or University and poses an awesome but welcome challenge for Hampton constituencies. With its existing fund-raising organization, and with a talented campaign staff, Hampton is positioned to attract increased support from its various publics. The university is currently in the silent or pre-public phase of this capital campaign, which will be formally launched during the 1997-98 academic year.

Our confidence is further buoyed by the impeccable planning that has been done for the campaign. The major building blocks for its success have been put into place. These building blocks are vision, statement preparation, prospect identification, a plan for donor cultivation, involvement opportunities for leadership prospects, communication, an organizational structure, volunteer recruitment, a solicitation plan, and stewardship.

Planned Giving

At Hampton, planned giving offers a myriad of opportunities for donors to provide for the university—opportunities over and above naming Hampton as a beneficiary of a will. Planned giving is a valuable tool in expanding opportunities for prospective donors to give more assets to Hampton than one might otherwise imagine. The attractiveness of Hampton's planned giving model lies in the donor's ability to retain his or her income and, in some cases, to increase that income through these gift opportunities. During the last five years, Hampton has received a little over $1 million from planned giving sources. Although this amount is far less than that received by many schools, it represents an auspicious beginning for an institution like Hampton University.

Under the $200-million campaign, Hampton's planned giving program is being expanded to enable prospective donors to make larger gifts to the university. Operationally, our planned giving program includes various means of educating trustees, volunteers, and prospective donors about such gift opportunities. These opportunities are provided through bequests, charitable reminder trusts, charitable gift annuities, pooled income funds, life insurances, and real estate.

The development staff has primary responsibility for planned giving, but works in conjunction with a volunteer committee on planned giving. Comprising a wide range of individuals, the planned giving committee brings expertise from accountants, attorneys, trust officers, insurance executives, and investment officers. The committee promotes each of the above gift categories. Moreover, it designs ways in which gifts of stocks, bonds, and real estate can be given to Hampton, with donors receiving tax and other advantages. The committee also assists with prospect building and cultivation, and with creating an environment in which planned giving is facilitated and encouraged. Prospects for planned giving fall into two categories—potential donors and professionals who advise or counsel individuals of wealth.

Publications and publicity are two important facets of our planned giving program. A planned giving newsletter provides information about gift opportunities and presents information on the tax ramifications of planned giving. A general brochure on planned giving and pamphlets on special subjects are also used. Planned giving dinners, luncheons, and seminars also provide opportunities to communicate with prospective donors. Finally, good stewardship is vital to the success of Hampton's planned gift program.

ALTERNATIVE SOURCES OF FUND RAISING

Endowment as a Fund-Raising Tool

The university also uses its endowment as a fund-raising tool. Until about seven years ago, Hampton had only one manager for its endowment portfolio. As a result of the efforts of board members such as Joe Wright, former director of the Office of Management and Budgeting (OMB); George Lewis, president and CEO of Philip Morris Capital Corporation; Ben Head, former chairman and CEO of the Republic Bank of Austin in Texas; and Wendell Holmes, chairman of the Board of Trustees at Hampton University, the board decided to diversify its holdings and secure the services of five different managers.

The university's portfolio still contains its traditional stocks and bonds, but has also diversified into other areas. These areas, although slightly more risky, provide the balance and the opportunity to generate more funds or to increase the corpus of the endowment.

One such arena is emerging markets. The Investment Committee decided to put some of its money into companies doing business in emerging market countries such as Poland, China, Russia, Vietnam, South Africa, and the countries of Latin America. Investments in those countries continue to be made in companies involved in banking, cement, beverages, telecommunications, oil, gas, and the like.

Alternative Asset Investing

Alternative assets, also known as "nonmarketable investments," include venture capital and other forms of private equity, real estate, and oil and gas. These investments are considered nonmarketable because the securities underlying them tend not to be freely tradable. Consequently, these investments are not liquid. The university has broadened its alternative assets to include certain "marketable investments," such as hedge funds, risk arbitrage, distressed securities, and specialty mutual funds.

A principal reason for investing in alternative assets is to achieve a higher return than that obtained on the domestic stock market. Other reasons to invest in alternative assets are to reduce the endowment fund's volatility and to assist in protecting the purchasing power of the portfolio during periods of sustained or hyperinflation.

While investing in alternative assets has its advantages, this choice, as with any investment vehicle, also has risks and disadvantages. The disadvantages include illiquidity, as mentioned above, often complicated fee or distribution structures, interim valuation difficulties, an occasional lack of current income, and flawed historical returns.

By any technical definition, investments are not classified as fund raising. However, if as a result of innovative investing, assets are increased, investments serve the same purpose. Hampton's standard fund-raising initiatives, its campaign objectives, and its innovative investment policy are designed to generate increased funds for student scholarships, faculty salaries, new facilities, and upkeep of the physical plant. Therefore, while technically not fund raising, our investment policy is also designed to protect assets and to generate additional funds.

Commercial Revenue

I have long advocated that colleges and universities seek alternative sources of revenue as a fund-raising strategy. One such alternative source for Hampton University is its commercially developed project called Hampton Harbor. The project's 60,000 square feet of retail commercial space and 246 two-bedroom luxury apartments set a new standard for innovative and efficient development of institutional physical facilities. Completed in 1990, at a cost of $12 million, Hampton Harbor, in its first year of operation, generated a positive cash flow for the university. Since its first full year of operation, profits from Hampton Harbor have exceeded $1 million per year. With the apartments 100 percent leased and the commercial space approximately 90 percent leased, the Hampton Harbor project is a positive model for other colleges and universities seeking alternative sources of revenue. Moreover, this alternative source of revenue gathering for the university is an outstanding and unique model of self-sufficiency for African Americans.

After-tax profits from the Hampton Harbor project are used primarily for student scholarships. The project has also created approximately 150 jobs, provided services, increased the number of African-American entrepreneurs, and expanded the tax base in the City of Hampton.

FUND RAISING: THE NECESSARY CONDITIONS

In the final analysis, successful fund raising is predicated upon effective management and leadership. Effective management dictates establishment of clearly defined measurable objectives, clearly delineated strategies, and a firm grasp by each participant in the fund-raising process of his or her role in helping to execute those strategies and to achieve the desired outcomes. Effective leadership involves facilitation of the above, but goes far beyond that role to include the effective creation and communication of a vision, and the ability to inspire others to share that vision and to help translate it into reality.

Role of the President

Effective presidential management/leadership is vital in the successful fund-raising enterprise. My own experience is that the president's role in fund raising is directional and multi-dimensional. For instance, my work demands overseeing the university's strategic planning process, speaking to alumni, cultivating potential donors, making solicitation calls, interacting with foundation officers and corporate executives, and testifying before congressional committees and various special interest groups.

The part of the fund-raising process that I particularly enjoy is the cultivation and solicitation of corporate and foundation executives on behalf of the university. This phase begins with research. The vice president for development provides information that gives me a full orientation on the corporation or foundation I am to visit. Thus, upon visitation, I have a full grasp of the entity's sales, profits, officers, and board members, and where each attended college, areas of funding interest, recipients of grants, and an estimated maximum amount that I should request. This knowledge facilitates my ability to engage initially in appropriate conversation, rather than launch immediately into what has been described by some corporate/foundation heads as "obtrusive begging."

Another important phase to which I devote considerable time is the formulation of a strategic fund-raising plan. Donors have become increasingly sophisticated about pursuing their own objectives. This sophistication translates into donor demands for definite information regarding Hampton's academic blueprint or strategic plan and an assessment as to the potential of their gifts to influence the university's strategic plan or to advance the campus master plan. In this regard, I, as president, work to ensure that strategic planning is firmly aligned with successful fund raising. The university's strategic plan, therefore, validates the rationale for soliciting purposeful and sustained financial support from Hampton's various publics.

A broad panoply of institutional needs emerged from our most recent strategic planning process. We prioritized institutional needs as they were translated into fund-raising objectives. The list of needs includes some items for which it is clearly impossible to generate funds. Other items have been identified as needs for which funding is only marginally possible. A third category represents those items for which the fund-raising potential is relatively good. Some needs, no matter how desirable, will not generate external funds. Of course, we made a responsible decision not to expend time seeking funds for those items.

We then moved to the institutional case statement as a salient document in setting forth a compelling argument for Hampton's educational goals and programs. In addition, we viewed the importance of the case statement in presenting our past and present accomplishments: the unique role that Hampton plays in higher education; our service to students and the community; our value to society; our future opportunities; requirements for faculty, students, facilities, and finances; and our plans for accomplishing future goals. Armed with compelling and convincing support for our case, the fund-raising team began to plan and organize the capital campaign.

In any fund-raising venture, the president must personify the goals and objectives of the institution. The president must also promote team management and concerted input and support from trustees, alumni, development professionals, deans, faculty, and students. The involvement and interaction of these various groups undergird the team management approach to fund raising at Hampton. A cadre of volunteers, along with strong, competent professionals with the competence to develop promotional materials and structure public relations events, to identify and cultivate potential donors, and to assist in cultivating and closing major gifts is a *sine qua non* for a successful fund-raising enterprise.

Role of the Board of Trustees

Trustees play a pivotal role in the overall effectiveness of Hampton's capital campaign. First and foremost, the trustees must be totally committed to the university's fund-raising effort. Trustee commitment translates into involvement in setting institutional priorities and fund-raising goals before the campaign and involvement in reaching the campaign objectives. Trustee leadership in support of the campaign must be tangibly documented, meaning 100 percent trustee participation in campaign giving. Further, all trustees must actively solicit support for the campaign.

Hampton's Trustee Development Committee has seven trustee members. Other trustees may attend the meetings of the Development Committee, which meets two times per year. During major campaigns, an Executive Campaign Committee, using an increased number of trustees, is established and meets four times per year.

Role of the Vice President for Development

In fund raising, many similarities exist between the role of the president and the role of the vice president for development. Supporting the president in fund raising is one of the primary roles of the vice president for development. At Hampton, much of the success of our fund-raising efforts can be attributed to Laron Clark, vice president for development.

The university's only chief development officer during my 19 years as president, Mr. Clark has distinguished himself as a consummate fund-raiser. He and I have worked closely together during those years. We plan and strategize together. We travel together. We make solicitation calls together. And, we rejoice in our success together.

The vice president for development also has a close working relationship with trustees and supports, in every way, trustee involvement in planning and conducting the campaign. An integral part of the vice president for development's role is making the best use of the president's time and identifying prospects from whom the president is likely to reap the most positive results. The vice president for development and the development staff make the appointments and arrangements for the president's fund-raising calls, arrange fund-raising calls for trustees and other volunteers, and develop a profile on prospective donors for the president's use. The vice president for development also makes calls on prospects and meets with alumni groups to present Hampton's programs and plans.

For the vice president for development, successful management of the development program includes establishing performance goals for his staff and setting annual goals and objectives for his department. The vice president must also implement procedures for staff follow-up in completing tasks and projects, and must organize the development staff so that effective back-up is always available for fund-raising volunteers.

Role of Public Relations

Hampton's University Relations Office helps to create or enhance the climate in which the institution's fund-raising activities take place. Early on in my fund-raising efforts, I recognized that a campaign cannot be successful without a significant contribution from the staff that must market the university to its many publics.

Hampton University fosters effective public relations in a variety of ways. Faculty are encouraged to give of themselves to their communities. Being of service is an honor. It is also good public relations. Therefore, Hampton personnel are encouraged to run for public office and to sit on community, regional, and national boards. These activities provide an additional avenue for keeping the public apprised of new developments and significant programs on Hampton's campus. These efforts are complemented through university publications, print and television releases, special events, alumni reunions and meetings, videos, parent programs, newsletters, and the Internet.

The staff members of Hampton's University Relations Office consistently meet with producers, editors, and reporters of local, regional, and national news outlets. They attend budget meetings at our local paper and are constantly cultivating relationships. During the 1996-97 academic year, Hampton University was featured 426 times in a variety of publications on diverse topics. Major feature articles included "The Museum Opening" (*Chronicle of Higher Education, Richmond Times Dispatch*, and the local *Daily Press*); the collaboration of the university physics program with the Thomas Jefferson National Accelerator Facility (*Richmond Times Dispatch*); the "Highest Graduation Rate" (*Black Issues in Higher Education, Roanoke Times, Virginian Pilot, Daily Press*), "John Templeton Foundation Honor Roll" (*U.S. News and World Report*), "National Science Foundation Awards HU $5 Million" (*Jet, Black Media News, Daily Press*), and "HU Raises Campaign Target" (*Chronicle of Higher Education, Daily Press*). During the 1996-97 academic year, Hampton University was featured 52 times on television, including worldwide exposure on C-Span.

Hampton is consistent in its efforts to fully inform faculty, staff, and students of the university's fund-raising efforts. Campaign goals and the impact of fund raising on facilities, teaching/learning, research, and institutional image are carefully outlined. Finally, communal spirit within the university, where all constituents share a sense of "ownership," is an ongoing priority in promoting fund-raising activities and in helping to ensure the university's continuing viability.

CONCLUSION

Development, advancement, and fund raising are words often used interchangeably by those who seek to secure resources for their institutions. At Hampton, the fund-raising process involves every administrative office, faculty member, alumni, trustee, and student. Successful fund raising, while not easy, has its own rewards. The concepts and strategies articulated in this chapter have brought to Hampton University unprecedented achievements in its fund-raising efforts. It is my belief that other institutions can also experience unparalleled fund-raising success if they appropriately adapt these concepts and strategies to their profiles and needs.

CHAPTER 11

Successful Fund Raising at an Independent School
Deerfield Academy

by David G. Pond and Eric Widmer

Deerfield Academy, an independent boarding school for 590 boys and girls, is located in the historic village of Deerfield, Massachusetts. The school will celebrate its bicentennial in 1997. The alumni office program was started in 1948, and the first formal Annual Fund drive commenced in 1952. The total budget for the alumni and development program represents approximately 7 percent of the total operating cost of the school. Each year, the annual support program provides approximately 12 percent of the annual operating budget, and endowment income provides approximately 25 percent.

During the 1995-96 year, approximately $2.7 million was raised through the annual support program. Although the specific amount in any given year varies tremendously, approximately $3 to $5 million per year is added to the endowment and given for other capital projects. The school's endowment is currently $133 million.

In recent years, Deerfield has successfully completed a capital campaign (1985-1988), and a capital improvements program for athletics (1991-1993). In each case, facilities were only constructed when it was clear that money had been raised in advance for those specific purposes. Deerfield has no outstanding debt.

On occasion, the Alumni and Development Office travels jointly with the Admissions Office; however, no formal, ongoing program exists. It is done more as a matter of convenience and cost saving. Deerfield does not maintain an office of public information or director of publicity. Whatever publicity work is done is generally reactive rather than proactive.

Alumni participation in the annual support program is approximately 50 to 55 percent each year among those alumni for whom we have current addresses. Parents of current students participate at approximately the 70 to 80 percent range. Because approximately 30 percent of our students are receiving some form of financial aid, this is an extremely high participation rate.

Our planned/major gifts program is focused on approximately 800 individuals and foundations, and approximately 90 percent of the dollars raised each year are given by that group.

ADVANCEMENT WITHIN DEERFIELD'S INSTITUTIONAL FRAMEWORK

Ongoing Objectives

Deerfield's advancement planning begins each year with an overall assessment of institutional needs. What are the annual support objectives for the operating budget, and what other development projects should we be attempting to support, either in the upcoming year or in subsequent years?

1. **Annual Support.** The chief development officer has a preliminary discussion with the business manager approximately nine months prior to the start of the new budget year. Following that meeting, an internal review occurs with alumni and development office personnel to assess potential among 1) reunion classes, 2) current parents, and 3) the Board of Trustees. Overall, these three groups each year account for approximately 60 to 70 percent of the total annual support dollars raised. Wherever appropriate, we also involve key volunteer leaders, be they reunion chairs, heads of the parents' committees, or the president of the Board of Trustees. The suggested goal is reviewed by the Finance Committee, which then makes a recommendation to the full board for final approval.

2. **Development.** Generally, our development objectives are part of a formal capital campaign. Deerfield had a successful campaign from 1985 to 1988, when over $36 million was raised as part of a comprehensive capital campaign. In 1989, a major infusion of capital was needed for athletic facilities. Therefore, a quiet campaign, The Athletic Resources Project, was launched in 1991 and completed in 1993.

Currently, Deerfield is in the early planning phase of a Bicentennial Campaign, the planning for which will be discussed below. We expect to publicly announce a capital campaign in the fall of 1998. Approximately two-thirds of the goal will be for endowment projects.

In addition to our regular, comprehensive, and well-defined campaigns, smaller initiatives, such as our annual Senior Parents' Campaign, are conducted each year. Nonalumni senior parents are also asked each year for a three-year capital pledge; since 1983, we have provided support for endowment initiatives, for technology, and for our physical plant. The Senior Parents' Campaigns have raised approximately $7 million over 13 years.

Development of Deerfield's Institutional Plan

An assortment of development needs are constantly being added to our list. At Deerfield, no central planning document is approved by all; rather, individual initiatives arise as a result of ongoing discussions. Examples of these initiatives include the following:

1. **East Campus Project.** This project, which is being overseen by the assistant head for student life, will include two new dormitories and significant refurbishments to several existing dormitories. The project will be completed over several years and will cost approximately $12 to $15 million. The project developed out of a two-year study to improve dormitory life for our boarding students.

2. **Ongoing Budget Discussions.** The business manager is responsible for initiating operating budget discussions each year, and for establishing the annual budget with the Finance Committee of the Board of Trustees. He has done projections of our budget on a *pro forma* basis through the year 2010. He is also the primary source for new development projects that will need support in future years.

3. **Endowment Initiatives.** The business manager and assistant head for alumni affairs and development have shared endowment needs projections for the future. Maintaining a level of affordability for our applicants is constantly on our minds. Our general assessment for the upcoming capital campaign suggests that our alumni and parents are interested in supporting a campaign with an emphasis on endowment needs.

4. **Salaries and Professional Development.** The dean of faculty, in his discussions with faculty members, has stated his desire to have the areas of professional development and salary growth receive highest priority for future budgetary growth. Those priorities continue to be part of our long-range thinking.

5. **Financial Aid.** The dean of admissions and financial aid oversees the various needs within the area of financial aid. Currently, 40 percent of our financial aid comes from endowed funds. We hope our upcoming campaign will allow close to 100 percent of our financial aid needs to be endowed.

6. **Technology.** The director of our technology initiative has projected our needs for the next several years. Those needs include funds to sustain appropriate and long-term growth in the areas of hardware and software. Given the speed with which changes are occurring, and given the changing demands of our students, that has been a difficult task. In an effort to review those needs on a regular basis, a faculty technology committee and a trustee technology committee meet regularly.

Deerfield, like all schools, is constantly striving to serve its students better. One of the ways in which that striving occurs is through the identification of and completion of various initiatives such as those outlined above. We are constantly bringing new ideas to the fore, and the headmaster must then provide encouragement and support for those initiatives that are most important to Deerfield's future growth.

THE RESPECTIVE ROLES AND RESPONSIBILITIES OF THE ADVANCEMENT TEAM

The chief development officer, the headmaster, and the president of the board compose the advancement team at Deerfield academy. If this group of three people is to work most effectively, the chief development officer must make it his highest priority. He must use the headmaster's and the president's time wisely and efficiently. In addition, this group must have regular opportunities to review development objectives and to discuss possible changes in those objectives. The role of each team member in the advancement process is described in more detail below.

Chief Development Officer

The assistant head for alumni affairs and development, as the chief development officer, is the primary planner and catalyst for our overall development plan. However, in an office of our size, he must involve all key development personnel in the plan's formation. As the catalyst, the chief development officer makes sure that the plan is occurring as anticipated, and he must be aware of the need for change. The chief development officer is always setting up appointments and establishing individual meetings. The chief development officer also summarizes meetings with notes for our files and develops follow-up strategies after the meetings have taken place. Overall, he encourages key long-term relationships and builds for the future.

Headmaster

The headmaster is the primary articulator of Deerfield's chief development needs. His role is also to establish key relationships with those individuals who are in the best position, and are most interested in, making a significant difference in the future of the school. The headmaster sets aside approximately four to five working days per month for those purposes. The dates (and likely destinations) are established as much as 12 months in advance.

President of the Board

Deerfield's board president, as the head of the board responsible for the long-term development and welfare of the school, must play a key role in articulating long-term development needs. The president can speak about the board's discussions and concerns with firsthand knowledge.

RECRUITMENT, INVOLVEMENT, AND SOLICITATION OF TRUSTEES

Recruitment

Deerfield's nominating committee (the Committee on Trustees) is the most important committee of the board. This committee will furnish the future lifeblood of the board and its committees. The process works in the following way. The Committee on Trustees meets three to five times per year. Names are submitted from several sources, including the Alumni and Development Office and other board members. Generally, the Committee on Trustees is looking for areas of expertise: architects, educators, financial types, physicians, etc. who can bring a special set of skills or knowledge to the board. The committee is also looking for other ways in which an individual can make a significant impact, e.g., as a donor or a leader in the community. Individual names are discussed for a year or more before an offer to join the board is put forth. Our school charter also states that a minimum of 50 percent of the trustees must be alumni, and that the president of the Alumni Association should be a member of the Committee on Trustees.

Involvement

When trustees join our board, they become members of at least two standing committees, which include Finance, Academic Affairs, Buildings and Grounds, Compensation and Personnel, Development, Investment, Trustees, and Student Life. Most committees meet actively between board meetings. Each trustee is also likely to be a member of one *ad hoc* committee. Current *ad hoc* committees include technology, affordability, and diversity. The full board meets three times per year, and over 90 percent of the board will be in attendance at any given meeting. Board members are also called on for less formal involvement, including the hosting of school functions and visits with prospective students.

Our board members have fully embraced the need for them to serve as leaders in all areas of solicitation. Each member recognizes that we cannot ask others to support a project before the board does. It is made clear to individuals when they are asked to join the board that Deerfield should become a high priority, whether in terms of time, work, or financial support.

Solicitation

Each board member is asked for his or her annual support gift each summer for the upcoming fiscal year. The request is usually made by the national chair of annual support, a full member of the Board of Trustees.

In the area of estate planning, we continue to maintain visibility of the program, and ask all to consider it. It is not an area that we generally discuss when trustees are asked to join the board, but we do emphasize the importance of estate planning and planned giving to the future long-range well-being of the school.

In our recent capital campaigns, generally 25 to 50 percent of what has been raised has been given by our board. That is still an unwritten expectation. Less would appear to be a sign of weakness and a sign that the school is perhaps not ready to undertake such a campaign.

As the involvement of each board member grows, so does his or her level of giving. We are continually trying to strengthen the board, an effort that we hope will have a trickle-down effect not only in the board, but in the school as well.

As of this writing, Deerfield is considering the possibility of reducing trustee terms from five to four years. Shortening terms will challenge our ability to involve people and will heighten the need to involve them earlier and more often. On the other hand, some prospective candidates may be more willing to consider a board position that has a shorter term—four years (or two terms totalling eight years) vs. five years (or two terms totalling 10 years).

THE DEERFIELD BICENTENNIAL—OUR INSTITUTIONAL PLAN FOR THE 1990s

In 1990, the Deerfield Board of Trustees began discussing appropriate ways of celebrating the school's bicentennial, which will occur in 1997. The bicentennial would clearly become the backbone of our institutional plan for the next decade. Due to the recent fund-raising campaigns (1985-88 and 1991-93), we determined after much discussion to undertake our Bicentennial in two phases—celebratory (1997-98) and fund raising (1998-2001). The remaining segments of this chapter will describe the thinking that led to our final plan and to the process that will unfold over the remainder of this millennium and the start of the next one.

Preparing for the Bicentennial Celebration (1990-1997)

In 1990, following a series of preliminary discussions among trustees, then Headmaster Robert Kaufmann and Assistant Headmaster David Pond organized a series of discussion groups in four major alumni and parent areas in the Northeast. The purpose of each luncheon was to discuss, with a cross-section of alumni, parents, current and former faculty, and trustees, ways in which the bicentennial should be celebrated. The specific ideas resulting from those luncheon groups included the following:

1. The bicentennial should be an occasion to showcase what Deerfield does well—educate boys and girls.
2. The bicentennial should be an occasion for Deerfield to give back to the town, community, and others who have been so helpful in its creation and growth.
3. Deerfield should consider a major fund drive as a means of solidifying its financial position as a leader among independent secondary schools.

In 1992, the Bicentennial Steering Committee was formed; it consisted of a cross-section of 15 alumni, parents, and current and former faculty. The committee's mission was to create a master plan of key events and a timetable for those events; their plan was approved by the board in 1993.

Coincidentally, the committee's plan came as Headmaster Robert Kaufmann submitted his resignation, effective in the summer of 1994. He had served the school for 13 years, having overseen the completion of the most successful capital campaign in Deerfield's history, and having put the school on solid financial footing. Headmaster Kaufmann had also guided the school through its transition from an all-boys' school to a coeducational institution. He also realized that by resigning at this time, the next headmaster could have input into the shaping of the bicentennial celebration and capital campaign.

The planning for the bicentennial continued. A director of the bicentennial was hired in early 1994, and she devoted her full attention to the important planning phase. One of her first tasks was to form three working committees to assist her. The committees were populated with tried and true veterans who had served in previous volunteer roles, and specialists in certain areas (such as book publishing and marketing) who could provide special expertise at appropriate times during the planning process. Those committees and their responsibilities were as follows:

- **Publications Committee.** Shared oversight responsibilities with the bicentennial director for all bicentennial publications, including Deerfield's first pictorial history.

- **Communications Committee.** Created additional options and ways to raise the awareness of Deerfield.
- **Educational Initiatives Committee.** Encouraged discussions among the Deerfield faculty to enhance the educational program. This committee included several former independent school heads and current and former college presidents.

Most importantly, these committees were opportunities for those alumni and parents who wished to be helpful as volunteers, but who did not wish to serve in a fund-raising role. The committees allowed us to involve more volunteers than we had ever been able to involve.

In the spring of 1994, as our planning gained momentum, Eric Widmer, formerly dean of admission and financial aid at Brown University, and a Deerfield alumnus (class of 1957) was named headmaster. Throughout the interview process, he was made aware of the approaching bicentennial celebration, and the importance that this event had in the history of the school. Headmaster Widmer, a trained historian, saw this as a special opportunity to enrich school life for our students. As he assumed leadership of Deerfield, he stressed three areas on which he wanted the faculty to focus and which will become the cornerstones of our bicentennial.

1. **Curriculum.** The curriculum is the cornerstone of our educational program. Although no formal curricular review was planned, Headmaster Widmer used the discussions of the Bicentennial Educational Initiatives Committee as a means of encouraging faculty to look at how they teach and what they teach.
2. **Outreach opportunities in the local community.** In recent years, Deerfield has offered its students a limited number of community service opportunities; an enlargement of those opportunities is a key element of Headmaster Widmer's agenda.
3. **Global perspective among our students.** As our world, through all forms of communication and transportation, becomes smaller, the need to live more harmoniously with our neighbors becomes more challenging. Two ways in which Deerfield hopes to prepare its students for that world are by providing overseas exchange opportunities and by increasing the number of visiting scholars and speakers to our campus. Deerfield must do everything it can to provide its students with insights into the world they will inherit.

By the fall of 1996, the celebratory phase of our bicentennial was about to begin. Six years of planning would be implemented over the next two years. (See Exhibit 11-1.)

THE DEERFIELD BICENTENNIAL
DEERFIELD ... DAYS OF GLORY

1996-1997

September:
. "1797" Topiary
. Alumni Directory
. 9/13 - Heritage Day
. Bicentennial Stationery

January:
. 1/17 - Press Kits

March:
. 3/1 - Bicentennial
   Charter Day
. Morning event 10-12
. Lunch

April:
. 4/17-4/19 Homecoming #1
   (1960-1968)
. Symposia: English Dept.
. 4/18-4/20
. Bicentennial Trustees' Weekend
. Premier of Bicentennial
   Composition, Deerfield
   Always We Remember
. Marx groundbreaking

May:
. 5/9-5/11 Spring Day
. Premier of Bicentennial
   Theater Production
. Bicentennial Composition

June:
. 6/1 - Commencement
. Bicentennial Theater Production
. 6/12-6/14 Homecoming #2
   (1981-1989)
. Symposia: Science
. 6/13-6/15 - Reunions 2's and 7's

August:
. 8/15 - *Days of Glory* mailed
   Article on Charter Day

1997-1998

September:
. 9/11-9/13 Homecoming #3
   (1928-1947)
. 9/12-9/14 - Convocation
. Ceremony begins Friday
   at dusk w/ parade
. Address

. Bicentennial Celebration Group
. Symposia - Math Dept.

October:
. Heritage Award
. 10/17-10/18 - Parents' Weekend
. no Bicentennial events
. Program -
   . Bicentennial logo
   . 1-page description
   . Bicentennial car sticker

November:
. 11/6-11/8 Homecoming #4
   (1948-1959)
. Symposia: Foreign Lang.
. 11/7 - Choate (H) 1998

January:
- First Bicentennial Newsletter
  - Update of what has happened
  - Convocation
  - 4 Homecomings

April:
. 4/23-4/25 - Homecoming #5
   (1969-1980)
. Symposia: Fine Arts
. 4/24/25 - Trustees' Weekend

May:
. 5/1-5/2 - Spring Day
. Bicentennial visuals
. Bicentennial Composition
. 5/30-5/31 - Commencement

June:
. 6/11-6/13 - Homecoming #6
   (1990-1995)
. Symposia: TBD
. 6/12-6/14 - Reunions 3's & 8's

July:
. Second Bic. Newsletter
. Cheek book
. Play up Final Celebration

1998-1999

October:
. 10/1 - Cheek book
. 10/2-10/3 - 1797 here
   Friday night
. Final Celebration
. Announce BEIC

THE DEERFIELD BICENTENNIAL

EXHIBIT 11-1

THE DEERFIELD BICENTENNIAL
DEERFIELD ... DAYS OF GLORY

. Kick-off Campaign
. Marx Dedication
. 10/16-10/17 - Parents' Weekend
. 10/30-11/1 - Trustees' Weekend

November:
. 11/14 - Bicentennial
    Choate Day
. All-school to Wallingford by train
    with marching band
* Bicentennial to NYC

December:
. 12/10 - Third Bicentennial Newsletter
. recap of celebrations
. mention Street Celebration 1/1/99
. announcement of BEIC
. focus now on Campaign
. 12/31 - Exhibition Ball

January:
. 1/1/99 - Street Celebration to
    celebrate anniversary of opening
    of DA

April:
* Bicentennial to Boston

June:
. 6/11-6/13 - Reunions 4's and 9's

July:
. Fourth Bicentennial Newsletter

1999-2000

Fall:
. BEIC start or 1997
. Opening of Heritage House
. Fourth Bicentennial Newsletter if not
    sent in July
  * Bicentennial to Chicago

Winter:
* Bicentennial to
    Deerfield/Western Massachusetts

Spring:
. Fifth Bicentennial Newsletter
* Bicentennial to
    Los Angeles
    San Francisco

2000-2001

Fall:
* Bicentennial to Philadelphia,
    Washington, DC

Winter:
. January - Sixth Bicentennial
    Newsletter
* Bicentennial to
    Atlanta
    Southeast

Spring:
* Bicentennial to
    Texas
    Southwest

Fall:
. Final Campaign Report in book form

* Regional Bicentennial
    Events to include 1 or 2 of the
    following:
- Archival Exhibit
- Bicentennial Video
- Presentation of Bicentennial
    Medals
- Student performances in
    music and theater
- Faculty/Alumni Symposia
- Bicentennial Dinner

THE DEERFIELD BICENTENNIAL

EXHIBIT 11-1 (continued)

To this point in our bicentennial, we had not asked any volunteer for fund-raising assistance, but we had involved over 100 alumni and parents in our planning. Several told us that they enjoyed their involvement and that we should use them again when the fund-raising phase begins.

Oversight responsibilities for the bicentennial rest with the Board of Trustees and the senior officers of administration. The board is charged with responsibility for the long-range health of the school, and has, as mentioned, several working committees. The president oversees the board; an Executive Committee is made up of the officers plus the heads of each of the individual committees. Each committee has a statement of goals and objectives, which is reviewed annually so that an action plan for the year can be established for each committee.

A general review of the bicentennial has occurred at each board meeting (January, April, and October each year). Reports are made by the assistant headmaster for alumni and development and by the headmaster. The first celebratory events occurred in early 1997, and brought with them a clear sense that we are moving from the planning phase into the active phase of the celebration.

Several senior officers of administration, in concert with the headmaster and the Office of Alumni and Development, comprise an internal oversight group. These individuals meet weekly to review the various initiatives and proposals that are part of the bicentennial, as well as other significant matters relating to overall school direction and policy.

Bicentennial Fund Raising (1996-2001)

As our bicentennial celebration commences, our fund-raising planning is gathering momentum. We have made good progress on each of the three bicentennial objectives noted above.

Our first objective was to make the bicentennial an opportunity to showcase what Deerfield does well—educate girls and boys. We will accomplish that goal in a number of ways, beginning with Charter Day (1 March 1997). A national speaker will address the school community and share some thoughts about the town of Deerfield and the school over its first 200 years. Our pictorial history, which is the first history of any kind written about Deerfield, will be published at that time, and will provide a wonderful overview of Deerfield, both the school and the town. A series of homecomings will provide alumni with an opportunity to visit the school while it is in session. (Reunion weekends are held in the summer when the students are not in attendance.) Our Bicentennial Convocation (September 1997), for which the speaker will be U.S. Senator John Chafee (class of 1940) will focus on community service and outreach—two areas to which Senator Chafee has devoted virtually all of his adult life. The final celebration (October 1998), to which we will invite all alumni, will be an excellent occasion for all to share, for one week, the school and its wonderful past, present, and future.

Our second objective was to make the bicentennial an occasion for Deerfield to give back to the town, community, and others who have been so helpful in its creation and growth. Deerfield's inaugural Heritage Day was held on 13 September 1996. On this occasion, all students and faculty devoted a day of service to others throughout the Franklin County area. The day was devoted to assisting local communities in whatever way we could. Following Heritage Day, the school has continued to embark on an expanded community service program for all students who wish to serve others, either during the afternoons or on weekends during the school year.

Our third objective was for Deerfield to consider a major fund drive as a means of solidifying its financial position as a leader among independent schools. During Eric Widmer's first two years as headmaster, and as discussions have continued among faculty, alumni, parents and others, a clear sense of the new headmaster's agenda is emerging. The bicentennial campaign will include a desire to seek funds for faculty salaries, for additional financial aid, for faculty professional development, for technology, and for outreach. The articulation of those needs has emerged from Headmaster Widmer's early agenda, and through our internal planning structure, which involves faculty, administration, trustees, and alumni. A major benefit of having spent the last two years preparing for a bicentennial celebration has been the wonderful input we have had from a variety of sources, and both individuals and groups have been kept apprised of our planning and our needs as they emerge.

The momentum generated by planning for our bicentennial has continued into our fund-raising efforts. A series of feasibility luncheons, at which Headmaster Widmer has shared his plans for the next decade, have been extremely well attended. At each luncheon, the headmaster has outlined his thoughts and his hopes for the next 10 years. The president of our Board of Trustees, Robert M. Dewey, has also spoken forcefully about the financial challenges the board sees on the horizon, especially relating to affordability for prospective students and retention of outstanding faculty and staff. The results of the feasibility luncheons were made available to the Board of Trustees in January 1997.

For the last two years, internal planning for a capital campaign has also taken place. Additional staff members have been hired to allow us to better prepare our internal systems and to identify additional major gifts prospects through the use of individual and group screening sessions. A key element of the identification of new sources of support has been our early bicentennial celebration discussions since 1990. The process of hiring staff and undertaking an enlarged capital gifts effort can also occur efficiently only if staff are hired early and given enough time to put appropriate systems in place and to meet with key prospects and volunteers. Team-building can be an important part of the process, and time working together is a key component.

The same can be said of our volunteer organization. Our efforts to establish a National Campaign Executive Committee have made clear how long it takes for some people who would like to serve to make room on their calendars for Deerfield. Therefore, approach prospects early and let them know what you want them to do, and in what time frame. The more lead time, and the more clearly defined tasks you can give, the better your chances of having a person serve in a key volunteer role. Prior to any public campaign announcement, our objective is to have virtually all volunteers for the public phase of the campaign in place.

The board approved a capital campaign in January 1997. We are now moving ahead with the solicitation of the board itself, and of other key alumni, parents, and trustees who should be included in our nucleus fund effort. We plan to be ready for a public announcement of the campaign in October 1998—the same evening that we will hold our final bicentennial celebration. On that evening, we will make the public transition from a bicentennial celebration to a bicentennial campaign. We will also then be in a position to announce our final goal to all alumni, parents, and townspeople who are able to be in attendance for that special occasion. The public phase of our campaign would then unfold over the next three to four years.

SUMMARY

At this point in our planning, we are well on our way to accomplishing the three objectives we identified in 1992. The consciousness level of the school will have been raised; Deerfield will have added significantly to the full educational program that it provides to its students; and a capital campaign will have been undertaken with every expectation of success. The juxtaposition of the bicentennial capital campaign following the bicentennial celebration is different from most traditional campaigns. However, we believe that it will prove to be a key component in whatever bicentennial successes we are able to achieve. A longer term achievement, from which we are likely to benefit for several years, will be the expansion of our volunteer base. All schools and colleges are today concerned about their eroding volunteer groups. Deerfield was also able to include its newly appointed headmaster's vision for the future into the bicentennial on rather short notice. Eric Widmer arrived just prior to the start of our planning. An expanded, thoughtful, and orderly planning process provided him with an opportunity to have a clearer sense of Deerfield as ongoing bicentennial planning discussions were taking place.

Finally, we believe that the decade-long bicentennial planning and implementation will solidify Deerfield's place as a leader among American independent schools.

BIBLIOGRAPHY

Prepared by the CASE Reference Center—November 20, 1996.

Ackerman, Richard H. *Making Sense as a School Leader: Persisting Questions, Creative Opportunities.* San Francisco: Jossey-Bass Publishers, 1996. 186 pages.

Adams, Michael F. "Teamwork at the Top: The Development Officer's View: How One Fund Raiser Works with His President to Do More Than Raise Funds," *Currents* 15, no. 7 (July/August 1989): 16-18.

Addy, Cathryn Louise. *The President's Journey: Issues and Ideals in the Community College.* Bolton, MA: Anker Publishing Company, 1995.

Alberger, Patricia L., ed. *How to Work Effectively with Alumni Boards.* Washington, DC: Council for Advancement and Support of Education, 1981. 81 pages.

Alfred, Richard, Paul Elsner, and Jan LeCroy, eds. *Emerging Roles for Community College Leaders: New Directions for Community Colleges, no. 46.* San Francisco: Jossey-Bass Publishers, 1984. 132 pages.

Anderson, Wayne. "Presidents Must Make Fund Raising Work," *AGB Reports* 26, no.6 (November/December 1984): 17-19.

Axelrod, Nancy R. *The Chief Executive's Role in Developing the Nonprofit Board.* Washington, DC: National Center for Nonprofit Boards, 1990.

————. *Creating and Renewing Advisory Boards: Strategies for Success.* Washington, DC: National Center for Nonprofit Boards, 1990.

Bauer, Hank. "Be Prepared: Also Honest, Open, and Supportive. That's What Trustees Expect from You," *Currents* 19, no. 8 (September 1993): 43.

Benezet, Louis Tomlinson, Joseph Katz, and Frances W. Magnusson. *Style and Substance: Leadership and the College Presidency.* Washington, DC: American Council on Education, 1981. 121 pages.

Bensimon, Estela Mara. *Redesigning Collegiate Leadership: Teams and Teamwork in Higher Education.* Baltimore: Johns Hopkins University Press, 1993. 182 pages.

Bensimon, Estela M., Anna Neumann, and Robert Birnbaum. *Making Sense of Administrative Leadership: The 'L' Word in Higher Education: ASHE-ERIC Higher Education Report, no. 1*. Washington, DC: George Washington University, School of Education and Human Development, 1989. 109 pages.

Bergquist, William H. *The Four Cultures of the Academy: Insights and Strategies for Improving Leadership in Collegiate Organizations*. San Francisco: Jossey-Bass Publishers, 1992. 250 pages.

Birnbaum, Robert. *How Academic Leadership Works: Understanding Success and Failure in the College Presidency*. San Francisco: Jossey-Bass Publishers, 1992. 252 pages.

Board's Role in Fund-Raising: How Your Board Can Strengthen Its Fund-Raising Effectiveness. Washington, DC: Association of Governing Boards of Universities and Colleges, 1991. Videotapes.

Boggs, George R. "Matching CEO and Board Expectations," *Trustee Quarterly* no.4 (1995): 8-14.

Boone, Jerry H., Sue Peterson, and Daniel J. Poje. "University Autonomy: Perceived and Preferred Location of Authority," *Review of Higher Education* 14, no.2 (Winter 1991): 135-151.

Borden, Samuel Edward. "Framing Board/CEO Interaction in Decision-Making," Ph.D. diss., Indiana State University, 1993. 162 pages.

Bornstein, Rita. "Muffled Voices: The Key to Liberating a College President to Serve Society as a Public Intellectual Is for the Board Explicitly to Endorse That Role," *Trusteeship* 4, no. 2 (March/April 1996): 11-15.

Briscoe, Marianne C. and Joanne Hayes. "Building Campaign-Worthy Boards: Board Members Are an Essential Ingredient in Capital Campaign Success. Here are Some Tips on the Roles They Should Play—And How to Encourage Them to Participate Fully," *Advancing Philanthropy* 3, no. 4 (Winter 1995): 44-45.

Brown, James M. "Duties and Politics of the Board of Trustees," *AGB Reports* 24, no. 5 (September-October 1982): 4-13.

Bryce, Herrington J. *The Nonprofit Board's Role in Establishing Financial Policies*. Washington, DC: National Center for Nonprofit Boards, 1996. 20 pages.

Carbone, Robert F. "What Your Development Officer Might Tell You," *AGB Reports* 30, no. 1 (January-February 1988): 21-23.

———. *Presidential Passages: Former College Presidents Reflect on the Splendor and Agony of Their Careers*. Washington, DC: American Council on Education, 1981. 91 pages.

Carver, John and Miriam Mayhew. *A New Vision of Board Leadership: Governing the Community College*. Washington, DC: Association of Community College Trustees, 1994. 130 pages.

Casteen, John T., III. "Ownership of What Ails Us: The Diagnosis of the Uneasy Relationship Between Chief Executives and Boards as an Ailment That Needs Attention Is Accurate and Nearly Universal in Its Long-Term Ramifications," *Trusteeship* 4, no. 2 (March/April 1996): 4.

Casteen, John T., III. "Withdrawal Pains: How Can Trustees and Presidents Satisfy Strict Standards of Accountability, Protect Donors' Legitimate Interests, and Avoid Binding the Future with the Cords of Today's Conflicts?," *Trusteeship* 3, no. 3 (May/June 1995): 4.

Chait, Richard. *How to Help Your Board Govern More and Manage Less.* Washington, DC: National Center for Nonprofit Boards, 1993.

———. *The 1990s: The Decade of Trustees: New Directions for Higher Education, no. 70.* San Francisco: Jossey-Bass Publishers, Summer 1990.

———. *The New Activism of Corporate Boards and Implications for Campus Governance.* Washington, DC: Association of Governing Boards of Universities and Colleges, 1995.

Chait, Richard P. and Others. *Trustee Responsibility for Academic Affairs.* Washington, DC: Association of Governing Boards of Universities and Colleges, 1984. 144 pages.

Chait, Richard P., Thomas P. Holland, and Barbara E. Taylor. *The Effective Board of Trustees.* Phoenix: ACE/Oryx Press, 1993. 140 pages.

Cheshire, Richard D. "Strategies for Advancement," In *Presidential Leadership in Advancement Activities: New Directions for Institutional Advancement, no. 8.* San Francisco: Jossey-Bass Publishers, 1980. 9-18.

Clark, Kenneth E. and Miriam B. Clark. *Choosing to Lead.* Greensboro, NC: Center for Creative Leadership, 1996.

Clark, Kenneth E.; Miriam B. Clark, and David P. Campbell. *Impact of Leadership.* Greensboro, NC: Center for Creative Leadership, 1992. 559 pages.

Cohen, Michael D. and James G. March. *Leadership and Ambiguity: The American College President.* 2nd ed. Boston: Harvard Business School Press, 1986. 298 pages.

———. *Leadership and Ambiguity: The American College President.* New York: McGraw-Hill Publishers, 1974. 270 pages.

Colson, Helen A. *Philanthropy at Independent Schools.* Washington, DC: National Association of Independent Schools, 1995.

Conklin, Richard W. "The Role of Public Relations," In *The President and Fund Raising.* Phoenix: ACE/Oryx Press, 1989. 91-101.

Conrad, William and William Glenn. *The Effective Voluntary Board of Directors.* Athens, OH: Swallow Press, 1983. 263 pages.

Cook, Weaver Bruce. "Courting Philanthropy: The Role of University Presidents and Chancellors in Fund Raising," Ph.D. diss., University of Texas at Austin, 1994. 667 pages.

Costello, Kathryn R. "What I Expect of My CEO: A Chief Advancement Officer Outlines the Qualities that Make a President or Head an Ally in Fund Raising," *Currents* 19, no. 10 (November/December 1993): 24-28.

Cowley, William Harold. *Presidents, Professors, and Trustees: The Evolution of American Academic Government.* Edited by Donald T. Williams Jr. San Francisco: Jossey-Bass Publishers, 1980. 260 pages.

Crowley, Joseph N. *No Equal in the World: An Interpretation of the Academic Presidency*. Reno, NV: University of Nevada Press, 1994. 300 pages.

Crowther, Connie. "Building a Better Board: How to Lay a Solid Foundation for Your Fund-Raising Board," *Currents* 15, no. 10 (November/December 1989): 22-26.

Dagley, Duane H., ed. *Courage in Mission: Presidential Leadership in the Church-Related College*. Washington, DC: Council for Advancement and Support of Education, 1988. 165 pages.

Daughdrill, James H., Jr. *Essential Ingredients for Success: New Directions for Higher Education, no. 61*. San Francisco: Jossey-Bass Publishers, 1988. 81-85.

Davenport, David. "Teamwork at the Top: The President's View: When the President and the Chief Fund Raiser Share Ideas and Ideals, Money Is Just One Result," *Currents* 15, no. 7 (July/August 1989): 12-14.

DeFazio, Frank A. "The Role of Public Relations as Perceived by Presidents and Public Relations Officers at Private Comprehensive Universities and Colleges," Ph.D. diss., Drake University, 1987.

Dodds, Harold Willis. *The Academic President: Educator or Caretaker?* New York: McGraw-Hill Companies, 1962.

Dorich, Dina. "The Making of a President 1991: A Follow-Up to a 1982 CURRENTS Survey Reveals that More and More Advancement Professionals Are Moving Up to Academe's Top Jobs," *Currents* 17, no.4 (April 1991): 6-11.

Dziuba, Victoria and William Meardy., eds. *Enhancing Trustee Effectiveness: New Directions for Community Colleges, no. 15*. San Francisco: Jossey-Bass Publishers, 1976. 109 pages.

Eadie, Douglas. *Beyond Strategic Planning: How to Involve Nonprofit Boards in Growth and Change*. Washington, DC: National Center for Nonprofit Boards, 1993.

————. *Boards That Work: A Practical Guide to Building Effective Association Boards*. Washington, DC: American Society of Association Executives, 1995. 163 pages.

Eells, Walter Crosby. *The College Presidency, 1900-1960: An Annotated Bibliography*. Westport, CT: Greenwood Press, 1978. 143 pages.

Estes, Ellen G. "The Role of Volunteers in Fund-Raising," In *The Volunteer Management Handbook*. New York: John Wiley and Sons Inc., 1995. 244-258.

Farley, Eileen. "Fund Raising and Public College Trustees," *AGB Reports* 28, no. 5 (September-October 1986): 22-23.

Fazio, Charles R. and Carolyn Raffa Fazio. "Memo to the Chief Executive: Straight Talk About Presidential Leadership from Your Development Counsel," *Currents* 10, no. 1 (January 1984): 10-12.

Ferrari, Michael R. *Profiles of American College Presidents*. East Lansing, MI: Michigan State University, Graduate School of Business Administration, 1970. 175 pages.

Fisher, James L. "The Effective College President," *Educational Record* 71, no. 1 (Winter 1990): 6-10.

————. "Establishing a Successful Fund-Raising Program," In *The President and Fund Raising*. Phoenix: ACE/Oryx Press, 1989. 3-17.

————. "Evaluating Presidents," *Educational Record* 69, no. 3-4 (Summer-Fall 1988): 26-29.

————. *The Board and the President*. Phoenix: ACE/Oryx Press, 1991. 176 pages.

————. *Power of the Presidency*. New York: ACE/Macmillan, 1984.

Fisher, James L. and James V. Koch. *Presidential Leadership: Making a Difference*. Phoenix: ACE/Oryx Press, 1996. 408 pages.

Fisher, James L. and Gary H. Quehl. *The President and Fund Raising*. Phoenix: ACE/Oryx Press, 1989. 238 pages.

Fisher, James L., Martha W. Tack, and Karen J. Wheeler. *The Effective College President*. Phoenix: ACE/Oryx Press, 1988. 224 pages.

Fisher, James L. and Others. "Profile of Effective College Presidents," *AGB Reports* 30, no. 1 (January-February 1988): 28-30.

Fisher, Mark A. "Seasoned CEOs: Now That They've Reached the Top Spot, Former Fund Raisers Tell What They Know Now—And Wish They'd Known Then," *Currents* 19, no. 10 (November/December 1993): 38-40, 42.

Fitzpatrick, Joyce L. *The Board's Role in Public Relations and Communications*. Washington, DC: National Center for Nonprofit Boards, 1993.

Flawn, Peter Tyrell. *A Primer for University Presidents: Managing the Modern University*. Austin, TX: University of Texas Press, 1990. 210 pages.

Forman, Robert G. "The Role of Alumni Relations," In *The President and Fund Raising*. Phoenix: ACE/Oryx Press, 1989. 109-116.

Francis, Norman C. "Fund Raising at a Developing Institution," In *Presidential Leadership in Advancement Activities: New Directions for Institutional Advancement, no. 8*. San Francisco: Jossey-Bass Publishers, 1980. 65-72.

Frantzreb, Arthur C., ed. *Trustee's Role in Advancement: New Directions for Institutional Advancement, no. 14*. San Francisco: Jossey-Bass Publishers, 1981. 103 pages.

Freelen, Robert E. "Tasks in Government Relations," In *Presidential Leadership in Advancement Activities: New Directions for Institutional Advancement, no. 8*. San Francisco: Jossey-Bass Publishers, 1980. 73-82.

Fryer, Thomas W. *Leadership in Governance: Creating Conditions for Successful Decision Making in the Community College*. San Francisco: Jossey-Bass Publishers, 1991. 214 pages.

Fujita, Eleanor McKee. "What Is a Good College President?: How Leaders are Judged by Constituents," Ed.D. diss., Columbia University Teachers College, 1990. 317 pages.

Gale, Robert L. "The Role of the Governing Board," In *The President and Fund Raising*. Phoenix: ACE/Oryx Press, 1989. 102-108.

Gaona, Seth. "Trustee and Trusteeship of Selected Private Universities and Colleges in the United States of America and Canada," Ed.D. diss., Loma Linda University, 1992. 337 pages.

Gaudiani, Claire L. "Lemon Spritzers and Thank You Notes: A New Job Description for College Presidents," *Educational Record* 73, no. 2 (Spring 1992): 52-55.

George, G. Worth. "Releasing Your Board's Potential: The Vexing Problem of Boards and Fund Raising Is in Reality One of Identification and Recruitment of Persons of Influence with Potential for Growth, Even If Not Possessed of Abundant Means," *Fund Raising Management* 26, no. 8 (October 1995): 50-54.

Goldman, Robin. "A Presidential Primer: A Study of the President's Advancement Role Takes a Close Look at a Broad Subject," *Currents* 15, no. 7 (July/August 1989): 55-56.

Green, Madeleine F. *Leaders for a New Era: Strategies for Higher Education.* 2nd ed. Phoenix: ACE/Oryx Press, 1996.

Green, Madeleine F. and Sharon A. McDade. *Investing in Higher Education: A Handbook of Leadership Development.* Phoenix: ACE/Oryx Press, 1994. 384 pages.

Green, Madeleine F. and Marlene Ross. *The American College President: A Contemporary Profile.* Washington, DC: American Council on Education, 1988.

Gurin, Maurice G. *Advancing Beyond the Techniques in Fund Raising.* Detroit: Taft Group, 1991. 149 pages.

Guskin, Alan E. "Soft Landings for New Leaders," *Trusteeship* 4, no. 1 (January/February 1996): 12-16.

Haak, Harold H. *Victim to Victor: A Year in the Life of a University President.* Washington, DC: American Association of State Colleges and Universities, 1988. 76 pages.

Haenicke, Diether. "Presidential Perspective," *Currents* 17, no. 1 (January 1991): 18-21.

Hahn, Robert. "Getting Serious About Presidential Leadership: Our Collective Responsibility," *Change: The Magazine of Higher Learning* 27, no. 5 (September/October 1995): 13-19.

Hall, Carol Ann. "The Role of Public Relations in Three Ohio Liberal Arts Colleges: A Qualitative Study of the Role of Public Relations in Three Prestige Schools That Compete for Students on a National Basis, with Focus on Presidents' Perceptions," Ph.D. diss., Ohio State University, 1985.

Hall, Margarete Rooney. "Gilt by Association: Trustees Can Double Their Effectiveness in Such Areas as Fund-Raising by Creating 'Sub-Boards' with Clear and Distinct Roles and Responsibilities," *Trusteeship* 3, no. 3 (May/June 1995): 35.

Hamlin, Alan. "The President as Salesman," *Educational Record* 71, no. 1 (Winter 1990): 11-14.

Hartsook, Robert F. "Success Busters: A CEO Can Make or Break a Fund Raiser. There Must Be the Kind of Support That Motivates and Encourages. If Not, the Fund Raisers Will Not Succeed," *Fund Raising Management* 27, no. 4 (June 1996): 40-41.

Hay, Tina M. "Taking the Blinders Off: What You Can Do to Keep the President's Eyes Open," *Currents* 17, no. 2 (February 1991): 12-15.

Hill, Jesse William. "A Profile of Trustees: Characteristics, Roles and Functions of Trustees in Ohio's Two-Year College System," Ph.D. diss., Ohio University, 1989.

Hirzy, Ellen Cochran. *Nonprofit Board Committees: How to Make Them Work.* Washington, DC: National Center for Nonprofit Boards, 1992. 16 pages.

Holland, Thomas P., Richard P. Chait, and Barbara E. Taylor. "Board Effectiveness: Identifying and Measuring Trustee Competencies," *Research in Higher Education* 30, no. 4 (August 1989).

Holmgren, Norah. *The Finance Committee: The Fiscal Conscience of the Nonprofit Board.* Washington, DC: National Center for Nonprofit Boards, 1995. 16 pages.

Howe, Fisher. *The Board Members' Guide to Fund Raising: What Every Trustee Needs to Know About Raising Money.* Washington, DC: Jossey-Bass Publishers and the National Center for Nonprofit Boards, 1991. 140 pages.

———. *Fund Raising and the Nonprofit Board Member.* Washington, DC: National Center for Nonprofit Boards, 1990.

———. *Welcome to the Board: Your Guide to Effective Participation.* San Francisco: Jossey-Bass Publishers, 1995.

Hurtubise, Mark. "An Analysis of Presidential Attitudes Toward and Participation in Fund Raising at Select, Small, Independent, Liberal Arts Colleges and Universities," Ph.D. diss., University of San Francisco, 1988.

Hurtubise, Mark and Laurence A. Bishop. "Who are 'Successful' Fund-Raising Presidents?," *AGB Reports* 33, no.2 (March-April 1991): 32-33.

Iannoli Jr., Joseph J. "Strike Up the Board: Motivating Trustees at the Start Means Morale, Momentum, and Money," *Currents* 15, no. 6 (June 1989):28-31.

Ingram, Richard T. *The Basic Responsibilities of Nonprofit Boards.* Washington, DC: National Center for Nonprofit Boards, 1990.

———. *Governing Independent Colleges and Universities: A Handbook for Trustees, Chief Executives, and Other Campus Leaders.* San Francisco: Jossey-Bass Publishers, 1993. 479 pages.

Ironfield, Elaine B. "Characteristics of Two-Year Public Colleges and Foundations with Successful Fund-Raising Programs," Ed.D. diss., University of Massachusetts, 1991.

Kerr, Clark. *Presidents Make a Difference: Strengthening Leadership in Colleges and Universities: A Report of the Commission on Strengthening Presidential Leadership.* Washington, DC: Association of Governing Boards of Universities and Colleges, 1984. 141 pages.

Kerr, Clark and Marian L. Gade. *The Guardians: Boards of Trustees of American Colleges: What They Do and How Well They Do It.* Washington, DC: Association of Governing Boards of Universities and Colleges, 1989. 239 pages.

———. *The Many Lives of Academic Presidents: Time, Place and Character.* Washington, DC: Association of Governing Boards of Universities and Colleges, 1986. 260 pages.

Lang, Andrew S. *The Financial Responsibilities of Nonprofit Boards.* Washington, DC: National Center for Nonprofit Boards, 1992. 32 pages.

Larson, Wendy Ann. "Team Spirit: At the University of Tennessee at Chatta-
    nooga, the PR Staff and Campus CEO Team Up to Improve Community
    Relations," *Currents* 15, no. 9 (October 1989): 32-35.

"Launching a Successful Career in Academe: 32 Administrators and Professors
    Offer Advice," *Chronicle of Higher Education* 31, no. 1 (September 4, 1985): 42-
    44.

Leatherman, Courtney. "Bitter Feelings in Boulder: Ex-President Judith Alvino
    Left the U. of Colorado Under a Cloud of Controversy," *Chronicle of Higher
    Education* 42, no. 14 (December 1, 1995): A26, A28-A29.

Legon, Richard D. "Fund-Raising: Trustees Make a Difference," *Educational Record*
    70, no. 2 (Spring 1989): 50-52.

Levin, John S. "The Importance of the Board-President Relationship in Three
    Community Colleges," *Canadian Journal of Higher Education* 21, no. 1 (1991): 37-
    53.

———. "The Paradox of the Presidency: The Difference a President Makes in
    Institutional Functioning at Three Community Colleges," *Canadian Journal of
    Higher Education* 22, no. 3 (1992): 28-45.

Lillestol, Jane M. "Blue-Chip Board: Take Stock of Your Alumni Board—And
    Then Increase Its Value with These Insider Tips," *Currents* 18, no. 2 (February
    1992): 22-26.

Lucas, Ann F. *Strengthening Departmental Leadership: A Team-Building Guide for
    Chairs in Colleges and Universities.* San Francisco: Jossey-Bass Publishers, 1994.
    295 pages.

Manju, Bala. *Leadership Behavior and Educational Administration.* New York: Deep
    and Deep Publications, 1990. 250 pages.

Marshall, Penny. "The Independent School Perspective: Alumni Administrators
    Can Play a Role in Choosing and Acclimating a New School Head. The Best
    Advice: Be Direct, Realistic, and Supportive," *Currents* 19, no. 2 (February
    1993): 52.

Mason, Philip R. "Just What Do You Expect?," *AGB Reports* 32, no. 3 (May-June
    1990): 16-18.

McCurdy, Jack and Donald L. Hymes, eds. *Building Better Board-Administrator
    Relations. An AASA Critical Issues Report.* Arlington, VA: American Associa-
    tion of School Administrators, 1992. 130 pages.

McDade, Sharon A. *Higher Education Leadership: Enhancing Skills Through Profes-
    sional Development Programs: ASHE-ERIC Higher Education Report, no. 5.* Wash-
    ington, DC: George Washington University, School of Education and Human
    Development, 1987. 125 pages.

McLaughlin, Judith Block. "The Perilous Presidency," *Educational Record* 77, no. 2-
    3 (Spring/Summer 1996): 12-17.

McMillen, Liz. "More Colleges Tap Fund Raisers for Presidencies, Seeking Exper-
    tise in Strategic Thinking about Entire Institution," *Chronicle of Higher Education*
    38, no. 3 (September 11, 1991): A35-A36.

Mercer, Joye. "The Fund Raiser as President: Rita Bornstein Is One of Several Chiefs to Move Up from the Development Office," *Chronicle of Higher Education* 42, no. 3 (September 15, 1995): A35-A36.

Mihalovits, Sheila Barons. "Preparing Your Board for Fund Raising: You Can Create an Atmosphere That Will Spark the Philanthropic Spirit in Your Trustees. Here are Some Things You Can Do to Ignite That Spark," *Fund Raising Management* 25, no. 8 (October 1994).

Miller, Michael T. *The College President's Role in Fund Raising*. 1991. ERIC document ED 337099. 20 pages.

Mills, Margaret S. *Board Involvement in Fundraising [Working Paper]*. San Francisco: Institute for Nonprofit Organization Management, University of San Francisco, 1993.

Moore, H. Martin. "A Model of Cooperation: A Survey of Presidents and Chief Advancement Officers Shows Four Types of Relationships," *Currents* 13, no. 7 (July/August 1987): 40-44.

Moore, Hollis A. *Defining Leadership*. Washington, DC: American Association of State Colleges and Universities, 1980. 49 pages.

Moore, R. Keith. "Positioning Your PR Office: Capture the Elusive Power of Clout with These Concrete Steps," *Currents* 14, no. 10 (November/December 1988): 16-22.

Murray, Dennis J. "The CEO's Role in Fund Raising: It's No Secret That Not-for-Profit CEOs Must Cultivate Major Gift Prospects. But That's Not Where an Executive's Development Responsibilities Should Begin—Or End. The CEO Must Communicate the Organization's Vision and Build an Effective Board. A College President Offers His Views of the CEO's Role," *Advancing Philanthropy* 2, no. 5 (Spring 1995): 19-23.

National Center for Nonprofit Boards. *Building an Effective Nonprofit Board: Creating a Cohesive, Knowledgeable, and Committed Governing Board*. Washington, DC: Jossey-Bass Publishers and the National Center for Nonprofit Boards, 1990. Audiocassette.

——— *Speaking of Money: A Guide to Fund Raising for Nonprofit Board Members*. Washington, DC: National Center for Nonprofit Boards, 1996. videocassette.

Neff, Charles B. "Clear Expectations: The Missing Piece in Board-Presidential Relations," *Trusteeship* 1, no. 3 (May/June 1993): 20-23.

Nelson, Judith. *Six Keys to Recruiting, Orienting, and Involving Nonprofit Board Members*. rev. ed. Washington, DC: National Center for Nonprofit Boards, 1995. 64 pages.

———. "Work, Headaches, and Rewards: When Less Is More: Small Organizations, Small Problems, Right? Don't Count on It, Says One Who has Toiled in Not-for-Profits of Various Sizes. Managers of Smaller Organizations Confront Most of the Same Challenges That Leaders of Large Groups Face—But with Fewer Resources at Their Disposal," *Advancing Philanthropy* 2, no. 5 (Spring 1994): 28-32.

Newton, Wayne. "The College President, the Board, and the Board Chair: Effective Relationships," *Trustee Quarterly* no. 2 (Spring 1995): 17-19.

Nicklin, Julie L. "Fund-Raising Master: In 18 Years as Cornell's Chief, Frank Rhodes Has Given His All to the Task," *Chronicle of Higher Education* 41, no. 40 (June 16, 1995): A31-A33.

O'Bar, Dairel Lee. "The Behavior of Community College Presidents and Board Members in a Formal Setting: The Board of Trustees Meeting," Ph.D. diss., University of Kansas, 1991. 170 pages.

O'Connell, Brian. *The Board Member's Book*. 2nd ed. Washington, DC: Independent Sector, 1993.

O'Shea, Catherine L. "Countdown to Success: With a Little Planning, You and Your New CEO Can Launch a Successful Fund-Raising Program," *Currents* 19, no. 10 (November/December 1993): 30-36.

Panas, Jerold. *Boardroom Verities: A Celebration of Trusteeship With Some Guides and Techniques to Govern By*. Chicago: Precept Press, 1991. 239 pages.

Peacock, J. *Fund-Raising Leadership: A Guide for College and University Boards*. Washington, DC: Association of Governing Boards of Universities and Colleges, 1989.

Peavy, Elizabeth A. "A Study of Historically Black College Presidents' Perceptions of Environmental Factors Influencing Their Institution," Ph.D. diss., Temple University, 1986.

Penney, Sherry H. "Five Challenges for Academic Leaders in the 21st Century," *Educational Record* 77, no. 2-3 (Spring/Summer 1996): 19-23.

Pocock, John W. "Fund Raising: The Board's Role," *AGB Reports* 27, no. 4 (July-August 1985): 40-42.

———. *Fund-Raising Leadership: A Guide for College and University Boards*. Washington, DC: Association of Governing Boards of Universities and Colleges, 1989.

Powell, James Lawrence. *Pathways to Leadership: How to Achieve and Sustain Success*. San Francisco: Jossey-Bass Publishers, 1995. 253 pages.

"Questions for Your Board Chairman, Realizing Your Board's Fund-Raising Potential," *FRI Monthly Portfolio: FRI Bulletin* 35, no. 3 (March 1996): np.

Quigg, H. Gerald. "Welcome Aboard: To Improve Your Board's Fund- Raising Results Educate and Support Its Members," *Currents* 15, no. 10 (November/December 1989): 28-32.

Razik, Taher A. *Fundamental Concepts of Educational Leadership and Management*. New York: Merrill Publishing Company, 1995. 588 pages.

Robinson, Maureen. *Developing the Nonprofit Board: Strategies for Educating and Motivating Board Members*. Washington, DC: National Center for Nonprofit Boards, 1994. 16 pages.

Ryan, Ellen. "Advice to the Fundlorn: Having Trouble with Your Trustees? Consultants Across the Country Offer Solutions," *Currents* 15, no. 10 (November/December 1989): 40-44.

Schulze, Charles Joseph, Jr. "The Role of the Community College President in Successful Fund-Raising," Ed.D. diss., Columbia University Teachers College, 1991.

Seiler, Timothy L. and Kay Sprinkle Grace, eds. *Achieving Trustee Involvement in Fundraising: New Directions for Philanthropic Fundraising, no. 4.* San Francisco: Jossey-Bass Publishers, 1994.

Shoemaker, Donna. "PR Perceptions: A Master's Thesis Reveals How Campus Pros View Public Relations—And Their Presidents," *Currents* 19, no. 9 (October 1993): 15-18.

———. "They Pledge Allegiance: PR People and Their Presidents Tell How They Forge a Bond Through Open, Honest Communication," *Currents* 19, no. 9 (October 1993): 20-23.

Short, Paula M. *Leadership in Empowered Schools: Themes from Innovative Efforts.* New York: Merrill Publishing Company, 1997.

Slinker, John Michael. "The Role of the College or University President in Institutional Advancement," Ph.D. diss., Northern Arizona University, 1988. 224 pages.

Smith, David H. *Entrusted: The Moral Responsibilities of Trusteeship.* Bloomington, IN: Indiana University Press, 1995.

Smith, G. T. "Chapter Fifty-Four: The Chief Executive and Advancement," In *Handbook of Institutional Advancement: A Practical Guide to College and University Relations, Fund Raising, Alumni Relations, Government Relations, Publications, and Executive Management for Continuing Advancement.* San Francisco: Jossey-Bass Publishers, 1986.

Sontz, Ann H. L. *The American College President, 1636-1989: A Critical Review and Bibliography.* Westport, CT: Greenwood Publishing Group, 1991. 176 pages.

Spangler, Mary Schuhsler. "The Role of the College President in Facilitating Organizational Growth Through Group Learning: A Qualitative Study of the Creation Phase in the Life-Cycle Process of a Community College Foundation," Ed.D. diss., University of California, Los Angeles, 1994. 161 pages.

Sturnick, Judith A., Jane E. Milley, and Catherine A. Tisinger. *Women at the Helm: Pathfinding Presidents at State Colleges and Universities.* Washington, DC: American Association of State Colleges and Universities, 1991. 103 pages.

Swearer, Howard R. "A More Perfect Union: Brown University President Tells Why It's Vital to Link Advancement to the Institution's Intellectual Life," *Currents* 14, no. 1 (January 1988): 8-9.

Tempel, Eugene R. *The Development Committee: Fund Raising Begins with the Board.* Washington, DC: National Center for Nonprofit Boards, 1996. 20 pages.

Terry, Robert W. *Authentic Leadership: Courage in Action.* San Francisco: Jossey-Bass Publishers, 1993. 315 pages.

Thompson, D. Thomas. "Turning Points for Successful Institutions: A Look at 18 Private, Christian Liberal Arts Colleges and Universities in California," Ph.D. diss., Pepperdine University, 1995. 259 pages.

Tierney, William G. *The Web of Leadership: The Presidency in Higher Education.* Greenwich, CT: JAI Press, 1988. 241 pages.

"Toward a Trouble-Free Board: Sure-Fire Solutions to Common Conundrums," *Currents* 18, no. 2 (February 1992): 32-36.

Townsend, Clark. "76th Annual Convention: Resources: Building Assets with Fund-Raising Team Leadership," *Community College Journal* 66, no. 5 (April/May 1996): 30-31.

Trachtenberg, Stephen Joel. "Life at the Top: It's a Heap of Trouble," *Currents* 13, no. 2 (February 1987): 80.

―――. *Speaking His Mind.* Phoenix: Oryx Press, 1994. 140 pages.

―――. "What I Expect of My CDO: A University President Describes the Basic Rules for Chief Development Officers," *Currents* 19, no. 10 (November/December 1993): 18-22.

Tucker, Barney A. An Activist Board Chair's Advice. AGB Priorities 31, no. 2 (March-April 1989): 26-27, 29.

Turner, Richard C. , ed. *Taking Trusteeship Seriously: Essays on the History, Dynamics, and Practice of Trusteeship.* Indianapolis, IN: Indiana University Center on Philanthropy, 1995.

Vaughn, George B. *Dilemmas of Leadership: Decision Making and Ethics in the Community College.* San Francisco: Jossey-Bass Publishers, 1992. 216 pages.

―――. *Leadership in Transition: The Community College Presidency.* Washington, DC: ACE/ Macmillan, 1989. 146 pages.

Vineyard, Edwin. *The Pragmatic Presidency: Effective Leadership in the Two-Year College.* Bolton, MA: Anker Publishing Company, 1993. 213 pages.

Wallace, Richard C. *From Vision to Practice: The Art of Educational Leadership.* Thousand Oaks, CA: Corwin Press, 1996. 218 pages.

Weaver, Gwendolyn A. "A Support System for Presidents: The Adage That Good Boards and Effective Presidents Go Hand-in-Hand Is Particularly True Today, as Presidents' Jobs Grow More Complex. Here Are Some Ways a Board Can Support Its Chief Executive," *Trusteeship* 4, no. 2 (March/April 1996): 5.

Wendel, Frederick C. *Outstanding School Administrators: Their Keys to Success.* Westport, CT: Praeger Publications, 1995.

White, Harry. "Excuses, Excuses: Why Trustees are Reluctant to Raise Money—And What to Do About It," *Currents* 15, no. 10 (November/December 1989): 34-38.

Whitt, J. Allen and Others. *The Inner Circle of Local Nonprofit Trustees: A Comparison of Attitudes and Backgrounds of Women and Men Board Members.* New Haven, CT: Yale University Program on Non-Profit Organizations, 1993.

Williams, Roger L. "Presidential Perceptions: A CASE Survey Reveals How Campus CEO's View Public Relations—And Their PR Staffs," *Currents* 17, no. 7 (July/August 1991): 52-56.

Willmer, Wesley K., ed. *Winning Strategies in Challenging Times for Advancing Small Colleges.* Washington, DC: Council for Advancement and Support of Education, 1993. 237 pages.

Wilson, Jeanne M. and Others. *Leadership Trapeze: Strategies for Leadership in Team-Based Organizations.* San Francisco: Jossey-Bass Publishers, 1995.

Witmer, Judith T. *Moving Up: A Guidebook for Women in Educational Administration.* Lancaster, PA: Technomic Publishing Company Inc. 1995. 387 pages.

Women Presidents in U.S. Colleges and Universities: A 1995 Higher Education Update. Washington, DC: American Council on Education, 1995. 5 pages.

Wood, Miriam M. *Nonprofit Boards and Leadership: Cases on Governance, Change and Board-Staff Dynamics.* San Francisco: Jossey-Bass Publishers, 1995.

Woodrum, Robert L. "The PR Officer's Survival Kit: A Former Corporate PR Pro Shares Strategies for Pleasing the CEO—And Hanging on to Your Job," *Currents* 22, no. 3 (March 1996): 46, 48-50.

Worth, Michael J. "The Fundamentals of Fund Raising: A Step-By-Step Guide to Development for Presidents," *Currents* 16, no. 3 (March 1990): 51-53.

————. "Presidents Under Pressure: A Controversial Book Says Boards Have Unintentionally Weakened the Presidency," *Currents* 18, no. 4 (April 1992): 45-46.

————, ed. *Public College and University Development: Fund Raising at State Universities, State Colleges, and Community Colleges.* Washington, DC: Council for Advancement and Support of Education, 1985. 164 pages.

————. "Boards of University-Related Foundations: Their Characteristics, Roles and Relationships to Presidents and Governing Boards of Host Institutions," Ph.D. diss., University of Maryland, 1982.

Zacharias, Donald W. "A Program of Substance: Advice from a CEO on Proving Your Worth to Your Alumni, Your Campus Community, and Your President," *Currents* 19, no. 1 (January 1993): 20-24.

INDEX

by Linda Webster